Perspectives on School
at Seven Years Old

Publications from the Child Development Research Unit
University of Nottingham

Studies in Urban Childhood
John and Elizabeth Newson, *Infant Care in an Urban Community*
(George Allen & Unwin, 1963; Penguin, 1965)
John and Elizabeth Newson, *Four Years Old in an Urban Community* (George Allen & Unwin, 1968; Penguin, 1970)
John and Elizabeth Newson, *Seven Years Old in the Home Environment* (George Allen & Unwin, 1976; Penguin, 1977)
Sheila Hewett with John and Elizabeth Newson, *The Family and the Handicapped Child* (George Allen & Unwin, 1970)
Sheila Hewett, *The Need for Long-Term Care: Factors influencing the admission of children to hospitals for the subnormal,* Occasional Paper 3 (IMMR, Butterworths, 1972)
Susan Gregory, *The Deaf Child and his Family* (George Allen & Unwin, 1976)

Other publications
Peter Cummings, *Education and the Severely Handicapped Child* (NSMHC, 1973)
W. E. C. Gillham and K. A. Hesse, *The Nottingham Number Test* (University of London Press, 1974)
W. E. C. Gillham, *Teaching a Child to Read* (University of London Press, 1974)
W. E. C. Gillham (ed.), *Psychology Today* (Hodder & Stoughton, 1975)
W. E. C. Gillham (trans.), Vurpillot, E., *The Visual World of the Child* (George Allen & Unwin, 1976)
John and Elizabeth Newson, *Toys and Playthings in Development and Remediation* (Penguin, in press)
John Newson and M. L. Matthews, *The Language of Basic Statistics* (Longman, 1971)
Lorna Selfe, *Nadia: A case of exceptional drawing ability in an autistic child* (Academic Press, 1977)

Perspectives
on School at
Seven Years Old

John and Elizabeth Newson
with
Peter Barnes

Child Development Research Unit
University of Nottingham

London
GEORGE ALLEN & UNWIN LTD
Ruskin House   Museum Street

First published in 1977

© George Allen & Unwin (Publishers) Ltd, 1977

ISBN 0 04 136017 6

Printed in Great Britain
in 10 on 11 point Times
at the Alden Press, Oxford

Contents

Acknowledgements

The people and bodies to whom we are grateful for their various kinds of help in making this book and the research it reports possible are precisely those whom we thanked in the companion volume to this, and our indebtedness to them is spelled out there; they will perhaps forgive us if we do not try to paraphrase our previous acknowledgement, but merely list them, with equal appreciation. They are: the Social Science Research Council, the Nuffield Foundation and the University of Nottingham; Dr William Dodd, Dr Wilfrid Parry, Mr W. G. Jackson, Mr D. J. W. Sowell, Mr James Stone, Mr B. O. Neep and the Educational Welfare Staff of Nottingham Education Authority; Diane Barnes, Jean Crossland, Jean Jacobs, Dady Key and Margaret Rose; Malcolm Fletcher and Frances Canning; Julia Hibbitt, Penelope Key and Veronica Mohammed.

Special thanks are due to Beryl West who, unflustered by constant interruptions from students, staff and the telephone, made a handsome typescript out of an almost illegible draft, and who remained cheerful through a dozen last-minute changes. We should also like to thank five Nottingham headteachers – Mr Evans, Mr Harwood, Miss Jones, Mr Stanton and Mrs Stephens – who, as they have so often done before, welcomed our request for help: on this occasion, to count temper tantrums occurring among seven-year-olds in their schools.

Parents, teachers and children are the dramatis personae of this book. It is dedicated to them.

Tables

The conventions observed in setting out these tables, together with the statistical procedures on which they are based, are explained on pages 15–19 and in Appendix II.

Introduction

This book is a study of those aspects of a child's educational experience which can only be understood by going into his home and listening to what his parents have to say. Parents as a resource for research data in education have been sadly under-used; this is largely because children undergoing education are for the most part conveniently grouped together in schools, making it possible for a respectable quantity of research material to be amassed economically and with relative ease in that environment. Parents, on the other hand, have to be sought out one by one on their own ground – a time-consuming and expensive business. None the less, parents possess information which is obtainable in no other way than by asking them for it.

When we started work on the seven-year-old age-stage of our long-term investigation of children growing up in Nottingham, we did not originally intend to ask questions about school; research in education, we thought, had far too long a history for us to contribute to it in any useful way from the indirect vantage-point of the home. It was in a spirit of curiosity, rather than serious research planning, that we included a section on school at the piloting stage of the interview. By the time the piloting was half completed, we knew (reluctantly, because it made the interview far too long) that we were tapping material that we could not afford to lose if we really wanted a rounded picture of the growing-up process. Indeed, to discuss the child's behaviour without mentioning his major occupation, to explore the mother's attitudes to his developing personality while ignoring her feeling about massive social and intellectual forces in that development, to identify ways in which she assumed an educative role without being interested in how she evaluated this role in relation to that of more formal educators, to pinpoint her anxieties about the child at home while excluding possibly more potent anxieties about the child at school: any of these omissions would have been dangerous sources of distortion to the full account which we were trying to achieve.

Moreover, it seems to us more and more urgent that those of us who are in any way professionally involved in the business of education should have the opportunity to look at ourselves from the parental perspective; it is only by comprehending each other's needs, and perhaps by trying to empathise with each other's misconceptions, that an effective job can be done for the child, who too often finds himself playing pig-in-the-middle of a parent–teacher confrontation. As J. H. Robinson wrote in *The Mind in the Making*,[1] 'Partisanship is our great curse. We too readily assume that everything has two sides and that it is our duty to be on one or the other'. Because parents and teachers have rather different motivations and roles in the child's development, there are good reasons for them to feel threatened by each other: all the more necessity, then, for each to make a *positive* effort to understand the other's outlook. Thus we are not here fundamentally concerned to present an objective view of schools (though we hope that our own comments are reasonably objective); rather, we have tried to create an opportunity for parents' subjective opinions to be listened to, in the hope that teachers will find them illuminating and helpful in broadening their own subjective views. It must be understood that in neither case do we use the word 'subjective' pejoratively; subjectivity is the stuff of parenthood and the humanising element in professionalism – without subjectivity there is no commitment.

The book can, then, be read on its own as a study in education; the usefulness and meaning of the findings it describes will (we think) be more than doubled if they are set in the context of the basic home environment which we have delineated in the preceding volume,[2] just as our studies so far of one-year-olds, four-year-olds and seven-year-olds will eventually be thrown into more significant perspective by bringing together the data from these and later age-stages on a longitudinal basis. Because the present volume reports only one part of a much larger and integrated programme of research, we do not propose to rehearse once again the theoretical implications of the approach we have taken nor the methodological problems which are involved. For discussions of our approach, we refer the reader to the first chapters of the two books which precede this one; in addition, both a broader outline of our interest in parents as a research resource, and a more detailed account of the interviewing method as we have developed it, will be found in Shipman's collection of case studies in the social sciences.[3]

We do think it necessary to give once more a guide to the way in which we have analysed and presented our material: rather than paraphrase for no sensible reason, the rest of this Introduction will repeat the explanation given in the companion volume.

PRESENTATION OF DATA

As before, we have had to cope with the basic technical problem of reconciling and blending different sorts of evidence to form an adequate perspective. On the qualitative side, we have verbatim transcripts of our tape-recorded interviews which show how the mothers received and interpreted our questions and what they actually said in response to wording that was expressly designed to provoke extended conversation. This in turn leads to quantitative evidence concerning the proportion of mothers whose answers fell into meaningfully different categories. To illustrate differences in attitude, we have again quoted extensively from transcripts; but we are obviously conscious that quotations can all too easily be selected so as to give credence to almost any theoretical generalisation. As a corrective, we need continually to refer back to the quantitative and statistical level of analysis. This enables us first to give an account of which things parents *typically* say and do in relation to seven-year-old children, and secondly to chart the variations in standpoint which characterise parents in different social circumstances.

From the earliest study, we were forced to recognise the pervasive influence of social class as a determinant of different patterns of child rearing. We had been very ready to recognise other factors, such as the child's sex or family position, as important; but at one and four years we could not identify either as a significant variable in relation to the questions we were asking. At seven, however, it quickly became clear that both sex and social class were operating at a high level of potency in the child's upbringing experience. We have therefore adopted a procedure for presenting our quantitative findings which allows us to observe the effects of sex and social class both separately and in combination.

Tables   In an effort to make the statistical findings easy to follow, we have set out tables in a standard form which is followed, more or less consistently, throughout this volume. A typical example is shown below in illustration. These tables are normally used to show the percentage of mothers who answered some particular question in a defined way; but the method of presentation lends itself equally to the display of other information about the sample, such as, for example, the number of high scores on some more sophisticated measure, derived from combining answers given to a group of questions which contribute towards a single theme: these combined measures we shall refer to as indices.

In the left-hand part of the specimen table, the results are broken down in two ways, showing the percentages for five different social groups and for boys and girls separately; the bottom line shows class proportions for boys and girls combined. Social class is, as previously, ascribed according to the Registrar-General's classification,[4]

Specimen table   *Children who own more than ten books of their own, analysed on the basis of sex and social class*

	I&II	III wc	III man	IV	V	I&II+ III wc	III man, IV, V	overall popn.
	social class					summary (middle class)	(working class)	
	%	%	%	%	%	%	%	%
boys	98	70	48	43	28	85	45	56
girls	95	69	50	44	10	83	45	55
both	97	70	49	44	19	84	45	55

Significance: trend ↘ ****   m.class/w.class   ***
(non-linear, p=0·06)
between sexes not significant, interaction class × sex n.s.

with the modification that Classes I and II (upper and lower professional and managerial) are combined, while Class III is divided into white collar and manual workers; foremen in industry are included in the III white collar group, and class affiliation in any individual case is determined on the basis of whichever of the parents' occupations is higher in the class scale.

If the combined proportions for boys and girls increase or decrease consistently as a function of social class, this indicates a trend which can then be tested for statistical significance (see Appendix II). The result of this trend test is indicated at the foot of the left-hand side of the table in terms of *direction* (upward from Class I to Class V ↗, or downward ↘) and of *significance level*: here we have used the convention of stars to indicate the order of significance (**** p < 0·001; *** p < 0·01; ** p < 0·02; * p < 0·05). The test used also allows us to say whether there is any evidence for non-linearity. In examining this half of the table, it is worth observing whether the boy/girl differences are consistently in the same direction throughout.

The right-hand part of the table first summarises the social class findings in terms of a broader comparison between middle-class children generally (Classes I & II and III white collar) and working-class children generally (Classes III manual (skilled), IV (semi-skilled) and V (unskilled)). It should be noted that our sample, while randomly drawn with respect to all other variables except the exclusions mentioned, is class-stratified: that is to say, it is weighted to include more of the low-frequency classes than would normally appear in a totally random sample.[5] In the summary table, the data is statistically treated to represent the proportions *which would occur in a fully random sample* (given the original exclusions), so that it now takes into account the fact that, for instance, most of the children in the working class belong to the skilled manual group. Similarly, the percentage figures given in the final column on the right provide a weighted estimate of what the proportions would be in a random cross-section of the overall population (again, given these exclusions).

The middle-class/working-class comparison is also tested for significance, and the result is given at the foot of this section. The overall sex difference is tested on the basis of the difference shown in the 'overall population' column. The summary table is also used to provide evidence of any significant interaction between the two factors of class and sex. If, for instance, a sex difference is in one direction among working-class children but in the other direction or absent in middle-class children, this would be noted as a class/sex interaction of a given significance level (an example appears in Table 23).

Taking the specimen table for comment, we can see that, in the first place, there is a very marked downward trend in the proportions of children who own more than ten books as we move down the social scale. Proportions decrease at every level from 97 per cent of children in the managerial and professional group (Class I & II) to a mere 19 per cent in the unskilled manual group (Class V). There is also some suggestion that the drop is not evenly distributed through the whole scale, the difference between Class III manual and Class IV being much smaller than that between any other two class groups. This slight irregularity in the downward trend is confirmed by the test for non-linearity, which nearly, though not quite, reaches significance level. Except in Class V, sex differences are very small indeed, and their direction is not consistent from one class to the next; the overall sex difference is not significant. From the summary table, we can see a clearly significant difference on this variable between middle-class and working-class groups as a whole: scanning this table (which now minimises the effect of the Class V sex difference, since Class V makes up only 11 per cent of the working class) there is obviously no sex difference between middle class and working class generally, and hence no class × sex interaction effect.

For future reference, it is perhaps worth noticing that in all these tables the size of sample is such that, broadly speaking, a difference between middle class and working class of 10 per cent or more is likely to prove significant; while a difference of the order of 8 per cent between boys and girls overall usually reaches significance.

Indices Every individual question contributes something to our understanding of the child-rearing process; but it is only when several related questions are considered together, and a pattern is seen to emerge from the responses, that the interpretation can be more confidently stated. We may do this simply by juxtaposing responses; a more useful method in some cases is to group different but related questions to provide an accumulation of evidence on a given theme for any given mother/child pair. An index is constructed by assigning scores to responses and summing these to give any individual child an overall score for that index. A potentially useful index is one which gives a reasonable spread of scores across the sample, and for the purposes of comparison it is desirable that the scatter of the scores should be similar. The index is operationally defined in terms of the questions that make it up; the label attached to it is an attempt to sum up this definition. Expressing the child's standing by this single figure allows for a more complex statistical treatment of the data, including the calculation of the degree of association between the various indices.

Indices of this sort, if they can be assumed to be valid as measurements which meaningfully distinguish individuals along a continuum, can be cross-correlated one with another and subjected to other forms of more detailed statistical analysis which are not generally possible on a head-counting or percentage-taking basis. There are, however, a number of problems which tend to arise when moving from the non-parametric domain towards methods where measurements on continua are deemed to be appropriate. First there is the question of deciding upon the rules which should be followed when attempting to put together separate pieces of information in order to arrive at a new dimension. The difficulty here is that there is no infallible and universally applicable set of statistical rules for arriving at forms of measurement which will turn out to be both meaningful and useful in promoting a deeper understanding of the theoretical questions at issue. In particular, we have yet to be convinced that procedures which rely on the selection of a few items from a larger pool on the criterion of maximising internal consistency within the chosen subset have any intrinsic merit. We are, in fact, inclined to the opinion that, in interpreting the answers given to the sorts of questions we are asking, the most prudent course may well be to rely most heavily upon a reasonably direct evaluation of the first-order data: the proportions of mothers whose answers fall into categories which have been defined in everyday common-sense terms. In other words, the further we move from results which are directly and intuitively comprehensible, the less secure we ought to feel about the interpretations we are making.

In practice, therefore, what we have attempted to do in compiling our indices is to put together all those responses which seemed to us, *on the grounds of face validity*, to have some bearing on a more general underlying attitude or characteristic style of behaviour. The only serious technical considerations were that each index should, as far as possible, be based upon answers given to a variety of questions, preferably with a discernibly different specific content, and that each index should have a dispersion or scatter compatible with a score range of approximately ten points. In practice, this also generally resulted in a distribution of scores which was unimodal and approximately symmetrical, which makes it permissible to use conventional statistical methods when comparing means.

A further and related problem with continuous measures established in this way is to choose labels which adequately convey what is being measured. In particular there is a risk of reification: that the giving of a name to a constellation or pattern of answers may artificially establish in the mind of both investigator and reader a conceptual notion of greater salience and definition than is strictly justifiable in terms of the specific questions asked and the way the actual answers were coded. Simply the use of a quantitative scale of assessment is likely to suggest that it is possible, merely through a refinement of technique, to measure an abstract conceptual notion with the same accuracy and precision with which we measure the physical properties of real objects. It is a comfortable and rather dangerous human propensity to impose patterns on perceptions and then to manipulate the patterns as objects in their own right; to press the analogy, the organisation of a constellation of items into a plausible whole is not totally unlike learning to see a particular pattern of stars as a Great Bear or (alternatively!) a Plough.

Thus we invite the reader to scrutinise carefully the questions which any index comprises, together with the way in which they are scored, rather than to rely uncritically on a summarising label. These questions define the dimensions we use.

Other conventions Finally, certain conventions which we have adopted in our reporting need to be restated.

All forenames and surnames used, both of members of the sample and of people to whom they refer, are of course pseudonyms. In the case of the 700 children, a name once ascribed is not used for anyone else in the sample: so that, for instance, 'Vicky' at seven is the same child as 'Vicky' at four and at one. We have found it necessary to duplicate sibs' names, though within families each sib retains its pseudonym through time. We have not thought it necessary to disguise names of places and shops, though we have done so with names of schools.

Occupations of fathers have been given with each quotation. We have not been altogether happy about describing individual women by the possibly diminishing term 'so-and-so's wife'. However, we have continued to do this because it in fact indicates their own status and life-style more economically than any other means available. Where the wife has a relevant or high-status training or job, we have usually mentioned this in addition. We do in fact have information as to the wife's educational level as well as any occupational training she may have received and we shall eventually use this information in conjunction with other data.

Some sharp-eyed readers may notice that certain children's fathers have changed their occupations; in these cases we have given the new occupation (and a new class-affiliation if appropriate). Two fathers are now labelled 'student'; both are mature students, of course, one moving into psychology, the other into teaching. Occasionally a class tag only has been given, where from internal evidence the mother would otherwise be identifiable by friends or relatives.

It goes without saying that nothing has been added to quotations from transcripts; occasionally repetitiousness has been abridged, and in half-a-dozen cases the sentences have been reordered to avoid utter confusion on the reader's part. We have used a five-dot ellipsis (. . . . .) to denote an editorial omission and a three-dot one (. . .) to denote a tailing-off of speech.

The interview schedule which forms the core of the interview is given in full in Appendix I. It should be borne in mind that this schedule has been devised to be used by highly-trained interviewers, and *not* as a straightforward questionnaire. While we do not object to its use in whole or in part by other research workers, we would also suggest that this should not be done without consulting the account of our interviewing method to which we have already referred.[6] In particular, we would explicitly condemn any use of the questions which contribute to our index scores in such a way as to derive such scores out of the context of the whole interview.

NOTES

1 J. H. Robinson, *The Mind in the Making* (London, Cape, 1923).
2 John and Elizabeth Newson, *Seven Years Old in the Home Environment* (London, George Allen & Unwin, 1976).

3 John and Elizabeth Newson, 'Parental roles and social contexts', in M. Shipman (ed.), *The Organisation and Impact of Social Research: Six original case studies in education and behavioural science* (London, Routledge & Kegan Paul, 1976).

4 General Register Office, *Classification of Occupations* (London, HMSO, 1968).

5 A fully random sample of 700 would include 350 in Class III manual and only 56 in Class V; in order to make statements comparing class groups, we need at least 100 in each. To achieve this in a totally random sample, we would have to double our sample size and interview 600 Class III manual mothers unnecessarily.

6 M. Shipman (ed.), 1976, op. cit.

Chapter 1

To Qualify Itself to Live in Society . . .

Now let us ask what are a child's rights, and what are the rights of society over the child. Its rights, being clearly those of any other human being, are summed up in the right to live . . . the right to be what the child likes and can, to do what it likes and can, to think what it likes and can, to smash what it dislikes and can, and generally to behave in an altogether unaccountable manner within the limits imposed by the similar rights of its neighbors. And the rights of society over it clearly extend to requiring it to qualify itself to live in society without wasting other people's time: that is, it must know the rules of the road, be able to read placards and proclamations, fill voting papers, compose and send letters and telegrams, purchase food and clothing and railway tickets for itself, count money and give and take change, and, generally, know how many beans make five. It must know some law, were it only a simple set of commandments, some political economy, agriculture enough to shut the gates of fields with cattle in them and not to trample on growing crops, sanitation enough not to defile its haunts, and religion enough to have some idea of why it is allowed its rights and why it must respect the rights of others. And the rest of its education must consist of anything else it can pick up; for beyond this society cannot go with any certainty, and indeed can only go this far rather apologetically and provisionally, as doing the best it can on very uncertain ground.

George Bernard Shaw, Preface to *Misalliance*

It is a duty required of parents of seven-year-old children that they submit their child to some recognised process of education; and it is generally considered both convenient and beneficial to the child that education should take place within schools – indeed, for fairly good historical reasons, it is made very difficult for parents to opt out of the school-based educational system.[1] In the companion volume to this, in which we focused on the seven-year-old's home environment,[2] we acknowledged that seminal statement of Ruth Benedict's: 'No man ever looks at the world with pristine eyes: he sees it *edited* by a definite set of customs and institutions and ways of thinking';[3] and we added that, if home is the medium through which the child acquires his first understanding of the world, the second edition is the school's. The school has often been compared with the family (in a thousand speech-day addresses!); and others have suggested its function as a microcosm of society. We would not be happy with either of these descriptions; but this much is true, that school does in fact serve as a link between the kinds of demands (and immunities) which are characteristic of family life and those which the child will discover in the wider society of adulthood. The primary school years in particular coincide with children's emotional and conceptual growth away from egocentricity and towards a more socially-oriented understanding; to reiterate, 'school is the context which crystallises the child's transformation into a social creature, which formalises his experience of the peer group and of outside adult authority, and which presents a new set of demands which may be totally alien to the expectations of home but which are too powerful for the child to reject altogether'. During these years, he may hardly be aware of whether there is indeed an alienation between school and home; yet such disjunction, however dimly perceived by him, can eventually become a major factor, whether constructive or destructive, in shaping his long-term purpose. How the child negotiates and achieves an adjustment to school life can hardly be usefully considered, then, without reference to the family life which both precedes and parallels it, and which will inevitably serve as a backcloth for his own perception of his approaching adult roles.

In the present study, we are concerned in particular with how children respond to ordinary educational provision as represented by local authority primary schools. The children of our sample all live (or lived when they first joined the sample) within the area administered by the then City of Nottingham Education Authority; only 2 per cent of them at age seven were attending private schools. Had we included some of the predominantly middle-class commuter villages falling within a wider radius, the percentage might have been slightly higher; but even taking Class I and II on their own, the proportion in private education only reaches 12 per cent.

Thus the basic facts of the situation are that children not only have to go to school but do not have much effective choice as to which school they attend; most of these children are in fact attending the primary school nearest to where they live. This being so, are they personally frustrated by these constraints? How happy are seven-year-olds at school?

We asked the children's mothers: 'We should like to know something now about how N gets on at school – does he *like* school?'; and this was the first of about fifty questions exploring the child's educational experience. Later on we shall look at the positive and negative factors which go to make up this experience; for the moment a more general view will serve for orientation. Overall, children seem to present their mothers with an impression of happiness: 55 per cent liked school 'very much' and 32 per cent 'well enough'. Ten per cent were negative on balance ('not much'), and 3 per cent 'strongly disliked' school.

'Very much'

Doctor's wife:
> Now that she is at school, she doesn't want to be home so much – she *adores* school, you see, absolutely.

Miner's wife:
> He'd rather be at school, rather than be at home. I think he occupies his mind more when he's at school, there's more to do at school.

Maintenance man's wife:
> He loves it. He tends to be a bit sulky when it's weekend time, you know. Saturday morning he'll get up full of bounce for school, and when you tell him it's Saturday – down in the dumps he goes, and starts throwing his weight about.

'Well enough'

Miner's wife:
> He doesn't dislike it, he likes it because he can do things, constructive things. Um – his reading and his writing – his teacher has got him into it, and he's progressing, I think, and he doesn't dislike . . . he's not madly keen, but he doesn't object to going.

Loco fireman's wife:
> He does like it, although like most children if he has the day off

he's delighted. I think really he enjoys it *once he's got there,* you know – when he first gets up in the morning, if he's got a bit of a cold he'd try and exaggerate it; but once he's sort of got ready, he's quite happy to go.

'Not much'

Sales representative's wife:
> She *tolerates* it – because she knows she has to go. She never fakes illness or makes out she doesn't want to go, she gets up and she says p'raps on a Monday, 'Oh, back to school again!' She knows she's got to go, and she knows if she plays up she's still got to go.

Mechanic's wife:
> He's not a lover of school, and he doesn't like doing his work – he's all moaning! – if his teacher makes him work extra hard, he'll come home and moan about it. He's not very thrilled about work, he just likes school because he likes the friends that are there.

Miner's wife:
> She sees no need why she should have to go to school weather like this [sunny and warm]. She doesn't mind going when it's raining.

'Strongly dislikes'

Lorry driver's wife:
> I've had a job with him, ooh I have. The first week, ooh . . . he ran off at dinnertime – I had to run him round that block there – oh and he cried! It upset me, I cried as well, I had to *drag* him to school; but I said to him, 'Well, you've *got* to, everybody else has to go.' Same as I say, he says he doesn't like it but he knows he's got to go. [How long did you have to drag him to school?] About a fortnight – oh, it upset me awful – cause I thought, well, he's got to go, I've got to take him whether he wants to go or not. But it doesn't matter who asks him if he likes school, he always says no.

Company director's wife:
> He's terrified of school. He's frightened to death of school. I think this is because he can't apply his mind to the subjects, and he goes to a state school where there's no individualistic teaching either – which is all to the good, I'm not against it, I'm very *for* it, because I think he must learn to mix with others; but he's frightened, you

see, that they can do it and he can't. He can't apply his mind to it, and that's his fear.

Combining the two groups of children with negative feelings towards school, and comparing them with those who like school 'very much', we can look at how these feelings are linked with the child's sex and social class. Table 1 shows this breakdown.

The table shows a consistent difference between boys and girls from class to class: girls are less likely to dislike school. Why this should be may be a fairly complex question: some of the sex differences which we discussed in relation to the child's home environment[4] seem relevant. For instance, boys were more likely than girls to be rated by their mothers as 'difficult to manage', which might link with their finding the demands of school unacceptable; girls were rather more likely to prefer indoor activities; boys were more likely to be 'wanderers', which might mean that they would chafe at being

Table 1   Children's liking for school

	social class					summary		
		III				I&II+	IIIman	overall
	I&II	IIIwc	man	IV	V	IIIwc	IV, V	popn.
	%	%	%	%	%	%	%	%
Likes very much								
boys	57	47	43	49	63	52	46	48
girls	75	55	61	59	64	66	61	62
both	66	51	52	54	64	59	54	55

Significance: trend U-shaped   **   m.class/w.class   n.s.
                                    between sexes   ****

Doesn't much like or strongly dislikes								
boys	10	14	17	10	11	12	15	14
girls	2	10	16	0	5	6	14	11
both	6	12	17	10	8	9	14	13

Significance: nil

confined to school; and boys were also markedly less accustomed (whether by their choice or their mothers') to being kept under adult surveillance. If boys normally spend more of their time 'out and about' than girls, away from both home and school control, the classroom-based world of school may more easily seem irksome: as Alex's mother says, 'he likes holidays – he likes to be outside; he says he's inside too much at school'.

Social class differences are less striking and rather more difficult to interpret: it appears that children at both extremes of the social scale are more inclined to like school than are children in the middle. It is commonly argued that because schools employ teachers whose values are naturally mainly those of their own class (i.e. middle class), school must appeal most to children whose parents hold similar values. This analysis suggests that it is equally popular, at this age at least, with children whose home environment is also most likely to be 'deprived' – and perhaps this is the answer to the question of why they should find school inviting even though alien in its values.

But just what is the school environment? In terms of hardware, in Nottingham it is (and was still more at the time of the interviewing) extremely varied. Despite an active building programme, a good many nineteenth-century school buildings are still in use:[5] built to last in the kinds of tile and brick and stone that make no concession to physical or visual comfort, their corridors and stairways seem mainly designed to resist any mark of the shoulder-rubbing, shoe-scuffing children they contain, yet give the impression of a permanent disinfected grubbiness. That they have stairways at all is, of course, characteristic of their date; later primary schools are single-storey and hence better scaled to the age group they serve (the teachers who have to contend with marshalling hordes of excited, short-legged children safely up and down stone stairs at playtime would add, better scaled to them, too). The classrooms are large and high-ceilinged, which means that there tends to be an expanse of upper wall unreached by the teacher's drawing-pins and sticky tape: the rooms would seem lighter were it not for this oppressive off-cream lid. The windows are usually large; but, built as they were for children whose eyes were supposed to be fixed on teacher, blackboard or copybook, they are not intended to be looked out of: with only a view of the sky, the outside world is not available to be commented on, until the first snowflakes of winter set off a glad shout of

> *Ally ally ăsta*
> *Snow, snow făster!*

Between-the-wars school buildings make more concession to the idea that the classroom can safely be opened up; often the rooms open from a windowed corridor on one side and, perhaps via folding glazed doors or french windows, on to the school garden on the other. Although these buildings are much less forbidding in scale than the older ones, they also have a certain inflexibility and lack of imagination: the purpose intended for each room by the architect is obvious, and it is difficult for schools to change things around to suit their own changing needs, though some of them make valiant attempts to metamorphose (for instance) a cloakroom into a cosy 'quiet room'. For many of these schools, as with older ones, playground space has dwindled as portable classrooms were installed during the period of rising numbers on the roll.

The schools built in the last ten years have a much warmer feel to them, partly because of the use of natural wood finishes and brighter colours. They are compactly built, yet have a feeling of space engendered by the 'open plan' type of design which tends to be a major influence, even where classrooms have doors. Often two classes will share a utility area, which gives much more sense of free movement about the school. Imaginative touches abound in the structure itself: a tiny courtyard with pool or fountain, sloping planes as well as horizontal and vertical ones, decorative surfaces which are interesting to feel as well as to look at. One thing that recurs in open plan schools is the use teachers make of spaces which were intended by the architects to be unimpeded: there is a strong tendency to use the furniture as walls and barriers, and to create enclosed areas in which small groups can make themselves comfortable and flitting children can be better contained.[6] One also has the impression (which it would be interesting to substantiate by controlled observation) that in the newer design of school the teacher is more on the move within the class area; for one thing, the children following their various pursuits are no longer all visible from the vantage-point of the teacher's desk, so that she is likely to abandon that erstwhile commanding position and to blend democratically into the many busy groups all over the working space.

Those schools which are housed in new buildings are also likely to have better equipment and more of it, because of the way equipment funds are allocated; in general, they would appear to offer the ideal environment for a seven-year-old's education. It is interesting, then, that these are not necessarily considered the most desirable schools by middle-class parents. The four schools whose grapevine reputation (largely based upon eleven-plus successes) was high enough for parents deliberately to look for houses in their catchment areas were all in pre-war or earlier buildings; and this was also true of private preparatory schools in Nottingham.

'It's supposed to be this new education . . .'
When we asked mothers directly whether they were pleased with the schools their children were attending, in terms of whether it suited the child's personal needs, the low priority which they gave to material environment – buildings and equipment – was very apparent. These were indeed hardly ever mentioned except incidentally to some other comment, usually about teachers, size or composition of classes, or teaching methods.

The question was in a sense a summing-up opportunity, since it came towards the end of a detailed discussion of the child's reactions and adjustment to school: thus a mother could pronounce herself in general very pleased with the school even though she might already have told us about a number of difficulties that had arisen on specific points. The fact that a massive majority of mothers are happy with the school their seven-year-old attends, and think it suits him personally, does not mean, then, that everything has been plain sailing for them.

Eighty-two per cent were very satisfied with the school; 11 per cent had reservations ('Well, it suits him but it doesn't suit me'); and only 7 per cent were strongly dissatisfied. No significant class or sex differences were found. Teaching methods or the general organisation of teaching attracted more criticism than any other feature of school, usually focused on the mother's anxiety about her child's reading skills or lack of them. Later on we shall be looking in more detail both at the way parents attempt to help the child (or wonder how to), and at the home factors associated with reading achievement. At this stage, we will merely quote, as a taster, two of the mothers who were concerned about the way the school approached the teaching of the basic skills.

Machinist's wife:
No, it doesn't suit him yet. He's only just really started to read. This is a thing against this school. I've had trouble with all of mine. When they first started school they was interested, they *wanted* to do it; but they hadn't got the time with them at school, and they gave them things to play with. But the last year in the infant school they seem to cram it all in at once; and they seem to stand their ground and they won't take it. We had the same trouble with John and the same trouble with Michael, and it's like starting from scratch when they get to the juniors. [You feel he was ready to read

at five, but they didn't do it?] I feel he was ready to, and I told Miss Williams this, and I explained to her that I thought they should start a little earlier in the infants – perhaps a term earlier, even – to start them reading, because it's not fair to expect them to take it all in like that. This last term seems to be *all* more or less reading – well, they've gone so wild for such a long time, you know, they seem to just stand their ground and they won't take it. You know, they *couldn't* have it when they wanted it, and now it's being crammed in, they just won't do it. I've found it with all three.

Labourer's wife:

Well, I don't think they learn them very much. The new scheme they've got up there – where they play and learn to do it with play, you know – the teacher thinks he'll benefit from it, but I don't think that they get anywhere. I mean I did know my ABC when I was seven, but he can't get his ABC at all; and it makes me wonder sometimes if it *is* a good scheme, and I think I'm a bit disgusted to think he can't say his ABC like that, you know.

Overcrowding was a lesser worry, but one which was also often attached to under-achievement in reading; sometimes this was coupled with a complaint about the number of immigrant children, who were identified by parents as a group demanding a disproportionate amount of the teacher's time.

Civil engineer's wife:

Well, I think really – she is sort of shy and quiet, and I think she really could do with that little bit of individual attention. The classes are so big, you know. On the whole I think she's quite happy.

Ashman's wife:

She doesn't read very well. It's the school itself though, it's not just Rosie. My sister, her little boy, he's been reading now, oh, about a year, and he's six months younger than Rosie; he's up at E—, and they've learned a new method. Well, it puts you to shame. He can pick the newspaper up and read it, he can read anything that's on the television, and big words, not just little words, you know. But it's the method he learned with there. But when we go and complain – there's that many coloured children; and they've got to learn the coloured children first – hygiene, what they should learn at home. Cause some of us have been down to the school, you know; and there's that many in the class as well. I mean, I think Rosie's behind for her age but it isn't just Rosie, she's not on her own, you see.

Tobacco worker's wife:
Mainly the overcrowding. I can't really blame the teacher – although last year she was on the top table for reading, but this year her teacher says she's average. I think she's dropped down, you see. [Do you feel that is because of the overcrowding?] I do – you see there's a lot of coloured children, and they take up more time, don't they? I can't really blame the teacher.

Surprisingly little blame was attached to individual teachers. Unsatisfactory teaching methods were more likely to be seen as a reflection of 'this new education' than as stemming from a teacher's personal incompetence.

Policeman's wife:
Well this is always a great thing with me, I'm always up in arms about reading at school, because I don't think they do enough. He's third in the class for reading, but they don't do enough reading so that they can transfer what they read at school into reading a book at home, you know; he was on one reading book, and he'd been on it for months. Anyway, I had to go into school to see Mrs Barker, so I mentioned to her about this reading; I said that he was bored, and that I didn't think he was doing enough, that he wasn't making any progress at all, you know. So she listened, and she explained to me how different they teach and all this, that and the other . . . This school suits him, but it doesn't suit me, I would say; but this is the modern method, and every school's the same, and they don't vary much in the first two years.

Complaints directed against the individual teacher were more often in terms of unkindness or favouritism.

Lorry driver's wife:
This child that goes with Sharon, she's very dirty as I've told you, and Mrs W, she's always saying to this child, 'Go away from me you smell' – which I think is a terrible thing. The child can't help it if it's dirty. I'm not saying the teachers aren't good, but they seem to be all for the people who've got cars. It's true, I mean the people on this street all say the same thing. If you've got quite a few children they'll look down on you, but if you're dolled up to the eyes you can have anything, the child can do anything. It's

surprising, but no matter where you go, money talks all the time – if you've got nothing they're not interested. [Do you feel they teach the children differently?] Yes, I do, definitely. If your face fits you're all right, but if it don't, you know, they can't be bothered. [Is it just Mrs W who's like that, or do you feel that about all of them?] Well, I think it's just Mrs W – well, Mrs W and one or two more, but the majority I would say are all right. Mrs C, her other teacher, she's an entirely different person to this one, she'd always go and sort things out with her; but Mrs W – 'I haven't got time' – 'I'm too busy, go away'.

Storekeeper's wife:
This teacher's inclined to have favourites, and I'm afraid the children know it, and Kirsty complains a little. All her favourites have long hair. I think this is very wrong. I can't wait for her to leave this school myself.

Cranedriver's wife:
[Does he seem to get on well with his teacher?] Well, just the usual. She's a horrible old teacher anyway – I think so. He got a slap one day off her. She's got a cane as well, and she *does* slap them across the face. I said, 'Did you get slapped?' and he said 'Yes, but not across the face'. Well, *I* wouldn't fancy being slapped across the face, would you? Poor little kids.

The last quotation is exceptional not just for the unpleasant picture it presents of the teacher, but for the mother's very low expectations in the first place: that a mother should evaluate a fear relationship like this one as 'just the usual' is very unusual indeed. It was notable, in fact, both how appreciative parents were of their child's happy relationship with his teacher (even though they accepted that it could have its ups and downs like other happy relationships), and how normal they also felt this to be.

Sales representative's wife:
They don't seem to complain a lot about what happens at school. I think they have a pretty easy time now at school, and everything is made so nice. I mean this school, Miss Nestor, she's very nice and very friendly and she does things for the children, and they love it.

Newsagent's wife:
Sometimes he loves her very much, sometimes he's disenchanted; I think it's quite a normal situation, he doesn't dislike her at all.

Grocer's wife:
> Perhaps for a few days before she saw what the new teacher was going to be like [on changing classes], she wondered. She *couldn't* be as nice as the old one! – but she was agreeably surprised to find that there was more than one nice person.

Self-employed craftsman's wife:
> He still has quite a hankering for the lady who taught him in the babies' class. If I say to him 'Do you like your new teacher?' – 'Oh yes, Mum, she's very nice'. 'Well', I say, 'Mrs James that you've just left was excellent'. 'I know', he says, 'but I really do like Mrs Tyndale better than anybody' – and he still has got quite a little, almost a little *love* feeling for Mrs Tyndale; she's motherly; Mrs Tyndale's still his favourite.

Postman's wife:
> He loves her, and she is leaving today. He says he's going on strike on Monday.

'I sometimes wonder if she realises the extent of her influence . . .'
The whole discussion of the child's adjustment to school was dominated by the figure of the teacher; and it is clear that, whatever criteria may be used to evaluate the success or otherwise of a school, when we come down to the individual child and whether he is happy there, the teacher and how she handles her relationship with him (both individually and as a member of the group) remains the crucial factor. At the primary school stage, liking school depends upon liking the teacher.

This is true partly because of the child's age and partly because of the way the teaching is organised. Most children starting infant school at five are, as we saw in our study of four-year-olds, rather unused to spending long periods of time being cared for by adults outside their family; nursery experience is still the exception rather than the rule, and the pre-school playgroup movement, which grew rapidly during the primary school years of our sample, does not offer in scale any approximation to the long school day. Thus the child on entry to school is likely to look for certain mothering qualities in his teacher, and to show towards her something of the emotional dependence that he is used to showing to his mother. It is the infant teacher's role to meet this dependence halfway and to encourage him gradually beyond it, by offering him independence within a relatively protected context.

She is enabled to do this by a system which tends to place one teacher in sole charge of her class for most of the school day and for a full year at a time. This is basically true for primary schools generally, not just for infant schools. Obviously there are variations in degree: for instance, in an open plan school, two teachers may share responsibility for two groups; or, at the other end of the scale, one teacher may retain her class for two, three or more years, 'moving up' with them. Vertically streamed classes are another variation which tends to lead to more prolonged contact with one teacher; while crises in teacher supply can result in rapid changes of teacher, or in a class being taken by two part-timers. None the less, from the child's point of view perhaps the major difference between the teaching at primary school and that at secondary level is that he moves from an almost full-time relationship with 'his' teacher to the much more diversified experience of separate subject teachers. Inevitably, the influence of the teacher in the primary school is much more pervasive and powerful; it is also much less escapable if the child and teacher come to be at loggerheads. A teacher he likes can bring out the sun on a child's whole school life; an uncongenial teacher can turn it sour. Where a secondary school child may want to stay away on Wednesday because of the RI teacher, the primary school child is turned against school itself.

Businessman's wife (herself a primary teacher):
He reacts to the teacher in how he likes school. The teacher before this thought the world of Oliver, and Oliver thought the world of her. Now this teacher he finds an anticlimax. There are many things he doesn't care for. I've known him not want to *go* to school with this one.

Instructor's wife:
He liked it very very much at first; but since he's been in this class, this last six months, he's been more troublesome over school than he has been . . . . . I don't know quite what happens here, I think he feels that she ignores him a little; it always comes up, this – he says she's not interested, and I think she *must* be, but of course you can't . . . I think probably before, the teacher, you know, took more notice of them as individuals . . . . . Well, of course, they have to do work, she can't be all nice all the time, can she? I mean she's got to treat them as a class, and I do feel that he doesn't like her when she tells him off you know.

Administrator's wife:
We had trouble for six months last year and this set him back.

This was at the beginning of the school year – six months – got to the stage when you were having to *take* him to school, and he didn't want to go; and he was screaming, you know, he didn't like the teacher. And then she left, and it's not just Sean, it's the whole class – it put the whole class back, so that this year the teacher has eighteen month's teaching to do in twelve months.

University teacher's wife:
She said a very revealing thing the other day, she said 'How nice it is to have a teacher that isn't always cross'. She used to be nervous in case her teacher lost her temper.

Lorry driver's wife:
I say, er, 'Well, she's p'raps busy, you know, she's a lot of children to see besides you'. But, you know, she'll say 'I don't *like* her'. And I'll say 'Oh, she's not as bad as you think she is'. But of course children don't . . . they either like a person or they don't, don't they, and that's it.

Table 2   *Children who 'get on very well' with their teacher*

	social class					summary		
		III				I&II+	IIIman	overall
	I&II	IIIwc	man	IV	V	IIIwc	IV, V	popn.
	%	%	%	%	%	%	%	%
boys	81	81	76	78	89	81	78	79
girls	97	84	83	87	97	91	85	87
both	89	82	80	82	93	86	82	83

Significance: trend U-shaped   ***   m.class/w.class   n.s.
                                between sexes   ****

Looking at the answers given to the question 'Does he seem to get on well with his teacher?' (Table 2), a very similar pattern emerges to that shown in Table 1, 'Does he like school?' Again, although the great majority (83 per cent) got on well with their teacher at this age, there is a U-shaped distribution by social class: the professional and unskilled class children are most likely to get on with their teacher and girls more likely to do so than boys. Only 3 per cent definitely get on very badly with their teacher, the 14 per cent in the middle categories giving 'not particularly', 'so-so' responses. Looking at this another way, nearly a quarter of working-class boys don't get on very well with their teacher, a quite sizeable group; whereas less than a tenth of middle-class girls have this problem.

In discussing the child's relationship with his teacher, we also asked about his reaction to change of teacher during the previous year; and mothers often spontaneously traced the child's reaction to different teachers through time. Here again we found a picture of the younger school child responding in an emotionally dependent way to his teacher, often forming an intense attachment which included a wish to remain physically close to her, to monopolise her attention and to take her little gifts or 'things to show' which bore witness to a tie which stretched beyond the school gates. Some parents found themselves being absent-mindedly addressed as 'Miss So-and-so' by a preoccupied child! Although the child is becoming more independent at seven, much of this emotional investment remains: these mothers were under no illusion that they were the only women in their children's lives:

Motor mechanic's wife:
Everything's for Miss Briggs – we have to take flowers for Miss Briggs, this, that and the other for Miss Briggs. She'll come home and say, 'Now, what can I take?' I say, 'Take me!' [laughed] *Everything* is for Miss Briggs.

Metal polisher's wife:
If you let him, he'd take the house and the lot and give it to his teacher!

Student psychologist's wife:
Oh my word, she's absolutely gospel, it's sickening! He comes home and makes statements she's made. Of course, *she's right*, and in fact if we think or say or suggest anything different, we – oh dear – we're terribly criticised. He thinks we're foolish. He accepts every word that comes out of her mouth. I sometimes wonder if she realises the extent of her influence.

University teacher's wife:
The teacher's infallible. It's very irritating to find that something which *we* have told him, he'll come back and deliver as something quite new which he's been told by the teacher.

Executive's wife:
He's very fond of his teacher – in love with her, I think. She's

lovely, and he's lucky with her [a difficult child]. The headmistress says he's lucky that his personality complements the teacher's; but the teacher says on the quiet that she's got a soft spot for him. I can tell she's very fond of him; but I don't know what he'll do in the Juniors.

Where such a strong attachment has been formed, the separation involved in moving up to a new class can indeed be quite traumatic; and this was a common cause of apprehension, in both mother and child, and a frequent source of actual unhappiness.

Caretaker's wife:
> It did upset him rather, because he'd had the same one for almost two years, and she was very understanding. I think it was rather a big uprooting – it was p'raps for the good of Ivan really – it's all right now, you know – but it did upset him.

Hosiery trimmer's wife:
> It took a long while for him to get used to her. The teacher previous to her, Mrs Gresham, she had a child of her own and probably that's what made the difference, but he really idolised that teacher. Well he doesn't like change, as I've said, and it's taking him a long while to get used to her, this teacher; since we had a little talk at his Open Day, I think he's got on better with her. Not that he disliked her, but she was a stranger again, you see.

Political worker's wife:
> It did upset her in September, because, er . . . unfortunately she was the teacher's pet, and she didn't want to leave that class; because this particular teacher kept saying 'Why don't you come and live with me?' – and Nanda thought this was wonderful, and this was one of the arguments I had, because she'd say 'I'll go and live with Mrs Bunting'. She wasn't *terribly* upset, but I felt she was in for a comedown when she went into this new class; because every teacher has a different opinion of what a nice child is, and she wasn't going to fit into the pattern of two of them.

Not all children form a bond with the teacher in such an emotionally charged way. Some are naturally reserved; some show shyness and withdrawal; others will try to 'keep a low profile' and get lost in the crowd. Some already seem to have absorbed a 'them and us' ethic about the teacher–pupil relationship, and make a point of not admitting to a detente even though they do not seem actively harassed.

Cycle assembler's wife (herself a 'dinner-lady'):
I'd say, 'How do you like your new teacher, Philip?' – and he'd say 'She's terrible'. 'Why?' – I'd say – cause I know she's a very nice teacher, you see; and two days after, I'd say 'How do you like your teacher now?' He says 'She's getting worser'. But I think he does like her; from what he tells me about, he likes her, you see, he just wants to *make out* he don't. She is a very nice teacher – cause I've met her, you see. It's just his way. I don't think he likes you to think he's being sloppy, sort of thing.

Prison officer's wife:
She's never any objection to going, and I think she really likes it but if you said to her 'Do you like school, Lisa?' she'll say 'No, I hate it!' That's what she would *say*. But really she's quite happy there, I know it.

A new reception class of infants, each one of whom has lived five years in the world, arrives at school not as a homogeneous mass of raw teaching material, but as a loosely bonded group of individual personalities, each shaped by a unique set of previous experiences, social and intellectual. Inevitably they will vary rather widely in what they need from the teacher during the first two or three years in primary school. Some children love to be mothered; others complain of the teacher 'babying' them in a way that hurts their pride – as Tony's mother said, 'she pampers them, you know, she speaks to them *down* as children. Well, Tony don't like to be that, he's your equal, and me and Grandma we talk to him like we talk to a grownup man, you know; but this teacher is a children's teacher, and Tony is resenting it, he don't like to be treated like that at school'. Some children expect to be warmly praised for every little thing they do; others thrive on being allowed to use their own initiative and take responsibility, and like the teacher to bring a genuine critical appreciation to their efforts rather than smother them with absent-minded approval. The shy child will want a teacher who can encourage him to be more self-confident within a framework which also makes allowance for his shyness; the rumbustious child may welcome most a teacher who can channel his energies into constructive and useful pathways without becoming upset and irritable. The child who is slow will respond to a teacher who can help him understand without making him appear stupid; the child with a quick, inquiring mind will appreciate someone who takes the trouble to find meaningful answers to his many questions, who can provide accurate and up-to-date information herself, and who is not threatened by his excursions beyond the limits of her own knowledge.

Some children will need pushing in order to get the best out of them: Wyn's mother, for instance, felt that her daughter had 'wanted someone stern' – there had been 'a lot of trouble' because Wyn thought she 'could rule the teacher', and the child had been moved to a different class with a stricter teacher and 'got on a lot better'; the school was not felt to suit her very well. Other children resent anything they see as pressurisation. We had many examples of children digging in their heels with real determination against certain demands such as being made to change for PE, joining in a dancing lesson or using messy materials like paint or clay: Ross, for example, sat at his desk for three months and refused to move away from it. Characteristically, resistance is passive; we had very few examples of children running away from school once they were actually there.

It is clear, then, that children do vary rather widely in what they need from the teacher during the first two or three years in primary school; some mothers in fact drew attention to this from their own experience with successive children in the same school, in that the style of a particular named teacher had suited one of their children but not another. The ideal qualities for the primary teacher are perhaps flexibility, sensitivity and responsiveness: an ability to be different things to different children according to their personalities. She must be prepared to get to know all her children as individuals; she must bring a fine judgement to the analysis of their idiosyncratic needs; and she must have the capacity to respond in such a way as to meet these differing needs, and yet to maintain an appearance of fairness to the class as a whole.

It would hardly be realistic to expect every teacher to be successful at all times in maintaining such a demanding role, and few teachers would claim this. Teachers differ in their talents and predilections, as well as in their training and experience. Inevitably the personalities of individual children will sometimes fail to harmonise with the personality of a particular teacher, even though she may try very hard to be equally sympathetic to all her pupils. Again, there are differences in the extent to which teachers approve of 'meeting children halfway', because they may find it difficult to handle this without laying themselves open to the charge of favouritism. They know very well that they do not naturally get on equally happily with every child. They can also feel insecure in their relationships with fellow-teachers, and they are no more immune than the rest of us from stresses and strains to contend with in their private lives. It is only to be expected that teachers will function better at some times than at others, that some teachers will be noticeably better than others generally, and that certain teachers will offer a much better 'fit' to the needs of certain children; as Nanda's mother has pointed out, 'every teacher has a different opinion of what a nice child is'.

In practice, what tends to happen is that the infant school allows for an initial 'honeymoon' period during which individual eccentricities or immaturities will be taken into account and dealt with tolerantly. Sooner or later, however, the child has to learn that life at school, because it is the life of a larger community than the family, is subject to manifold organisational restrictions; he discovers that, as a properly conforming member of that community he must put up with certain constraints upon his own individual freedom for the benefit of the group as a whole. This concept is, of course, not new to him: he has normally learned within the family organisation to eat when he is not necessarily hungry because it is 'dinner-time', or say 'thank you' or 'sorry' to neighbours when he is neither grateful nor contrite, for the sake of his family's good name. But because the child is a much smaller cog in the school organisational machine than he is in relation to the family, and because the school is very much less closely geared to his individuality, the message that he will have to accept group rules before he is entitled to group rewards is a very powerful and convincing one.

A number of different factors contribute to the process of adaptation and settling-in. One, of course, is the child's own personality; and we distinguished in our preceding study of these children a group who tended to be negativistic and difficult, and to meet life with suspicion, claws out.[7] We also saw that a few of those same children had been lucky enough to meet up with a congenial teacher who knew how to deflect the claws and engage the child's interest and loyalty, so that he was transformed to 'a different personality at school'. The majority of children seem to find a good-enough fit between their own needs and what the school offers, so that socialisation into the school community runs an acceptably smooth course with reasonably good will on the part of mother and teacher to straighten out minor snags; for these children, the acquisition of new rules of behaviour is relatively painless and imperceptible. The process becomes painfully clarified by more-or-less accidental factors, when the child has to cope with a really unsympathetic teacher or when he has to adjust and readjust to a series of teachers in a short space of time. It is at this point, when school is no longer seen as a colourful world of rich opportunities in which he is allowed to participate, but as a succession of frightening demands which he would like to escape but may not, that for some unfortunate children the *compulsory* nature of group socialisation is spelled out. For these children, assimilation into the school ethos happens more in terms of resignation to the inevitable than through joyful acceptance of a well-adapted rule-structure. *All* children, however, as they grow older, will experience a decreasing tolerance for their fads and fancies, an increasing pressure to meet group norms and an acceptance which becomes more and more conditional on their behaviour.

'School's not the same as home, when all's said and done . . .'
The teacher, then, as well as being the key figure in the child's introduction to formal learning, also mediates his experience of the school world in which that process of learning takes place; and the school itself serves (for most children) as the earliest model of the complicated patterns of behaviour and social interaction which evolve in the institutional or organisational settings that will continue to be important to a greater or lesser extent as the child grows up – later models to include more advanced varieties of school or college, hospitals, work environments, leisure-time and voluntary organisations, armed services, prisons and so on. It is part of the teacher's role not only to identify herself with the school, but to cause the child to do so too, usually via the transitional stage of himself identifying with her. If the child's relationship is only with the teacher and not with the school beyond her, she has failed to wean him from the purely personal bond of which the mother was the first model. Eventually the child must familiarise himself with the corporate entity of the school, come to feel that he belongs to it and it to him, and learn in his turn to initiate younger children into its customs and values. In becoming socialised in the school as social institution, children are carried onward by repeatedly experiencing the rhythms and rituals of the school day and the school week, as well as by innumerable encounters with other people who themselves have a known place in the pattern: children from their own class and their own year, children from the 'babies' class' or the 'top class', in-between children who are not 'the big ones' but yet are bigger than themselves, teachers who are soft and motherly from looking after the little ones, teachers who are bright and brisk from keeping nine-year-olds in order, the head and the deputy head, the school secretary, the dinner-ladies and the caretaker. Through such encounters, in which he may be either participant or observing bystander, the child begins to appraise his own position within the hierarchical age-graded structure of the school as a whole.

Probably no one person has full knowledge of all the customs, beliefs and practices which make up the social organisation of a single primary school. In our daughters' school, for instance, it was only the lower junior girls who knew about the Green Lady behind the cupboard in the hall, and how she needed to be propitiated; and no doubt any group one could identify, among children and staff alike, would be found to have its own beliefs which contribute to the total social edifice. But even understandings which have the status of 'common knowledge' must be acquired gradually over time by any given child, by piecing together a thousand scraps of experience. In this way, children get used to the idea that they are destined to move up into new classes and have different teachers. By witnessing small acts of deference, they sense that their own class teacher is considered less important than the headteacher. They may hear comments about Miss A, who talks in a loud voice and is very strict; and about Mr B, who talks in a still louder voice but is soft as butter to his own class. They learn that in the Juniors you do hard sums; in the Juniors the boys play proper football; when you go up to the Juniors, you'll have to try harder than *this*, you know. In the playground they notice who does the pushing around and who gets pushed; who always has a bosom friend or two and who has none; who are the rough and noisy ones and always get told off. They are told that when you talk to Jesus you must shut your eyes, and when you go to the toilet you must shut the door. They discover that one of the dinner-ladies is another child's Mam and that the oldest of the teachers taught Billy's Daddy when *he* was in Class 4. They learn that telling tales isn't approved of, but that there are ways of laying a complaint if you choose your words carefully. They begin to distinguish between events that are routine and normal and those which are exciting or worrying because they are unusual. And through repeated observation and personal involvement, they discover the values to which teachers and pupils subscribe in the world of school: what is regarded as especially clever or especially praiseworthy; what is considered babyish or 'mardy'; where teacher–pupil values overlap, and where they separate or contradict each other (as in 'who-can-pee-highest-up-the-wall', an ability much prized by little boys but notably under-valued by teachers and dinner-ladies).

From all these diverse sources of information, then, children gradually absorb a rather different set of standards from those which have come to govern their behaviour in the intimate family environment. Because the seven-year-old is an extremely social animal, the child approaching this age will be very responsive to a philosophy of 'This is the way we all do it, so this is how it has to be'. Schools are thus enabled to guide and mould the behaviour of their children in hundreds of different and subtle ways, often without resort to any coercion other than the social pressure which is implicit in the example of the majority being willing to conform to group expectations. The compelling difference between home socialisation and socialisation to the school lies in *the degree of tolerance accorded to egocentricity*. At school, egocentricity must fairly quickly accept subordination to group needs. Obviously the pre-school child *is* developmentally more egocentric than the primary school child; but it is not just a question of age. Obviously, too, parents subscribe in general terms to the idea that one child cannot be allowed to dominate the whole group; it is their own conscious endeavour that one member of the family should not ride roughshod over the others. None the less, children of any age, including adolescents, do dominate their families egocentrically for brief or longer periods according to their special problems or needs or preoccupations of the moment; and it is perhaps the family's special function to put up with such episodes of domination because they are necessary to the child's development at the time and because no other institution in society will tolerate them.

In fact, although children of seven still respond to their teachers in a highly personal way, it is a mistake to suppose that the relationship between teacher and pupil is at all similar to that between parent and child. The teacher's role, however democratic or benign he or she may be, is deliberately formalised; and in the school environment all sorts of social forces are in operation to constrain the behaviour of both adults and children. Teachers themselves naturally assume – and are indeed accorded – a respect proper to their status within the institution, which is quite different from that which parents would nowadays expect from their own offspring at home. Related to this is another consideration: that teachers behave, and are expected by parents to behave, according to a code of professional conduct. Thus they must set limits to their emotional involvement with individual children, and they must attempt to be reasonably neutral and impartial on all sorts of religious, political, social and even quasi-moral issues, notwithstanding their own personal views. Basically, this is because they are not supposed to risk giving offence to individual parents when values inevitably vary between the families of all the different children whom they teach. Parents, by contrast, are expected to pass on their own personal convictions, values and attitudes to their own children as a matter of principle: the parents of the 'Spock-marked generation' are widely criticised because (it is said) they assumed that respecting the child's opinions, as Spock enjoined, meant subjugating their own judgement to the child's, and thus failed in a basic parental responsibility.

Often it is only when teachers themselves become parents that the difference in roles is fully brought home to them. They quickly discover that if their own offspring are badly behaved, it is as parents rather than as teachers that they can expect to bear the brunt of society's disapproval. For all the emphasis placed by educational theorists on the education of the whole child, it is only the *academic* failings of children which are ever seriously laid at the door of teachers; and even these tend to be rationalised within the profession as being due to inadequacies, real or imagined, in the children's home backgrounds.[8]

The development of group norms of acceptable school behaviour is a factor of considerable practical importance, since it is only this development which enables such a small number of adults to cope effectively and benignly with such large numbers of children. Many parents express deep admiration for the way teachers surmount what appears to be the almost impossible task of controlling such an enormous 'family', and it is clear that their admiration stems from this false comparison with their own parental role. Surely teachers must be almost superhuman if they can deal with thirty children single-handed! Imagine what it would be like if their own families were to be increased by a factor of ten! It is this mixture of awe and sympathy which can lead parents to ignore their children's complaints, feeling that they themselves could not do such a job and therefore have no right to criticise if something goes wrong. This is interesting, since not being able to do a job ourselves does not normally prevent our criticism of, say, an inefficient television repair or an inept comedian; and it does appear to be the sense of comparability, *coupled* with parental feelings of inadequacy, which produces this reaction.

Machine operator's wife:

> I do think teachers have got a big job to do, especially when you think how it is looking after one, let alone a class with about twenty or thirty! And I wouldn't take a child's complaints really seriously . . . I think the teacher – you've no right to interfere with their job, I don't think so, oh no.

What needs to be understood, however, is that the attempt to teach such a large group of children would indeed present an impossible task were it not that they are already, by the time they reach junior school age, in bond to a substantial network of group conventions. The average benign primary school is a complex social institution with a tightly knit and well-ordered social structure. The hierarchy is dominated at one level by older children whose own status is served by assisting in the socialisation of the younger ones; and at another level by experienced adults who are deliberately accorded considerable power over the children in their charge. As in most social organisations, the participating members, whether higher or lower in the hierarchy, are constrained within a system of values and customs which govern when, where and how the participants are expected to behave towards each other. Some few of these customs will be made explicit as school rules or school information, to which the attention of children and parents will be deliberately drawn; but many more will be absorbed through the pores, as it were, as 'natural' and established usage – the accepted ways in which pupils and teachers do behave in school. The child imperceptibly comes to adopt and make his own a quite complicated notion of a dynamic social structure and his own evolving status within it, by a long accretion of incidental learning.[9]

When we say that children adjust or 'settle down' to school, then, we may be in danger of missing the crucial point: that they are being subjected to a compelling socialisation process, much of which offers persuasive rewards, but as a result of which they learn to accept their place as very junior members of an elaborate social hierarchy. This is by no means to say that the child simply learns passive conformity to rules and conventions: on the contrary, the power of the system lies in the fact that the child internalises its values in a very active sense. We have already seen how some children accept their teachers' statements as unquestionable and infallible; but even those who are not totally in thrall to the teacher can be scandalised and awestruck when another child challenges her authority by refusing to comply with a request or throwing a tantrum in the classroom: these are things which are simply 'not done'. (A spot check of five primary schools in Nottingham, taking the previous week as a sample period, produced the grand total of one incident of open display of rage and temper among seven-year-olds; compare this with our finding that 22 per cent of these children 'get into a real rage' once or more per per week at home.) Teachers tend to encourage the rest of the group to feel outraged by the bad behaviour of an individual, even though they may resist actually holding him up to public shame and ridicule; the dramatically raised eyebrows, the emphasis of an astonished 'I *beg* your pardon?', the expression of long-suffering patience – all these are partly for the benefit of an attentive audience, who are implicitly ('We're all still waiting for you, Kenny') or explicitly ('. . . aren't we, children?') invited to identify with virtuous authority. Thus it is not just the teacher's own personality but the social forces that she can muster in her support that can make children feel that rebellion is almost unthinkable. It becomes socially impossible for most to refuse a direct request, even when they have reasonable grounds for objection; moreover, because the child is conscious of the existence of rules of behaviour, but does not always know precisely what they are, many worry that they will accidentally transgress.

Loco fireman's wife:
>He gets a little bit frightened – he's just changed school, he's gone to junior school now, and he was looking forward to going to junior school, you know, sort of step up if he was going to be a Junior, not an Infant; but when it got towards it, he was getting a bit scared, you know: 'I shan't be able to do the work – I don't know where to go and I don't . . .'; he doesn't refuse to go, just sort of frightened that he isn't going to be able to cope.

Electrical engineer's wife:
>He does worry – things at school bother him, things that you wouldn't think were important. There was a time he cried every night and he kept saying he hadn't done very much story – as I say, he's a perfectionist, he can't write as he would like to write . . . . . I tried to get at what was wrong; and the next day he was very worried . . . . . Well, this went on for, ooh, a fortnight, and he was coming to the end of the book, and when he got to the end of his book, he said, his teacher would see it, and then she'd know he'd only done a little story, and one page only had the date on. So I said, well, if he's really worrying about it, I'll go to school; and I found that the head had been in and told them that they must fill up the pages, they must use the paper. And apparently they were all doing this one sentence on one page, and it was nothing more than that; but they would have to go to the head to get the new book. Only a little thing, but . . .

Turf accountant's wife:
>He doesn't really like going up to the teacher if anything goes wrong. Just little things – you know, if he wanted another writing book or jotter, he didn't like to say. Oh, and she gave him the wrong book once, and he didn't like to tell her – he did worry about that! And to stop him worrying, I went with him – I didn't tell her, I said 'Russell has got something to tell you'. So he did tell her while I was there. And she did laugh, the teacher did – she thought it was really funny.

Labourer's wife:
Now the class where Molly's in now, there's the yellow table –
the top table – and the red table, and so on; and she says 'So-and-
so, he's at the bottom table, you know'; she says, 'I was on the top
table today, that's cause somebody wasn't at school' – she's on
the next table really; so she said, 'Mammy, the teacher said I was
fit for top table, but there's no room at top table yet, there's too
many'. So she has to sit at the other table. This I think does worry
her at times, that she's not; cause she tries to be at the top. I say,
'Well, Molly, you've not been going to school as long as some'.

Schools today, as parents often pointed out, offer much more
freedom of choice than many of these parents themselves remember
from their own early schooldays. The style of control has changed;
the atmosphere is more child-centred and permissive. Harshness of
punishment or threat of punishment is only rarely encountered. This
does not, however, mean (as some parents supposed) that children
can do whatever they like, or that teachers have given up any control
over their pupils: only that teachers, like parents, have moved
towards a democratic image, and have learned to use group forces, at
least in the primary school, to maintain an illusion of democratic
choice within a relatively unyielding framework. Within this framework, parents and teachers are at some pains to keep the child
contented, and with goodwill and easy communication can often
smooth the difficulties which the child encounters. However, problems of communication can arise, both between parents and teachers,
and between parents and their own children: home and school *are*
different worlds, and the two worlds foster myths about each other
which may not be helpful to the child moving between them. Certain
facts, beyond the myths, have to be lived with. Teachers have always
been aware that some parents provide a frankly damaging environment for their children, and that these children will continue to be at
risk however compensatory the education that may be devised for
them. It is also true that some teachers are incompetent and that
some are unsuitable for their profession and damaging to the children
they teach: when this happens, both parents and children are likely
to find that there is very little to be done to change the situation, other
than to sweat it out as best they can. It is here that both communication for parents and democratic choice for children break down.
    In this introduction to the parents' perspective on school, we have
attempted first of all to present the school situation from a more
objective perspective than parents are usually themselves able to
take: they are, after all, usually too immediately concerned with the

individual personalities involved and the actual activities being undertaken from day to day. We have tried to show how the child extends his horizons from home and family, to school, peers and less intimate authorities, and how his adaptation to the more formal social system takes place. In his first months in the infant school, the child's teacher will make considerable allowance for his individual quirks and foibles: less responsive than his mother to his egocentricity, she is still a tolerant, nurturant figure, to whom he can ascribe a mothering image and who can offer him a protective transition from home to school expectations. Loving his teacher uncritically, yet also compelled to share her with a greater number of peers than he has been used to, he learns two massive adaptations: he identifies with his teacher, and thence with the school world which she represents; and he is introduced to a discovery for which he is now intellectually ready – the discovery that group co-operation brings its own rewards in greater achievement and more complex and satisfying play. These crucial social lessons of the infant school, mediated chiefly by the teacher herself, allow him to become fully integrated with the peer group and with the school as social institution, and bring him under the powerful influence of both: and in this way he is enabled to wean himself from the protective nurturance of his teacher, and become an independent 'junior'. At this stage, while retaining a close and friendly relationship with his class teacher, he is also more able to look beyond her to other teachers with whom he enjoys more casual contact; and, detached from his personal dependency, be begins to show the emergence of 'us and them' loyalties in relation to peer group *vis-à-vis* teachers, turning more frequently towards other children as a source of comfort and support in meeting difficulties at school. Socialisation takes on a new emphasis.

NOTES

1 Even the 'de-schoolers' still expect alternative kinds of groups rather than private tutoring or nothing at all. The so-called 'free schools' are an obvious example. Ivan Illich moves furthest from the idea of teaching in schools when he complains that 'Free schools . . . . . produce the mirage of freedom', and suggests access to facts, use of tools and 'the ability to convoke peers to a meeting' as the prerequisites to educational opportunity and 'conscious personal growth'. However, what he presents as an attack on schools as such, with their 'hidden curriculum', merely refuses to make explicit the fact which he finally cannot escape, that some people have more knowledge than others even if we do accept each other on a peer basis. There seems no insoluble reason why schools should not in principle be capable of undergoing such a revolution. (Ivan Illich, *After Deschooling, What?* (Writers' and Readers' Publishing Co-operative, 1974.)

2 J. and E. Newson, op. cit. (1976*b*).

3 Ruth Benedict, *Patterns of Culture* (London, Routledge & Kegan Paul, 1935).

4 J. and E. Newson, op. cit. (1976*b*).

5 In 1974, eleven junior schools (not counting voluntary schools) were still housed in nineteenth-century buildings, which the surveyor to the Education Department described as trouble-free in terms of their resistance to either wear and tear or vandalism: several were to be replaced in the following two or three years. Only one was single-storey.

6 There does not seem to be adequate communication to architects of the practical needs of teachers. This is still more true in special education, where open plan design can be disastrous for the teacher trying to cope with, say, a hyperactive child. In a study of thirty-three classes for severely subnormal children in five different LEA areas, Theresa Scott found only five 'quiet areas' available and *no* withdrawal room ('a small room off the main classroom and specially designed for individual teaching') which are regarded by Mittler as essential requirements for ESN(s) classrooms. T. L. Scott, 'The teaching day as described by some teachers working in ESN(s) schools', MA thesis, University of Nottingham Child Development Research Unit, 1974; P. Mittler, 'Towards educational responsibility', *Teaching and Training*, 7 (1969).

7 J. and E. Newson, op. cit. (1976*b*), pp. 40–2, 294 *f*.

8 The enormous interest generated by the public inquiry into the running of the William Tyndale Junior School, which was accused of failing to provide an adequate education for its pupils, attests both to public consciousness that education *can* be inadequate and to the rarity of specific examples being set out for detailed scrutiny. A major point of interest in this case was the reluctance of the education authority involved to interfere. Two accounts of the case are given in J. Gretton and M. Jackson, *William Tyndale: Collapse of a School – or a System?* (London, George Allen & Unwin, 1976) and in T. Ellis, J. McWhirter, D. McColgan and B. Haddow, *William Tyndale: The teachers' story* (London, Writers' and Readers' Publishing Co-operative, 1976).

9 This is one part, in fact, of Illich's 'hidden curriculum' – the 'structure of schooling, as opposed to what happens in school'; like most socialisation issues, it has political consequences which Illich chiefly emphasises. I. Illich, op. cit. (1974).

Chapter 2

How Willingly to School?

Problems of school refusal as they appear in the literature, whether in terms of truancy or 'school phobia', tend to be concerned with the secondary-age child. Partly this seems to be a question of who writes the literature and how their samples are obtained: most of the studies of school refusal come from psychiatric, psychological or social work sources, where the referrals will tend to be those who are more clearly seen as 'problem children'. Children of primary school age are less likely to be seen as in need of specialist psychiatric help because they refuse something they don't like, even if they do have complicated emotional reasons for doing so; the problem will probably be contained within the family and its normal sources of advice, i.e. schoolteacher and family doctor. A rare general-practitioner study, by Max Clyne, reflects this: in a series of fifty-five school refusers seen in his practice over a five-year period, children under nine years were twice as numerous as those over nine, with a mean age of seven years and nine months.[1]

Simple attendance rates are not very easy to interpret in terms of the factors contributing to non-attendance. Both Douglas and Ross in the 1946 cohort study[2] and Fogelman and Richards (1958 cohort)[3] found better attendance at the upper primary level than in the earlier years: in the latter study, twice as many children had a less than 85 per cent attendance at seven as at eleven years, although poor attenders at eleven were not necessarily predicted at seven. On purely physical grounds, however, one might expect an improvement in attendance over the primary years, as children put the common infectious diseases behind them. It is also true that younger children are more likely to have mothers at home full-time with pre-school siblings, so that absence from school with a slight cough or malaise can readily be catered for; once the mother is at work, sheer administrative problems will encourage her to make light of the child's milder symptoms – nor will he be so tempted to nurse his cold at home if he is only to be kept an eye on by a neighbour rather than cosseted by his mother with a younger sib for company.[4] Comparison of attendance figures at different ages, then, are not particularly good indicators of the child's willingness to go to school at these developmental points.

The National Survey of 1964 (Plowden)[5] found that 4 per cent of absence at primary level was for reasons which the child's teachers considered unsatisfactory. This immediately raises the issue of the distinction between truancy, where the child chooses not to go to school, and emotional school refusal or 'school phobia', where the child finds itself unable to face school. Hersov[6] and others have offered tables of differentiating points of symptomatology in order to distinguish between these conditions; but perhaps their areas of overlap are as significant as their differences. Thus Kahn points out that 'truancy is a *social* problem which, nevertheless, has consequences for the personality development of the individual concerned. School phobia is a *clinical* problem but it has social implications. When absence from school is a symptom of disturbance, it cannot be kept secret within the family in the same way as night fears, bedwetting or food fads. Society as a whole has a share in the problem.'[7] Clyne, too, although he regards the difference between truancy and emotional refusal as 'fundamental', is also interested in the parallels between the two, which as a family doctor he takes to be confusing both diagnostically and for remediation: 'In my initial contacts with parents and teachers I noticed a confusion between medical ideas, such as being ill, well, or incapacitated, and moral concepts, such as parental authority, the child's duty, or laziness, which confused me too, and made dealing with the child on a medical level even more difficult'; and later:

It is true that there is in [emotional] school refusal an element of challenge to parental authority in so far as the child resists successfully a demand by his parents. But this is merely the outer appearance of a complex interplay of the emotional forces of love and hatred, of control and submission, and not simply or chiefly the expression of rebellion against established authority, as in truancy. In any case, accepting for the moment that cultural changes in parental attitudes to discipline, punishment, and authority are responsible for the existence of an increase in school refusal, as physicians we should still be concerned rather with the *medical* problem of understanding and treating the breakdown of the school-refusing child within his existing environment, than with impressing our own views about social patterns upon our patients.[8]

Attendance figures give us percentages of children who have poor attendance records, but they are contaminated by social factors which affect both physical illness and parental pressure to attend school; and clinical records are concerned only with children who are a problem in that their refusal is persistent. Clinic referrals for school refusal may also contain a hidden social component, in that referral may itself take place on a socially selective basis: for instance, it is not unknown for a psychiatrist to refuse working-class 'school phobia' referrals, as having a lower prognosis for success, leaving them to be dealt with by the Educational Welfare Office under the 'truancy' label.

Thus even the frank problems of school attendance, which inevitably attract most attention in the literature, are beset with difficulties of classification. Looking as we were at a sample of 'ordinary' children, we were less concerned with cases where a problem had been already identified clinically or socially than with the day-to-day indications of unwillingness to go to school which the mother herself was dealing with. We were not only interested in the children who had on occasion refused to go to school; we wanted to know about the extent of reluctance expressed in grumbling, grizzling or crying, what proportion of children would attempt to stay at home by manufacturing symptoms of illness, and how mothers met and coped with their children's reluctance.

In so far as parents do not have much practical legal alternative to sending their child to school, they are not of course totally free agents; Shakespeare's much-quoted 'whining schoolboy . . . creeping like snail unwillingly to school' would not really have put his parents into quite the position of the parents of school refusers under compulsory education. It is interesting, however, that modern parents also do not expect to have to compel their children into unpleasant experiences; the image of school as something inevitably disliked by normal children is extremely rare, at least at this age. Andrew's mother, a fitter's wife, is very unusual in her opinion:

> I don't think any child really enjoys school terribly much. I think they're all bound to hate the teachers and hate the school in general at some time in their school life, so I don't really take their complaints too seriously.

The norm among parents is that they are enough aware of modern educational ideas and ideals to start from the assumption that children will find school a positive and rewarding experience. Taking it for granted that a child will enjoy going to school, if their own child is not happy to do so they conclude that something must be wrong, which needs at least a monitoring eye and possibly rapid intervention. They may be aware of special sensitivities in their child to which they will have to alert the teacher; they are conscious that misunderstandings may arise which may need sorting out before pressures build up irretrievably.

University lecturer's wife:
> Well, Charles has been very fortunate – I've had every confidence in the teacher in handling him. There was a short period when he had another teacher who didn't understand him very well, and he was obviously a bit upset about this, he could sense it, I think; and I thought, before we start a lot of trouble I would go and see her, and I explained what sort of a child he was [temperamental, fairly difficult]; and although he didn't like life as much under her, there was no positive complaint and no trouble. But I could imagine you might get a teacher who didn't know how to handle a particular child, and . . . um . . . I think you *can* have genuine trouble; and if I thought there was something that could be put right, I would do something about it.

Unemployed labourer's wife:
> Well, there must be summat, what makes 'em don't want to go to school – there must be summat wrong.

Actor's wife:
> Especially with Juliet, who *doesn't* try to stop off school – I would certainly go up straight away, because I would think it was that important.

Discovering what has gone wrong is not always easy, of course. Children of this age may not be able to express their difficulties explicitly or coherently; and perhaps if they were more competent in verbalisation, they would not need to state their anxieties in the more general terms of school refusal or reluctance. Sharon, who accidentally coloured her drawing black instead of the yellow that was required by the worksheet, and Clive, who had the bad luck to drop his underpants in a puddle on the lavatory floor, might have ridden out the embarrassing consequences had they been more verbally and socially adept; as it was, both refused the next session of school and had to be 'sorted out' by their respective mothers. These children were at least able to explain to their mothers what had made school frightening to them; but a child must often also sense that his parents may not fully appreciate the fearful element in experiences which they do not share – where, indeed, they have already abandoned him to face alone the powerful social forces which operate in the school situation. Moreover, the child may doubt his parents' power to intervene effectively, particularly since they were not usually physically present last time a problem arose and are unlikely to be there next time it recurs. This is of course a realistic doubt; and it is reinforced by parents themselves, who may point out to their children that it is a legal requirement to go to school, or may play down children's complaints of unfairness by stressing the teacher's responsibility for keeping discipline. A child may therefore feel that he needs to express his protest rather dramatically before his parents will take him seriously; in turn, refusal comes to be accepted as a gesture signalling real distress as opposed to mere discontent.

Only 5 per cent of the sample had refused school at some time during the twelve months between their sixth and seventh birthdays, and a further 8 per cent had done so since starting school, but not during the past year. It must be remembered that the children who have been known to refuse to go to school (or who have run home, having once set out) are not necessarily 'school refusers' in the sense of presenting a long-term problem recognised as such by their parents and teachers. There are no significant class trends to be found in the data, although among Class v boys the proportion for the past year rises from 5 to 11 per cent. Boys are consistently more likely to refuse school than girls in every class (7 compared with 3 per cent overall in the past year), but with these rather small numbers significance only reaches 0·05; this finding perhaps needs to be taken in conjunction with another, to be presented in Table 3, that rather more girls than boys are allowed off school without having to dig their heels in and refuse.

The examples illustrated below give an idea of the range of problem. The first child has always been a refuser until six months ago when a new teacher transformed the situation for him. The second is a spasmodic refuser – there are a number of these, some whose refusal, like this one's, seems linked to the start of the new term, others for whom things become too much from time to time without obvious cause. The third child, Valerie, also presents intractable problems of food refusal;[9] school refusal, at present only a 'panic' reaction, is to become a repeated pattern throughout her school career. The last girl, Sharon, is here seen truanting, but this is also the child who panicked after getting her colouring task wrong; both these girls, now and later, show the difficulty in drawing hard and fast lines between emotional and social reasons for refusing school.

Baker's wife:
Oh, I'd an awful job to get him to school. He used to wake up in
the night with it. Last term he's gone to school all right, but he
used to be awful. I took him to see the Education Officer – that
made no difference – I took him all over, and, you know, I talked
to him: 'Now you've *got* to go to school' – 'I'm not going, I'm not
going'. I've got him up there, although he's kicked and you know
how they are when they get these tempers; and I've had to bring
him down again. Sometimes I've smacked him before he'd go in.
Ever since he started – he's run up the woods – oh, it's been
murder. But now, oh, he's no trouble at all, he loves school; he's
got on well with this new teacher; he just settled down like *that*,
and in the holidays this Christmas he kept asking, 'When is it time
to go to school?'

Stoker's wife:
Yes, often. It's about every three months he starts. He comes down
feeling sick, well he's not actually sick, but . . . I think he *makes*
himself sick. Now last time he says 'I'm not going to school', I
just put me coat on and took him. I think it's when they've had
time off school; they have that many holidays, you know, he
doesn't want to go back after the holidays . . . . . When he was five
I used to take him up to the gate and see him in the door and he
used to run down there after me, but I used to turn round and take
him back. Two or three times the teacher's fetched him back.

Electrical engineer's wife:
It bothered her when she went from the infants to the juniors, and
the first time when I took her from the infants, when you take them
to the juniors you have to leave them in the playground. Well,
Valerie came home – she ran back. Mind you, I took her back
again, and they said it was all right, it was natural for her. Sudden
panic. I think it was panic, to be with all the children; she got into
the hall to be sorted out into the classes and then decided that was
it, she must come back. I said 'What have you come back for?'
She said, 'I don't like it'. I says, 'You haven't given yourself a
chance, you haven't even been in a class yet'. But we took her back,
and I went to see the headmaster and he said it was quite a natural
thing, and she didn't do it again.

Lorry driver's wife:
She played truant last week. I don't know really where she went.
She went with this other girl . . . . . [How did you find out?] Well,

Sharon went out of the house at half past one, I thought she was going to school. I came back from my errand at about quarter to three, and Sharon was in the back yard eating rhubarb – she'd got a bag of sugar, and she was eating the rhubarb sticks. When I came in, they scooted out the back . . . . . This is the second time. [Does the school know?] Well, er . . . the little girl that did it with her went to school the next day and told the teacher 'I didn't go to school because I didn't want to'. So I suppose the teacher must have known, cause they were in the same class. [You haven't seen the school about it?] No – I had to write a letter to say she hadn't been because she'd sprained her wrist, I'd got to lie, you see. The first time she'd only been at school five weeks, and she played truant with this girl. I went down to the shops to get something and she was playing on the street; and I says 'What are you doing here?' She says 'Well, I didn't want to go, I didn't feel like it'. She says, 'Me and Diane's had the afternoon off'. So I says, 'I'll give you afternoon off, go on, get in that house!' Course, you know, we had a bit of a stink about it; but she soon forgot about it.

'He'd have to convince me that it was for real . . .'
It is made very clear to children who refuse school that their stand is not legitimate: it happens in defiance of parents' persuasion, reasoning, demands or actions, which are all normally (at least overtly) directed at getting the child to the school and ensuring that he stays there. Often, in the course of the dialogue which takes place, parents also make explicit the circumstances in which absence from school *would* be considered legitimate: 'You're perfectly well, off you go'; 'I don't think your cold's *that* bad'. Children also know that excuse notes brought to school to explain absence are almost invariably in terms of medical needs: 'Jane had a sore throat yesterday', or 'Billy has a dental appointment on Thursday'. Parents, too, tend to be reluctant to offer such excuses as 'she seemed tired and overwrought', 'things have got on top of him and he needs a break as a safety-valve', but will play safe with vague talk of headaches and feverishness. In this context it is hardly surprising that children attempt to legitimise their wishes by feigning medical symptoms, i.e. malingering; while the subjective magnification of existing twinges can be well enough rewarded to develop into a fairly intractable psychosomatic problem. The process whereby the thought 'if I were ill' moves through 'I wonder if I *am* ill?' and 'I really don't feel well enough' to 'I've got an awful tummy-ache and I feel sick' will be familiar enough to those who have in their time suffered the Monday-morning syndrome (for aetiology, the definition of 'mondayish' in

the *Concise Oxford Dictionary* is commended); in practice, especially with children, there is considerable overlap between malingering and psychosomatic illness. Some examples of this continuum, beginning with a wish verbalised but not carried through, follow; we also have at least one child who has deliberately tried to produce a real illness, in his case by swallowing paper.

Milkman's wife:
  The other week he came home and said 'I wish I could fall down and cut me'. I says 'Why?' He says, 'I wouldn't have to do PE this afternoon!'

Cotton winder's wife:
  Ooh yes, yes! Oh we get that *very* often and . . . um . . . ooh! he's got a headache; then you'll put the telly up just that bit more, you know, or the wireless in the morning, put it a bit louder, and he'll suddenly start jiving and jumping, and he'll forget all about it. And I'll say, 'Er – does the – er – sound bother you? Is it too loud?' – 'No' – 'All right, you've got no headache!' Oh, then he's got a stomach-ache, it's killing him – and I can tell when he *is* bad, you know – and I put his food out, and he'll eat it, and I'll say '*You've* got no stomach-ache, come on!' Then he'll grin, and he'll say, 'You know I'm doing it again, don't you!' He just gives in, if it's a losing battle he don't bother.

Structural cleaner's wife:
  Oh yes, most mornings – headaches – pains in his legs, can't walk. I kept him off one day when he started it – about 10.30 he was running wild in the yard! He was watching the time, though, and at 12 o'clock he was back in the house, and at 2.30 he was out playing again. I knew from that day onward what it was – I haven't took much notice since.

Salesman's wife:
  . . . a few days prior to her starting school, she was playing with a little boy and he cut his ear rather badly . . . . . the child's mother got some cotton wool and started to clean up [the blood], and she heard a little thud beside of her, and there was Moira on the floor . . . . . it had just made her feel funny. Well – the day she went to school, she was so happy, her face was smiling as she walked up, and there was Miss Gregory, the headteacher, with her arm bandaged from top to bottom. Of course, she took one look at the bandage and started to feel funny; and Miss Gregory walked over

to her, held out her hand and said 'Come along, then', and got hold of Moira with the bandaged arm. Well, her face went like a ghost; as I say, she was so happy up till then, she was really thrilled – but of course that finished her completely. She started to cry and cling on to me; I just had to push her into the classroom and leave her. I saw the teacher take her out to the toilet . . . . . [later] oh, to get her there in the morning, I used to nearly throw her out of the house – she had diarrhoea, tummy-ache, cried when she was left . . .

Manager's wife:
The first couple of years he used to get up in the morning, and as soon as he had anything to eat he was sick. I had this day after day, week after week – this went on up to six months ago, on and off, this sickness. But I realised what it was, he didn't want to go to school, and after he'd been sick he'd eat another breakfast. It seemed as if he'd just got to get that off his chest – or stomach! It was something he woke up with every morning . . . . . mostly it was the teacher shouting; I know that did upset him, because this teacher came in the morning, and he had another one in the afternoon. Well, I had no trouble with him in the afternoon, it was just the morning, and I think it really was this teacher shouting. Now I think he's become immune to teachers shouting!

Five per cent of our children have 'often' pretended to be unwell in order to be excused school; and 22 per cent have 'sometimes' done so. Class differences are not consistent or significant; but boys are more likely to feign illness sometimes than girls (25 per cent compared with 18 per cent), and this difference is marked in the two Class IIIs (III wc 30%:18%; III man 27%:17%). We deliberately directed the question towards malingering rather than psychosomatic problems, by using the wording 'Does he ever *pretend* he's not well, so as to stay at home from school?'; thus the last of the above children would not be counted. In doing this, we are of course falling into the trap to which Clyne draws attention: that to ask first of school absence 'Is it genuine?' turns school refusal 'into a moral instead of a medical issue'. But this is indeed the first reaction of most parents: faced with a child who says he is ill and presents subjective symptoms which are difficult for them to verify by objective signs, their immediate concern is to evaluate the 'genuineness' of his complaint. We were in fact interested in whether parents would accept as genuine a malaise which they believed to be non-physical; very few expressed this point of view:

University teacher's wife:
    It has happened, and what I would do would rather depend how
    often it was happening. The first time I should probably say 'Oh
    well, you do look a bit pale' or something like that – *manufacture*
    for her a not-well excuse, I think, probably, and keep her at home.
    If it kept on happening, then I would look into it much further and
    see whether there was some serious reason. But I do like to keep an
    open door for this sort of thing – I think there are times . . . there
    are days when a psychological upset is just as important as a cold,
    shall we say. And although I think children have got to learn to
    face things, I also think that stresses arise at school sometimes
    which are beyond reason to expect them to face at this age, and I
    think you don't help them to face things in life by just flinging them
    in regardless.

It has also to be remembered that both children and adults
commonly react to general stress by producing 'genuine' symptoms
of a physical kind which cannot be traced to any physical aetiology.
For instance, Apley investigated a series of 200 children suffering
from recurrent abdominal pain; in only 7 per cent of these cases
could a causative organic disorder be found.[10] Similarly, pains in the
limbs, such as our grandmothers knew as 'growing pains', are estimated to occur in 1 in 25 school children: out of 213 such cases, only
7 were found to have a serious physical disorder – as Apley and
Mac Keith nicely put it, 'Bodily growth is not painful, though
emotional growth may well be'.[11]
    Thus it is not simply a question of deciding whether the child is
actually experiencing pain. Again, many of the symptoms of somatic
illness are at an early stage only recognisable in subjective terms,
since the best test of their physical origins is whether they develop
further. Parents are therefore in a real dilemma when the child says
he feels ill and can only produce subjective symptoms: if they keep
him at home and he turns out to be perfectly fit, they may be judged
(not least by themselves) as fussy and over-solicitous, while if they
send him to school and his condition deteriorates there, they may be
criticised as not only hard-hearted to the poor child but thoughtless
for the welfare of the school.

Foreman's wife:
    That's it, you see. He said he wasn't very well, and of course about
    half past nine he was right as rain, you see, so I made him go to the
    end of the week; on the Saturday and Sunday he was lively as a
    cricket so of course I made him go Monday morning. Any road,

Tuesday morning he come into our bedroom covered in spots, and he'd had measles a week, and it finished up nearly all the kiddies in the class got it; so now if there is a bit of doubt, I keep him at home.

Mothers tend in the first instance, then, to resort to various stratagems designed to test the child's claim that he is unwell. These are basically of five kinds, which may be used singly, in combination or in sequence.

(1) The mother invites the child to reappraise his claim, emphasising that there is no advantage in staying at home. She points out that if she lets him stay at home, he will have to remain in bed quietly, without television, and that school would be more entertaining. If he persists, she may deliberately make his day as boring as possible, with an eye to next time.

(2) She uses her own powers of detection designed to catch the child out in betraying that he feels better than he claims. Covertly encouraging the child to run about, show enjoyment of television or radio or eat a good meal, all of which are taken to be signs of rude health, she then faces him with this as evidence that he is 'swinging the lead'.

(3) She appeals to some established objective criterion of whether the child is unwell enough to stay at home: his temperature is the most usual one, but others are pallor, a convincing cough, behaviour the previous evening and lack of sleep the previous night. The child has to pass the test of objectively discernible symptoms (which may include distress beyond mere complaining) before he will be allowed off.

(4) She appeals to professional authority: 'Well, we'll have to get the doctor in'. Often this is used ostensibly as a message to the child that she is taking him seriously, but in fact as a test of his own seriousness: the reasoning is that if the child is consciously malingering he will be afraid to expose his fraud to professional eyes; or, in a number of cases, that the child dislikes seeing the doctor, and will avoid doing so unless he really feels unwell.

(5) Overtly, she accepts that he has some minor symptoms, but does not accept their sufficiency. However, she also accepts that they may become worse during the day, and therefore suggests that his teacher may reappraise his condition later on. In fact this solution is usually not quite so viable as the mother presents it to be: unless she is both on the phone and at home all day, the teacher will not in fact be able to summon her to take the child home, and to suggest that the teacher will bring the child home (to a house which might be

empty) places a heavier onus on the school than the mother really wishes to impose. Behind this strategy, therefore, lies the expectation that once the child is at school his mind will be taken off his symptoms if he has any, or he will be resigned to the situation if he has none: either way, he will be more reluctant to 'try it on' with his teacher.

Examples of these strategies in action follow.

(1) *Emphasises disadvantages*

Diesel engineer's wife:
> Well, I said if she wasn't very well she could stay at home, but she'd have to stay in bed because you don't stay at home to play – I said if you're well enough to play when you're at home, you're well enough to be at school, and she realises she can't . . .

Clergyman's wife:
> I'd pop her into bed without any books and give her a thoroughly boring day.

(2) *Detective methods* (and see cotton winder's wife, page 57)

Insurance clerk's wife:
> Well, I watch her after I've given her a couple of Disprins, and then I sort of note, and in a few minutes if she's jumping about I know the headache isn't very bad, or whatever she's suffering from, you know, and judge from that.

Representative's wife:
> He'd had a tummy upset, and on the Monday I didn't know whether he was going or not, and he did get up. 'Am I going to school, Mummy?' he said; I said, 'Well yes, you seem all right'. And he cried. And I says, 'Now you *are* going, if you hadn't have cried I might have kept you off. You cry because you don't want to go to school, not because you don't feel well', I says, 'You're going and that's it, so I don't want to hear any more'. Course, that was it, he went and he was all right – and when he came home at dinner-time, he said 'I was pleased I went, Mummy, it was ever so nice'.

(3) *Objective criteria*

Threader's wife:
> Oh well, I've got a thermometer and I always say 'This can tell me

if you're really ill, you know'. He realises he can't get away with it now.

Greengrocer's wife:
If I was quite sure he was all right, I wouldn't fall for it. Um . . . we have got Lorna [sib] right in the brake to go, and she's been so upset that I've said 'I don't think she really *is* well, you know', and we've taken her out again. But the point is we'd got her right into the brake ready for her to go to school – er – we'll play it out right to the limit. If we have a doubt we'll play it out to the end – we wouldn't send them if we thought they weren't well, but I mean they've got to *convince* us.

(4) *Appeal to professional*

Executive officer's wife (herself a nurse!):
He's a terribly good actor. I take his temperature and tell him it's normal, and then I say 'I'll ring the doctor' – and he's got his coat on in a flash, he's miraculously cured.

Bus conductor's wife:
I'd tell her I'd take her to the doctor's – that'd soon rally her round, she don't like doctors.

Class III wc widow:
She did after her father died . . . 'Ooh, I've got an awful headache', and she'd sound so convincing. I said 'Well, we'll have the doctor in, darling, because it's worrying me' – 'It's going a bit now'. You know, you knew damn well it was that, and I used to say 'The next time you have a headache we *will* have the doctor'.

(5) *Reliance on teacher*

Cabinet maker's wife:
I sent him off – I think if you give in once . . . I said 'If you *really* don't feel well, you ask the teacher and she'll pack you off home'.

Cold food packer's wife:
I say 'If you're not feeling well at school, go to the headmaster'. Well, you can always tell when a child is really poorly – well, I can, like – and I'll say 'Well, if you're not feeling well at school, go and tell the headmaster, and he'll let you come home' – which if he is poorly he will do, and if he isn't he won't!

HOW WILLINGLY TO SCHOOL? 63

'He's got to go – like Daddy's got to go to work . . .'
Malingering and refusal are emphatic expressions of unwillingness.
Bearing in mind that parents and educationalists alike expect primary
school education to be a very happy experience, we wanted to know
what proportion of children were sometimes just reluctant to go to
school without necessarily feigning illness or refusing. On the basis of
the question 'Does he ever say he doesn't want to go to school
today?', a tenth of all the children were said to do this 'often', and
there were no sex or class differences. Not all of these children have
a special fear of school, though obviously the persistent refusers and
malingerers will come into this group; some, however, are simply
children for whom school holds no delight, and who would prefer to
be elsewhere. In addition, 36 per cent of the children are 'sometimes'
reluctant to go to school, without presenting real problems. Table 3
breaks down the combined 46 per cent of children who are 'at least
sometimes' reluctant, in terms of class and sex; it will be seen that
this data confirms the tables on children's liking for school and
teacher (pp. 26 and 35), in that the children at the top and bottom of
the social scale show the least reluctance. A sex difference only
appears in the semi-skilled and unskilled groups, where considerably
fewer girls than boys show reluctance.

Table 3   *Children who at least sometimes express reluctance to go to
school*

	social class		III				summary	
	I&II	IIIwc	man	IV	V	I&II+ IIIwc	IIIman, IV, V	overall popn
	%	%	%	%	%	%	%	%
boys	37	49	53	57	49	43	54	51
girls	37	45	46	40	21	41	42	42
both	37	47	50	48	35	42	48	46

Significance: trend non-linear   ***   m.class/w.class   n.s.
                                between sexes   *

If almost half the mothers in the sample are having to deal with
this sometimes (and many more have experience of the same situation with other children), the question 'What do you think you would
do if he did?' is almost as realistic as 'What do you do when he does?'
We asked these questions as appropriate.

The answers were classified on a three-point scale: those who allowed the child to stay at home, those who showed sympathy for his reluctance but still made him go, and those who 'packed him off' without any sympathy. We do not present this as a linear scale of anything other than the degree to which the child's wishes are accommodated: that is, we have elsewhere[12] used the mother's willingness to show sympathy in this situation as part of an index of child-centredness, but we would not regard mothers who allow the child off as more child-centred than those who merely show sympathy, given that in the end children must by law attend school, that it is considered in their interest to do so, and that creating a sympathetic atmosphere in which they can bring themselves to go reasonably happily may in fact demand more in the way of thought and empathy from the mother. The following examples illustrate the three categories.

Allows off

Fitter's mate's wife:
> He used to hide his shoes and that, not just lately, but he's often done that; you know, 'I can't find my shoes', and after 9 o'clock he'd find them. Once it had gone 9 o'clock they'd turn up, and he wouldn't go if he was late, so . . .

Teacher's wife:
> I'd be most surprised for a start. I wouldn't persuade her. I'd be so surprised, to be quite honest, that I'd be inclined *not* to persuade her to go because I'd think there'd be some real reason for it; but I'd certainly get down to the reason or at least try to.

Sympathetic, sends nonetheless

Asphalter's wife:
> I ask her why – she just says 'I don't want to go'. I say 'Everyone has to go to school'. I say 'It'll be better when you've cleaned your teeth and gone out in the fresh air'. I make a bit of a fuss of her, and then she goes.

Businessman's wife (herself a teacher):
> I suppose I would try to cheer him up with the thought of something in the future – I'm afraid at the moment I'm cheering him up with the thought of going up to the juniors. He's getting a bit browned off at the moment.

Unsympathetic

Cycle worker's wife:
'You're going – don't be silly.' It was a bit hard, but if I give in
now, he's never going to want to go.

Scientific research worker's wife:
Say 'You're in perfectly good health, so you go to school, no
argument'. (See also page 79.)

Credit collector's wife:
She complains that it's hard work. We said 'Wait till you're
seventeen, and it *will* be hard work'. Some things are best ignored,
aren't they? [What do you do if she says she doesn't want to go to
school today?] Smack her bum.

Table 4 shows the variation in mothers' attitudes to school reluctance according to social class. As one might expect, only a small
minority of 5 per cent will allow the child off just because he is
reluctant; but it is interesting that this group is not mainly composed
of mothers who do not value education (the usual stereotype), but
more typically of those who value it so much that they do not want
it to be soured in any way for their child, and therefore feel that
reluctance needs to be treated positively. A further 37 per cent would
be sympathetic but still make the child go; here again, mothers at
the upper end of the scale are more likely to show sympathy so that
the child's reluctance is somewhat mitigated before he leaves for
school. The final part of the table shows the results when mothers
whose children haven't yet shown reluctance are excluded; compared
with the first two sections combined, the differences are remarkably
small, with two exceptions: when it comes down to hard fact, fewer
Class I and II mothers are sympathetic to their boys than think they
would be in theory, and the same is true of Class V mothers with
respect to their girls.

The transcripts throw further light on the feelings behind this data.
Although all parents want their children to be happy at school, most
expect them to be and many treat their reluctant days with sympathy,
higher up the social scale there seems to be more anxiety about any
suspicion that the child might become disenchanted with school life.
'I'd look into the school very seriously', says a director's wife, 'and if
I thought she wasn't happy, I'd certainly change her school'. Further
down the scale, there is also a good deal of concern expressed, but
with less real expectation of being able to put things right: '. . . but

Table 4   *Mothers' reaction to school reluctance, actual or hypo-thetical*

	social class					summary		
	I&II	IIIwc	III man	IV	V	I&II+ IIIwc	IIIman, IV, V	overall popn.
	%	%	%	%	%	%	%	%
Allows off								
boys	6	4	2	2	0	5	2	3
girls	15	4	9	1	0	10	6	7
both	11	4	5	2	0	7	4	5

Significance: trend ↘ ****   m.class/w.class   n.s.
between sexes   ***

Sympathetic but sends								
boys	55	49	33	30	33	52	33	38
girls	43	41	31	48	28	42	34	36
both	49	45	32	39	31	47	33	37

Significance: trend ↘ ***   m.class/w.class   ***
between sexes   n.s.

Unsympathetic – residual to 100%

'Allows' and 'sympathetic' combined, actual cases of reluctance only (n = 313)

boys	40	50	32	28	25	45	31	35
girls	62	50	35	40	12	56	33	40
both	51	50	34	34	19	51	32	37

Significance: trend ↘ ****   m.class/w.class   ***
between sexes   n.s.

what can you do?' It is more often lower down the scale that a kind of fatalism is expressed in terms of school being something you have to put up with if you don't like it: 'Oh well, I just point out all the sorts of things I don't like and Daddy doesn't like doing, you know, but people have to do things and, you know, you get used to them' (tobacco worker's wife). It is probably true to say that while mothers in general adopt the attitude of 'We've *all* got to get up in the morning, like it or not', working-class mothers are more likely to extend this parallel to the whole work or school situation, whereas middle-class mothers are unwilling to suggest that there might be anything intrinsically unpleasant about either.

University teacher's wife:
   This is a sort of ritual, in the same way as we all say we don't want to get up. He usually says, if he's in the mood for this sort of conversation, that his head hurts and his tummy hurts and I'd better take his temperature – and everybody knows that there's nothing to this at all, but he sort of tries it on. I say *my* head hurts and *my* tummy hurts, and that I don't want to get breakfast.

Lorry driver's wife:
   'Oh belt up, go on, you'll be late' – 'I've got ear-ache' – 'Here, have a drink of cocoa'. She has ear-ache, headache, all sorts of aches, but when she goes she's all right, as gay as anything once she gets going. I think it's just the thought of going. I says, 'You don't do things because you like doing them, you do it cause you've got to' – I says 'You don't think I like stopping here doing all this lot!'

Cotton winder's wife:
   Well, I just say to him, 'Well you've *got* to – Jim's been and you've got to, and you know when Marilyn starts, if she suddenly says she don't want to go, you'll have to take her yourself'. So he understands now; and sometimes I say 'I don't want to go to the Raleigh [factory] today, but if I don't go to Raleigh we'll have nothing on the table, and no toffees, and no holidays, and no nowt'.

The inevitability of school can be emphasised to the child by appealing more precisely to the forces in society which back it up; but here again differences can be discerned in the way this is done. Middle-class mothers, where they draw attention to this at all, do it in general terms of 'the law', while working-class mothers are more inclined to warn the child of the actual sanctions which might operate and of the authority figures who might carry them out.

Police officer's wife:
   It was over sums – they'd just started doing this different sort of thing, and she didn't really like it. I said 'I'm afraid the law says that you've got to go to school now. You've been going for two years and you've found it quite congenial before, so there's no reason why you shouldn't find it quite congenial from now on.

There are things you'll have to get used to, and you'll find they come easy to you when you've had a little bit of practice'. And she went, and she had a little practice, and she got on all right.

University teacher's wife:
He hasn't refused – he knew that this was required by law from a very early age. He has a respect for the law.

Welder's wife:
Well, I'd do to her what I'd do to the youngest boy, tell her that a policeman will come and take *me* away if I don't send her to school.

Miner's wife:
I say 'You have to go to school if you're not poorly, *or*', I say, 'someone'll come to see your Mum and Dad', I say, 'and then we'll have to go away'. I know it's awful, but I do. Then I say 'You *must* go to school to learn to be clever' – and he says 'Why have I got to learn to be clever?' he says, 'because *I'm* not bothered'.

Labourer's wife:
. . . she was sick every morning at breakfast, you know, just got herself worked up and didn't want to go . . . . . on the Friday morning she was crying. 'Molly, it's no use, you've *got* to go to school or else the man from the Education will be here'. They're afraid of him, you know. He used to come next door. 'Well, I suppose I'll have to go to school' – and I've never had this trouble after that morning.

Nylon winder's wife:
He sometimes cracks on he's got a headache. I say, 'Come on, you'll have the school board man after me' – because we did, over the girl of fourteen – 'and if *he* keeps coming, you know, you'll have me in prison'. And he bucks up straight away as soon as he hears that.

In the last two quotations, the Education Welfare Officer is no stranger to the neighbourhood; and perhaps one reason for working-class mothers being more ready to bring him into their strategies for getting children to school is that he is a part of reality to them. He is also, of course, an external authority figure, and we showed in the previous study that there is a very clear class trend in the use of such figures to back up parental discipline (from 6 per cent in Class I and II to 27 per cent in Class V, leaping to 40 per cent for Class V boys).[13] But in any case, middle-class mothers would find it much less appropriate to present themselves to the child as powerless in the face of either teachers or other employees of the education authority; they tend to have reasonable confidence both in their own ability to make sensible decisions for their children (including keeping them at home from school if necessary), and in being able to justify those decisions to anyone who might question them.

Despite the class trends, on reading the transcripts one is struck by the ways in which the individual nature of the situation in the end determines how the mother handles it. How she sets about coping on a bad Monday morning is coloured by the personality of the child ('He says these things for the sake of saying them more than anything'); the mother's knowledge of the school ('I know his teacher, she'll find him a little job to do and she'll soon sort him out once he's there'); her previous experience ('Well, I *should* be concerned because she normally can't wait to get there'); and the child's usual health record ('These asthma children blow up so easily, you know') – as well as by whether the atmosphere between mother, child and school is one of mutual trust or mutual suspicion, and whether the mother basically sees school as a rich experience which no child would willingly forgo, or as a chore which children will naturally try to evade on the least excuse. It must be borne in mind that this latter attitude may in fact be justified where the school in question is incompetent in the sense of failing to provide adequate motivation through imaginative and empathic teaching.

'Children sometimes exaggerate, but I think they should be listened to . . .'
We have hardly considered as yet what children complain of in school other than expressing a general unwillingness to go. Often their reluctance is indeed not specific; but there are inevitably certain quite clear-cut complaints from the children themselves, some recurrent, most of which do not in fact culminate in a wish not to go to school. In a short series of questions which preceded and followed those on school reluctance and refusal, we explored children's complaints and mothers' responses.[14]

99. Do you know what he *doesn't* like [about school]?
100. Does he seem to dislike talking about school?
101. Did [change of teacher] upset him at all?
102. Does he ever complain about anything special at school?
    What do you say to him about that?
109. How do you feel about children's complaints of school?
    Do you think you should take them seriously?

At seven one of the most obvious potential sources of difficulty comes with the transition from the infants department, where 'learning through play' is emphasised, to the junior school, where the teaching situation becomes progressively more formal and where more pressure is exerted on the child to acquire the basic skills of literacy and numeracy. These new intellectual demands need not prove a source of stress to the child, and indeed many children very much enjoy the stimulus of a rather less free-floating day. In practice, however, junior teachers' educational aims tend to be rather more specific than those of the infant school teacher, and it is almost inevitable that they will be more conscious of the curriculum, feel more pressurised themselves and convey this pressure to the child. Moreover, in a large mixed-ability class it will tend to be the pace-setting bright children and the especially dull who will most urgently claim the teacher's attention; too often the mediocre child who is beginning to flounder is the one who most needs a rapid salvage operation, yet does not get it because of his habit of keeping a low profile. The stepped-up pressure to work, and to work persistently, is a focus for worry and complaint for children in all social classes.

Plumber's wife:
    'Oh Mum, I've got a headache, I'm not going this morning.' I says, 'Well, Una, if you don't go today, you've still got to go the next day – you might as well go, and you'll be all right'. She says, 'I know, Mummy, but we've got to do harder work'.

Nylon winder's wife:
    He sits there and he's quiet, and I say 'What's the matter, Tony?' Then he always bursts out crying and says 'Our teacher's always gi'ing me hard sums'. 'Come on', I says, 'I'll give you one or two to do'. He seems to get through what *I* give him . . . he says 'It's not reading, Mam, that bothers me, it's these hard sums our teacher gives me'. 'Well, you *will* now, duck', I says, 'you *will* have hard sums'.

Cotton winder's wife:
    I don't think he likes writing – well, he likes it, but it's too slow for him to stand there with a pencil. If the pencil'd just get up and walk around, you know . . .

University student's wife (herself a student; see also the next group):
    Generally speaking his attitude is extremely enthusiastic. His fears are attached to not being able to understand . . . there is no doubt

that when he is introduced to these new things at school, that he isn't quite coping. This must qualify his enjoyment of school at this time.

Tobacco worker's wife:
I think it's pretty general with the kiddies that they *know* that once they get into the juniors they've sort of got to work at things, most of their play is over – because they do an awful lot of play in the infants' school, don't they. I think when they see sort of older children, you know – one or two along here with satchels and, you know, homework. I think this is all sort of revolving round in their minds – I think that was Nigel's worry, that he was sort of going straight into this.

A second group of complaints, connected with work but in a rather different way, comes from children who are strongly work-oriented but find themselves frustrated in meeting the standards they have imposed upon themselves. Sometimes it is the school which, usually for perfectly sensible reasons, frustrates them, as in the first two examples below; more often it is one or more of their peers. These children tend to be middle-class.

University student's wife (herself a student):
He dislikes things which don't contribute to this pushing forward – um – he gets very annoyed, he says he gets taken off his work because he has to go and practise hymns and prayers, and he regards this as a complete waste of time: an interruption to what he regards as the real purpose of being there. Funnily enough, he even regards something that I would have thought he would have appreciated for itself, this sort of PT they do, as a waste of time because it takes him off what he thinks he ought to be doing. [Is this rather what you and your husband are like?] Well, this is certainly how I feel about things. We've tried desperately hard not to . . . er . . . communicate an attitude which in fact values this. We try to be a little more general in our appreciation of things it's possible to do . . . but as you say, I suppose we're always to be seen scribbling at our desks, and so they probably do think this is the most worthwhile and important thing to be doing. We can't *help* communicating this.

Scientific research worker's wife:
He doesn't like writing – *because* he writes beautifully well, but it

takes him a long, long time; and I think that his teacher insists that he write *more*, and I think she pushes him, and that he doesn't like. He seems to have an urge to have everything neat and tidy, and if he has to do it quickly he *can't* do it neatly, and he doesn't like it.

Professional engineer's wife:
Christina did get quite worried about this little boy – two or three times over the last holiday she's gone to bed crying because she thought that when she went to school this little boy would be nudging her and spoiling her writing – things like that. I did mention it to the teacher last night, but she said 'Well, I don't know', and we looked through her writing books, and it's all ever so nice. So I think it's just a little bit of Christina getting over-worried about things.

Sales representative's wife:
He was always coming home and saying the boy sitting next to him wouldn't let him get on with his work. Well, knowing Gordon, I said 'Probably you're as bad', and I never took any notice. Well, he told me this quite a lot. Well, then I went to Open Day. A little boy came to him, and he really was a nuisance, and wouldn't let Gordon tell me anything . . . well, then when we got to Gordon's desk, he went on and on and I had to say 'You get on with your work and let Gordon show me'. Well, when we came home, I said 'Well, Gordon, that little boy was a nuisance'. He said, 'Well, I've been telling you, Mummy, he never lets me get on with my work'. And during that time, Gordon's work went down, and I blame myself.

Sales director's wife:
She only complains that she wishes the class was more well behaved. The other morning she came home and said 'Oh, we missed time in music this morning cause of a lot of silly kids' – you know the way kids go on – 'It took Mrs Clark such a long time to sort them all out and get them quiet that we missed time in music cause the time had gone'. So I said 'Well, you'll always get *some* naughty children'.

This last child was also upset because the class as a whole had a reputation for bad behaviour – 'the worst class in the school' – whereas she herself was a well-behaved child, and was distressed by the group reprimands that were her daily experience: the unfairness exacerbated the discomfort of 'being shouted at'. The shouting which some teachers resort to as a feature of teaching groups of juniors was the biggest complaint for many children, and certainly the most frequent single complaint by children against teachers.

Soap processor's wife:
> One thing that upsets her, if the teacher shouts at the other children, like, shouts at the class. That upsets her, especially if she isn't doing anything wrong . . . . . He had them all in the hall, he was telling them all off, and yet she'd done nothing wrong, and I think that's what . . . you know, I think that hurts a bit, that does.

Commercial traveller's wife:
> Only that . . . well, this teacher is not well-liked, I think. It's unfortunate that she's, er . . . she shouts a lot at the children. I mean, her shouting doesn't mean anything, but at this age it upsets, because he's a sensitive child.

Chemical worker's wife:
> She was very upset. I had 'I don't want to go to school today, Mummy', and that sort of thing. She was a different type of teacher and a bit harder class as well. It went from playing to . . . er . . . a different type of work altogether. And it was a big jump, that jump from a softer teacher to a shouting teacher.

Other complaints refer to school dinners, the state of school lavatories and having to get undressed for PE. School dinner complaints are typically potential rather than actual, since many children are allowed to come home for lunch because they resist the idea of staying or like a little cosseting from their mother in the middle of the day. Where children do stay they tend to have needed persuasion in the past, though they usually have now come to enjoy it.

A remarkable number of complaints had to do with the child's modesty being threatened by faulty locks on the lavatory doors, wet floors in the lavatories which could result in the child's own clothes being soiled and consequent embarrassment, and in particular being expected to show their pants or even change altogether for dancing and PE. As one might expect from the marked class differences in these children's training in modesty at four,[15] such complaints come mainly from working-class children and their mothers tend to agree that their complaints are valid.

Lorry driver's wife:
> She's not very fond of PE because they make them take their

clothes off, and she don't like that – well, naturally they don't. I don't think they ought to do. If she can keep her frock on and she's done one over the teacher, she always tells me. 'Kept me frock on today', she says. It's only cause they have to undress that she don't like it.

Export packer's wife:

He's never seemed to like the idea that if they had – well, in the infants they called it 'Movement', you know – to get undressed and that – he's quite upset about that. The thought of taking his trousers off, and that's it.

Bleacher's wife:

In the juniors it's mixed of course, and when they change for PE they expect them to do it in the classroom – change. Well of course he gets very upset about it. Course, I said 'Go to the toilet and do it there'. 'They won't let you, Mum, the teachers have found out, and anyway the boys jump over the top.' And I said, 'Well, you'd have thought they'd have had a – even a partition; or let the boys six at a time go and change them there'. It really did upset him, and I said 'Would you like me perhaps to have a word – perhaps the teachers *don't* realise, and they would do something about it if . . .' – 'No, no, don't bother, Mam, it's all right'.

This last mother is concerned about her son's complaint and proposes to enter into negotiation about it; but, as often happens, the child is more perturbed by this prospect than by the original situation. We were interested to find out how far mothers were generally prepared to listen to their children's complaints of school and take them seriously, or whether some of them might think it unwise or inappropriate to do so. We approached this in two ways: by asking what the child complained about and how the mother responded to this specific complaint, and by later asking how she felt generally about such complaints, and whether she felt they should be taken seriously. Mothers fell into three categories. Some (54 per cent overall) were receptive to complaints and discussed them with the child, perhaps going on to suggest ways of helping, either from a distance by counselling the child himself or by negotiation with the school. A smaller group (11 per cent overall) listened to the child's complaint but did not overtly take it seriously; although they might well act upon it, often through negotiation, they did not feel that the child should be aware that they were concerned, for fear that 'give him an inch and he'll take an ell'. Many of this group felt that the authority of the teacher might be undermined if the mother was seen to be intervening. The third group (35 per cent overall) were unwilling to intervene at all, and tended to regard this kind of complaint as similar to tale-bearing about the child's peers – to be discouraged.

Openly takes seriously

PO driver's wife:
> Well, it's serious to the child, we know. I think you've got to sit and talk to them about their little problems, you haven't got to pass them off at all.

Twist hand's wife:
> Yes, sometimes I think it helps the child: I mean, if it gets worried about something at school and you don't try to help it, then it'll worry them all the more.

Sales representative's wife:
> I take them all seriously. I should have to listen and see what was wrong. All the same, he's got to go, hasn't he? But I have every sympathy for him. I used to try anything myself to get out of going to school. I used to hate school – they say it's the happiest days of your life, but not mine. I hated school from first to last. I have no illusions, I'm very sorry for him, I know just how he feels.

Teacher's wife:
> Yes, very seriously. I think it's so easy to think 'Oh, what a silly thing to complain about', but it's so *big* to a child of that age, and I think we've got to remember that it's big to them although it's of no importance to us.

Takes seriously but hides this from child

Scientific research worker's wife:
> Teacher is always right with me, on principle; I don't think one should discuss teachers with the children. [. . . take complaints seriously?] Oh, I do, and I often take a point up with the head-mistress; but I mean, as for talking to the children *themselves*, I never criticise a teacher; because I think if you start, you undermine their authority, and it's difficult enough for them, with classes of forty-odd children. But I have often seen the headmistress or the teacher herself, and talked to them. [And you wouldn't let Jeremy know you were going to do this?] Oh no.

Service layer's wife:

This little girl was always tormenting her at school . . . . . it seemed to be getting her down; so I went down and I asked the teacher, and she told me, you know, that she had an idea that this little girl was tormenting Kathleen; so her teacher said 'I'll have a word with her', and she was as right as rain. Of course, I never told Kathleen I went to the school. I pretended she'd sorted it out on her own – cause it gives them their own little independence then. Well, I think it does with her. It's hard on her – their little minds, they've got to try and sort out so much, haven't they? And that's why I want to *try* and leave things to her and see what a job she makes of them.

Executive officer's wife:

'Oh', he said, 'Mummy, I am sick of sitting next to that Jimmy Todd' – he says – 'I don't mind him, but he's always bobbing about and interfering with my work and nudging me, and my writing's going all funny'. So I said, 'Oh well, perhaps they'll move you, I don't suppose it'll be too long – perhaps she's just feeling her feet and finding out where you're best'. Anyway, he told his Daddy, and his Daddy said to me, 'I'm not having that, he's moving – I'm not having his work spoiled because a child's fidgeting about like that all the time, it's not necessary'. Well, Guy takes a little envelope on Monday morning with his dinner-money, and inside my husband put this little note – Guy wasn't aware there was a note. We asked if the child could be removed because our child felt it was affecting his work and would she not say anything about it, so he wasn't aware. It was three or four days after before I said 'Er – how are you going on?' – 'Oh', he said, 'Fine, I got moved just as you said I would'.

Does not take complaints seriously

Casual repairer's wife:

No, not at his age, because I mean a child has got a vivid imagination, and the least little thing they sort of can make it bigger than what it is. I mean, if you're going to worry about everything a child tells you goes off at school, you're going to be up and down at the school and you're going to cause more trouble than a little, so . . . If it was anything *really* big that was *really* upsetting him, I would go and investigate if it was really worthwhile; but little things that they come home with, you know, teacher's said this and teacher's said that, I just don't bother, because I know a child at school needs a lot of discipline, and there should be more. I think if a teacher was allowed to keep a child under more, there'd be a lot less trouble in schools. I mean if parents are going interfering with a teacher's job . . . she's got a job to do, and why shouldn't she get on with it. But if it came to where he was *marked* . . . if a teacher marked him or bruised him – anything like that, I wouldn't *bother* going to school, I'd take it further, and I should want to know what actually happened. But a smack is nothing to . . . a smack on the arm is nothing if the child asks for it. I know that from past experience of myself!

Electrician's wife;
When they're at this age I don't think so, because they've got such young ideas. One day they might like doing something, and the very next day they might hate doing the very same thing, and when they come home if you took notice of everything they say . . .!

Machine operator's wife:
No I don't. They've got to get used to things in life, and get used to its rough and tumble.

Table 5 gives the breakdown of this data. Combining the first two categories, we can see that the majority of parents do take their children's complaints seriously. The size of this majority increases, however, at the upper end of the social scale, where parents are less concerned to maintain images of authority and adult/child differentials, and also less fatalistic about the immutable nature of institutions. While sex differences are not very consistent, there is some evidence of interaction between sex and class, in that sex differences are more marked in the middle class than in the working class; so that middle-class boys stand out as being particularly likely to have their complaints taken seriously (81 per cent, compared with 70 per cent of middle-class girls and 61 per cent of working-class children). This provides another indication of middle-class parents' special concern over the socialisation of boys, and, perhaps, reflects their determination that nothing shall interfere with boys' progress through school.

There is an interesting parallel between these class differences and those we found when the children were four in the way mothers dealt with the child's complaints about other children. Again there was a similar increase at the upper end of the scale in the number of mothers who were prepared to listen to and discuss complaints. At

Table 5   *Mothers' response to children's complaints of school*

	social class					summary		
		III				I&II+	IIIman,	overall
	I&II	IIIwc	man	IV	V	IIIwc	IV, V	popn.
	%	%	%	%	%	%	%	%
Openly takes								
seriously								
boys	62	67	50	59	56	65	52	56
girls	60	55	51	51	44	58	50	52
								—
both	61	61	50	55	50	61	51	54
								—

Significance: trend ↘ not quite sig.   m.class/w.class   *
(p = 0·06)
between sexes   n.s.

Seriously, but								
hides from child								
boys	20	12	6	7	9	16	7	9
girls	11	14	14	9	10	12	12	12
								—
both	16	13	10	8	9	14	10	11

Significance: trend   n.s.   m.class/w.class   n.s.
between sexes   n.s.

Not seriously								
boys	18	21	44	34	35	19	41	35
birls	29	31	35	40	46	30	38	36
								—
both	23	26	40	37	41	25	39	35
								—

Significance: trend ↗   ***   m.class/w.class   ****
between sexes   n.s.

that time we felt that these children were, in effect, being rewarded
for putting a good case and expressing themselves well verbally, so
that this kind of class difference has important implications for
cognitive and linguistic development, not just for the socialisation
process. This would still seem to hold true at seven.

Although we have talked in terms of combining the two groups
who fundamentally take the child's complaints seriously, whether
overtly or covertly, it must be remembered that *to the child* the feel

of the interchange may be very much altered according to whether the sympathy his mother feels is overtly expressed. The scientific research worker's wife quoted above, for whom 'teacher is always right on principle', felt that her child did not talk to her about school so much as formerly: 'as he gets no sympathy from me, he keeps it more and more to himself'. This mother's basic assumption that the teacher is right contrasts with an architect's wife's equally firm assumption that the child is right: 'I always do, and I always back the child up, and I think this is why she's ready to go, because she knows if there's anything really wrong, we'll be on her side'. Many grey issues arise in between these two whole-hog approaches, however: fairness to both teacher and child, demarcations of responsibility, the wish to convey either an authoritarian or a democratic ethic, considerations of courtesy and tact, considerations of openness and frankness, the mother's long-term knowledge of the child's personality and idiosyncrasies and her shorter-term knowledge of the school.

University teacher's wife:
> I'd certainly take them seriously; but here I'm in flat disagreement with the headmaster, though he doesn't know it and probably I shan't raise it. He said the other day, in fact, at Open Day, that parents should never criticise teachers to children. I think that's nonsense, *mainly* because I want her to be discriminating in her judgement of people as I want her to be discriminating in other things. I'm not saying I should encourage her to be destructively critical, I'd try and help her to see both sides, as I would if we were discussing anyone else; but to pretend that teachers are beyond criticism is nonsense, like saying children mustn't criticise grownups. In any case, when you're building a relationship where there's free discussion of anything the child wants to raise, you can't suddenly clam up on this one subject and more or less say 'Here I'm only going to talk pleasantries'. The child would see through you at once – I hope!

Student's wife:
> I can imagine circumstances in which it would be highly essential for something to be done about them, yes. I mean, I don't think one is justified in taking the view that, simply because it is a *child* that is complaining, there's no real grounds for their complaint. After all, teachers are human, and schools are institutions that give a lot of scope for things to go wrong . . . . . I wouldn't dismiss in a light-hearted fashion *every* grumble that came home . . . . .

People who come to me with grumbles – I tend on the whole not to sympathise directly, but to say 'Oh yes, tell me more about it', sort of 'explain your grumble in full'; and very often this is sufficient, having done this they feel better about it. And in this way you don't have to commit yourself to saying their point of view is reasonable, but at the same time they get the chance to tell you all about it and get it off their chest. There are many reasons, I think, why I don't want to be too sympathetic with James's grumbles; because he is inclined to think that the world owes him a living a bit, you know! And to be too sort of smothering and maternal about this encourages it a bit, I think.

'After all, half their life is school . . .'
Thus far in this book we have been looking at various ways in which the child indicates to his mother how well he likes his school: her general impressions of his adaptation to school and teacher, his reluctance or refusal to go to school, his attempts at malingering in order to escape. In order to examine more sensitively the sex and class differences in children's acceptance of school, we devised a measure to combine these various indications: this we have called the CLS index (an index of the child's liking for school). Table 6 shows

Table 6   *An index of children's liking for school*

Item		*Based on question*	*Response*	*Score*
(1)	95.	Does he like school?	Very much	3
			Well enough	2
			Not much	1
			Strongly dislikes	0
(2)	101.	Does he seem to get on well with his teacher?	Yes	2
			So-so	1
			No	0
(3)	104.	Does he ever say he doesn't want to go to school today?	Never	2
			Sometimes	1
			Often	0
(4)	106.	Does he ever pretend he's not well, so as to stay at home from school?	Never, or not now	2
			Sometimes	1
			Often	0
(5)	108.	Has he ever *refused* to go to school?	Never yet	1
			Has done	0

Possible and actual score range 0–10

how the index is made up. The distribution of the resulting scores is in fact J-shaped, with more children scoring the maximum of 10 than any other single category; and it seemed reasonable to assume that scores of 9 and 10 meant that those children (52 per cent) liked school quite a lot, whereas scores between 0 and 6 indicated children who on the whole rather strongly disliked school (17 per cent). Table 7 shows the class and sex differences between these two high- and low-scoring groups.

Table 7   *High and low scorers on the index of children's liking for school*

	social class					summary		
			III			I&II+	IIIman,	overall
	I&II	IIIwc	man	IV	V	IIIwc	IV, V	popn
	%	%	%	%	%	%	%	%
High scorers (9–10)								
boys	59	48	41	44	61	54	44	47
girls	74	57	49	57	69	66	53	57
both	67	53	45	51	65	60	49	52

Significance: trend non-linear ****   m.class/w.class ***
                              between sexes ***

Low scorers (0–6)								
boys	23	21	21	27	16	22	22	22
girls	2	8	15	13	8	5	14	11
both	12	14	18	20	12	13	18	17

Significance: trend n.s.   m.class/w.class n.s.
                              between sexes ****

The result of this analysis again confirms the findings in Tables 1 and 2 showing that children at both extremes of the social-class scale are more likely to be favourably disposed towards school than children in the other half of the population (skilled manual). With more information, however, it is now possible to see that this tendency is not at variance with the statement that on the whole more middle-class than working-class children like school. There is also clear confirmation that school is significantly more acceptable to girls than to boys. In terms of those who show a pronounced aversion for school, the results are not so clear-cut, since neither the social class trend nor the middle-class/working-class difference is significant. However, it remains true that significantly more boys than girls are strongly averse to going to school.

Children who are alienated from school are often said to have reached that point, not so much because of any shortcomings in the school, as because the home has failed to provide the back-up and support that teachers would like. This view makes the assumption that the two worlds of home and school cannot successfully operate in separate orbits, but that one must positively support the other: interestingly enough, this support is more often discussed as being needed from home to school rather than the other way round. In the next chapters, we will examine how parents see their role in the child's education and what they look for in the relationship between home and school.

NOTES

1 Max Clyne, *Absent* (London, Tavistock, 1966).
2 J. W. B. Douglas and J. M. Ross, 'The effects of absence on primary school performance', *Br. Journ. Ed. Res.*, 38 (1965).
3 K. Fogelman and K. Richardson, 'School attendance: some results from the National Child Development Study', in B. Turner (ed.), *Truancy* (London, Ward Lock, 1974).
4 In our own sample, 52 per cent at age seven years had pre-school siblings; by the time they were eleven, only 25 per cent had pre-school siblings.
5 *Children and their Primary Schools* (Plowden Report) (London, HMSO, 1967).
6 L. Hersov, 'Refusal to go to school', *Journ. Ch. Psychol. and Psychiatr.*, I (1960).
7 J. Kahn, 'School phobia or school refusal?', in B. Turner (ed.), op. cit. (1974).
8 Max Clyne, op. cit. (1966).
9 J. and E. Newson, op. cit. (1968), pp. 215–16; Penguin edn pp. 226–8.
10 John Apley, *The Child with Abdominal Pains* (Oxford, Blackwell, 1959).
11 J. Apley and R. Mac Keith, *The Child and his Symptoms*, 2nd edn (Oxford, Blackwell, 1968).
12 J. and E. Newson, op. cit. (1976*b*).
13 ibid.
14 See full interview schedule, Appendix I.
15 At four we found that, on the issue of whether it was permissible for the child to see his parents undressed, the attitude which was most characteristic for Class I and II mothers (that he could see either of them – 59 per cent) was in fact a minority attitude for the population as a whole (32 per cent). Forty-six per cent of the total sample thought children should see *neither* parent undressed, rising steadily from 19 per cent in Class I and II to 68 per cent in Class V, p < 0·001. J. and E. Newson, op. cit. (1968).

Chapter 3

The Prosthesis of Culture

Man is not a naked ape but a culture-clothed human being,
hopelessly ineffective without the prosthesis provided by culture
J. S. Bruner, 'The psychobiology of pedagogy'[1]

By the time he goes to school, the human child is already a product
of his culture if only by virtue of the fact that he has been reared by
adults who have themselves, for two, three or four decades, been
exposed to cultural pressures. It is not possible to envisage a culture-
free child: the 'child of nature' (whatever that may be) must reflect a
culture in which 'nature' is tolerated, just as a test-tube child would
reflect a culture that had produced laboratories.

Children brought up in a nuclear family, in a commune or by an
unsupported mother must subtly adjust to the way their adult care-
takers see their position in a society which has views about the
normality and acceptability of nuclear families, communes and
mothers on their own. In many other ways, long before he is necessarily aware of a world beyond his family, the child's notions and
expectations are shaped by an enormous variety of manifestations of
his culture as mediated by his parents. His mother's choice of his
first feeding medium, whether human nipple or rubber teat; the kinds
of dirt (agricultural or industrial, say) that his skin is exposed to, and
how or whether they are cleaned off; what is considered 'naughty' –
whether anything is considered naughty – and how the notion of
naughtiness is conveyed; the spoken language he hears around him –
whether it reflects a technological society and closely approximates
to written language, whether its roots are wholly oral, or whether his
parents, though living in a culture which is dependent on written
language, belong to a subculture which is comfortable only with the
oral form: these diverse experiences are only a few examples of the

means by which the culture makes itself felt at a quite implicit level in child upbringing.

Parents cannot help being the carriers of implicit cultural messages; but they do have some choice in how far they explicitly offer the child experience of institutions and concepts which belong to the world beyond basic family subsistence. We cannot imagine a culture-free child, but there is such a thing as a culture-deprived child: we can discern many possible degrees of contact between children and those activities and ideas which are provided by the culture in the community but not immediately available in a closed family unit. The young child is dependent upon his parents to welcome and seek such experiences for him.

The experiences we have in mind are of very various kinds. Some involve the formal coming-together of groups within the wider culture for a specific purpose: for instance, theatres exist to put on plays, variety shows and pantomimes, and audiences convene to watch these events; parents may or may not think it important that their children should take part in this kind of extra-familial cultural activity.[2] Religious services, the screening of films, dog-shows, trade exhibitions, Nottingham's Goose Fair, football matches, race meetings – all these are examples of cultural events which cannot be fully simulated within the family, and through which parents can therefore choose to widen the horizons of their children or not. Other formal manifestations of the culture include those permanent shrines of our values, interests or beliefs which can be visited by members of the culture without reference to specific events: museums, art galleries, stately homes, cathedrals, monuments, zoos, and places of sentimental or historic association such as Big Ben, Robin Hood's Major Oak or Carnaby Street.

These experiences are necessarily formal for the child in the sense that a deliberate effort has to be made by an adult in order to seek them out – and indeed they take on the status of 'outings' and 'treats'. But there are also day-to-day ways in which parents can welcome the outside culture into their child's home life. One is by the provision of books and comics, which offer the child a different view of the world, whether through the eyes of David Copperfield or Desperate Dan. A less obvious way of opening the family to the culture is by answering children's questions. The mother who takes the child's questions seriously – listens to them, thinks about them, and tries to furnish him with a satisfying answer – not only gives him further information about the world but, by treating his inquisitiveness as natural and sensible, and his questions as interesting to her, expresses to him her own involvement with the culture.

This is perhaps the crux of what parents are doing when they take an active role in introducing the culture to their child. By taking him on visits to places of interest, making sure that he has access to the written media, answering his questions and searching for the answers elsewhere when her own knowledge is inadequate, the mother repeatedly characterises cultural interests as *relevant to herself* and, by identification, to the child as well. Values which are both taken for granted (rather than stated) and demonstrated in action are likely to have a special potency for a child during these formative years. Consider the difference in the hidden messages reaching the child in these two families: both quotations are in answer to the inquiry 'Can you always answer his questions? . . . What do you do if you can't?' The first shows lively minds through three generations.

Building Foreman's wife:
    Well, I explain it as far as I can, and then I say 'Now look, I don't understand' – I *tell* him I don't understand it. Well, me Dad's pretty up on them sort of, you know, as I'd term it, general knowledge, you see. Well, he'll praps be able to answer them. Or what we can't answer, we try and find out. [Where from?] Well, books, or praps verbal if we can find an explanation about it. I mean . . . you know . . . when you're going to Birmingham there's a big gravel pit. Now it's full of water. Well then, when we went by one time, it was all grass all over it, you see, so I says to me Dad 'Weren't that full of water?' So he said 'Yes'. So Barry said 'Well *why*, Grandpa? – cause you said gravel pits are very deep, well *why* isn't it deep now, cause what have they done with the water?' So me Dad says, 'I don't know, me duck, but I'll see what I can do'. And do you know what they'd done? You know from the power station, they'd had the ashes blown in, you know, instead of taking them with the lorries – it had saved them, oh, he did tell Barry how many pounds it had saved them – they'd done this pipeline across and filled it. Now you see, he went and found out for him. [Where did he find out from?] I don't know, but I know when I was a child, he . . . you know, even now we'll be going along and I'll say 'What's that?' Me Dad'll say 'Do you think I'm a walking encyclopaedia?' But he always seems as though he can find it out, such things as that. But my kiddies have never gone to sleep in the car, you can go from here to Kingdom-come, and they'd never sleep; and me Dad says no, you don't expect them to, and we've always tried to make the ride interesting. Me Dad's a van driver, and on Saturday morning Barry will go with me Dad, and the things he sits down after and he'll be telling

you! They'll pass something, a building, you see, and me Dad can tell him. Ever so interesting, and me Dad's as interested as Barry is.

Unemployed labourer's wife:
Not always – I've lost my schooling now! I mean you don't keep it up, do you, what you learn in your own schooldays, I mean I'm forty-six, and I think you don't sort of keep that interest. He was on about Nelson or something the other day, wanted to know if it were true, but I can't remember all that. I just said 'I don't know owt about it, duck, you'll have to ask your teacher'.

It was because the active participation that spells out relevance seemed to us the vital factor that we did not include television as a way in which parents involve children with their culture. Television is almost universally provided, and therefore does not readily distinguish attitudes; and simply witnessing a programme together may or may not convey parental values to the child. The mother who has tears in her eyes as she watches news reporting of some human disaster expresses without words her involvement in life beyond her own street; the mother who chats gaily through the same news sequence identifies the suffering of others as removed from, and irrelevant to, her own conception of reality. Recognising these subtle differences as important, we yet did not feel competent to gauge them adequately within the limitations of this study.

Once the child inhabits another environment than home, the issue of relevance is brought to a new level of emphasis. From his first day at school, he will perceive the activities and values of school life within a work of reference that has been gradually built up by home-based experience. It is logical to suppose that a child will adapt more successfully to this necessarily novel situation if it includes some points of similarity to well-established home activities. Every reception-class teacher is familiar with the child who has to be *taught* how to listen to a story, turn the pages of a book, hold a pencil and scissors, and give his attention to a puzzle for as long as five minutes, because all these basic skills have been totally outside his previous life-style. For such a child, the classroom makes demands which are alien in terms of concentration, mobility control and fine motor co-ordination, before one even approaches the question of styles of communication and formal teaching goals, and how alien they too may be. Children who are used to looking at books themselves, and seeing adults also consulting or enjoying them; who have used paints, crayons and plasticine to produce decorative or representational effects; who have followed the sequence of events in a story, and learned to stay listening until the denouement; who have discovered the pay-offs of concentration – that sticking with a toy leads to more and more ideas for exploiting it: these children enter school to find many points of reference with previous interests to soften the unfamiliarity. Indeed, they are likely to discover that school picks up home pursuits and refurbishes them with greatly enhanced facilities – a more opulent choice of media for drawing, painting and modelling, more books, and a teacher with a new repertoire of stories, many and various puzzles, and constructional games against which to pit their wits. Such children undoubtedly have a head start in the formal learning process, which may well even be traceable back to the first year of life.[3]

By the time we reach the seven-year-old stage on which we are focusing here, school is no longer an unfamiliar environment, and we are not so much talking in terms of preparation for the school world as in terms of how the home backs up and sustains the school's professionally educational role. It is a reasonably well-documented assumption, to take British studies only, that some form of home back-up is in fact important through the child's primary school years if he is to be successful in this part of his education. Douglas, whose work has been particularly influential in drawing attention to parental interest in their children's education as a salient factor for subsequent academic achievement, used a rather simple measure of 'interest'; he based it partly on 'comments made by the class teacher at the end of the first and at the end of the fourth primary school year, and partly on the record of the number of times each parent visited the school to discuss the child's progress with the Head or class teacher'.[4] The National Child Development Study added parental aspirations for the child to these indices.[5] Plowden also used attendance at Open Days together with other indices such as provision of books and helping at home with school work.[6] Young and McGeeney, in a study of one junior school that illustrates many of the attendant difficulties of action research, none the less were able to show certain significant differences within the school in achievement between children whose parents made use of the school's intensified communication efforts and those whose parents did not.[7]

One difficulty with measures that rely strongly on parent attendance is that they tend to confound parental interest in education as such with parental pressure on schools to ensure that their child's needs are receiving the attention they expect. Parents who actively 'push' in this way put teachers on their mettle by subtly indicating to them that what they are doing for the child is being closely monitored and evaluated. Douglas also noted that, higher up the social scale, more fathers tend to visit the school; and it may well be that this adds a delicate status difference to the pressure which is brought to bear. Parental influence on schools can be seen both at individual and at community level, however; schools with catchment areas in which high expectations are shared by a majority of their parents will find themselves under constant and sustained pressure, and of a relatively informed kind, to achieve 'good' results, whatever the current criterion of 'good' may be. (In the case of this sample, schools could be conveniently and explicitly evaluated as 'good', 'bad', or 'only average' in terms of eleven-plus selection results. This is no longer so, and it will be interesting to see what new measures parents evolve over the years for judging the efficacy of primary schools.) For complex reasons, then, individual parental interest is difficult to separate from community pressure to maintain and improve the general facilities and teaching standards in schools located in middle-class catchment areas.

Taking as a starting-point the unquestioned fact that middle-class children are more academically successful than working-class children, the factors that bring this about in terms of direct influence from home and family on to the child are still not clearly delineated. We have suggested the influences which give some children a head start before they set foot in school in terms of the relevance of pre-school experience and parental attitudes. We have also seen that middle-class children seem happier in school than working-class children generally, *with the exception of unskilled workers' children*; but it may well be that the potent mixture for academic success is enjoyment of school *plus* a certain pressurising from parents towards taking all educational activities, both at home and at school, more seriously: certainly many middle-class mothers express the view that happiness on its own is not enough! The work of Bernstein and his colleagues has drawn attention to a further array of influences by suggesting that many working-class children experience severe communication difficulties at school, in the sense that they are ill-prepared, language-wise, to appreciate or express more abstract concepts, which tend to be articulated in elaborate linguistic structures;[8] and our own study of these children at four found many examples not only of verbal experience being richer and more copious higher up the social scale, but also of the child's verbal expression and facility being repeatedly rewarded by middle-class parents as a direct consequence of their child-rearing attitudes and values.[9] Yet another line of explanation that we should keep in mind derives from our own findings on child-centredness at both four and seven.[10] If child-centredness increases markedly as one ascends the social scale, it may be that middle-class children acquire a firmer confidence in their own worth, their own capabilities and their own rights to the attention of adults: which may add up to a powerful motivation towards active learning and the discovery of concepts and ideas for their own sake. And this brings us close to the thorny question of the improvability of the child's 'intelligence'. Bruner has quoted P. M. Greenfield as questioning, in a conference paper: 'If a mother believes her fate is controlled by external forces, that she does not control the means necessary to achieve her goals, what does this mean for her children?'[11] We would extend her question: if a child does not believe in his own intrinsic worth, in his own basic *considerability*, how can he be motivated to achieve his goals, or indeed to set himself goals at all?

In practice, all the factors that we have discussed so far in this chapter, and perhaps many more, are likely to be simultaneously at work: not only that, but almost inextricably intertwined. It is probably in the nature of the human social condition that problems of this kind simply do not have clear-cut answers, and certainly any single-factor theory tends to lead to a quite unhelpful oversimplification. Our own data may, however, illumine a little further some of the ways in which parents' and teachers' roles complement or run counter to each other; and may possibly help to dispel some of the wilder misconceptions about the home life of ordinary children. In the remainder of this chapter, we will look at the extent to which the seven-year-old child is involved with his parents in various cultural activities within the wider community. In the following chapter, we shall move closer to the school and explore what we shall call home–school concordance – by which we mean parental support within the home for the child's school-based activities; and we shall then consider from the parents' perspective the sensitive area of children's achievement or otherwise in reading skills.

'We go out together . . . we get toffed up . . .'

We asked a number of questions about whether the child had experienced, *with his parents*, various outside events or visits to places of cultural interest; in addition, we included a question about extra-curricular lessons; which usually do entail attendance at a dancing studio, music teacher's house or at a gymnasium or swimming lido, and which meet our criterion of involvement with the outside culture organised, and therefore endorsed, by parents. Schools themselves, of course, try to provide all children with a basic common denominator of such experiences by arranging not only school assemblies and formal concerts, but also trips to museums and theatres, visits to factories and fire stations, and so on; but we are not here attempting to measure the child's *total* experience of such things, but how far the limited school provision of them is actively affirmed and backed up at home. Thus Saturday morning children's film shows, which children attend unaccompanied, would not rate positively in Question 139 below.

The questions as asked follow; their context can be seen by referral to the interview schedule (Appendix i).

133. Do you pay for any extra lessons for N – music or dancing or anything else at all?
      Does anybody give him any special lessons that you *don't* pay for?
139. Do you ever take him to the pictures?
140. Have you ever taken him to a theatre or a concert?
141. What about museums and art galleries – has he been to any with you or his Daddy?
142. Is there any other exhibition or show or anything like that which you've taken him to?
      [prompt] Has he ever been to a zoo or a circus with you?
143. Does he ever go to a football match, or any other sporting event?
144. Does he ever go to a church service with you or his Daddy?

The data derived from the answers to these questions will be presented below in a series of short tables, for clarity, each accompanied by brief comments; these individual patterns are finally combined in an index of general cultural interest shown by the family in relation to this child.

Table 8   *Children whose parents arrange extra-curricular lessons for them*

	social class					summary		
			III			I&II +	IIIman,	overall
	I&II	IIIwc	man	IV	V	IIIwc	IV, V	popn
	%	%	%	%	%	%	%	%
boys	9	5	3	2	0	7	2	4
girls	34	10	9	8	8	23	9	12
both	22	8	6	5	4	15	5	8

Significance: trend ↘ ****   m.class/w.class ****
(non-linear ***)   between sexes ****   interaction sex/class *

Overall, the proportion of children who have additional lessons of any kind is rather low; but sex and class differences are highly consistent and significant, and there is a very striking tendency for professional and managerial class girls to be encouraged in this kind of interest (Table 8). It is undoubtedly the prevalence of dancing lessons which causes girls to predominate. In Class I and II, dancing usually means ballet; in the other classes, too, ballet is popular, but there is also a group of very dedicated ballroom dancers, who are much more consciously being groomed for stardom. Ballroom dancing involves children on a competitive basis from a very early stage; not only do they work for a series of grades of 'medal', but they also attend sessions of competitive dancing against children from other dancing schools and other districts. Good boy partners are at a premium, and partners may even be advertised for; while parents invest both time and money in making extravagant costumes and escorting children to competitive events.

Music lessons – mainly piano or violin at this age – are also more popular with girls than boys, but boys are more likely to learn an instrument than learn dancing. Here again, even at seven, 'working for grades', i.e. public examinations, is usual, and probably as often puts children off for good as provides a stimulus to keep them going. Like the 'eleven-plus' for schools, grades serve as a short-cut measure of music teachers' and dancing schools' success: when the results come out, a crop of advertisements appears in the *Nottingham Evening Post,* all in the vein of 'The Nadia Critchley School of Dancing congratulates the following pupils on their wonderful results . . .'

Other kinds of lessons are rather few and far between. Judo enjoyed a short vogue for young children as well as older ones, a little while after the time of the fieldwork; by the early 1970s it had been overtaken in popularity by karate, where children of this age were seldom involved. Swimming and boxing, while available, are again more sought after for older children.

It might be thought that working-class families would patronise the cinema at least as often as the professional and managerial group; but there is in fact a clear class trend showing that this is not the case (Table 9). The reason is probably partly economic. A family outing to the pictures, particularly to the larger city-centre cinemas, can be a very expensive occasion, and prohibitive to families on a low income – especially when bus fares and ice-creams are included as necessary extras. However, the economics of entertainment are not a simple question of higher incomes being correlated with more outings.

Table 9   *Children whose parents sometimes take them to the cinema*

	social class					summary		
			III			I&II+	IIIman,	overall
	I&II	IIIwc	man	IV	V	IIIwc	IV, V	popn
	%	%	%	%	%	%	%	%
boys	86	78	76	59	44	82	69	73
girls	94	92	65	59	51	93	62	70
both	90	85	70	59	48	87	66	71

Significance: trend ↘ ****   m.class/w.class ****
                between sexes n.s.   interaction class/sex **

When these children were babies, we noted that nearly half the working-class parent couples went out together in the evening once or less in a year, whereas this was true of only a quarter of the professional/managerial group; and working-class mothers frequently commented that they were happy enough to watch television at home.[12] In the subsequent period of increasing ownership of colour television rather than black and white, it has been very obvious to our interviewers that colour television became the norm in working-class households long before this happened in professional families. Perhaps the pattern of home entertainment laid down for these mothers while the children are very young, and backed up by making sure that the television set is an up-to-the-minute model, tends to reduce the attractiveness of an outing to the cinema.

The fact that in the middle class more girls than boys are taken to the cinema, whereas in the working class this trend is somewhat reversed, is difficult to explain; but it may be that middle-class parents more often deliberately avoid taking children to films which include an element of violence – Westerns and war films – and that this restriction makes middle-class boys less interested in the cinema than middle-class girls, who can uninhibitedly enjoy the singing, dancing, costumes and romance in those of the big spectaculars that are considered suitable for children.

Bleacher's wife:
　　Ooh yes, I do take her, ooh and she *does* cry! She does, and about things that . . . Snow White . . . but she cried because it was . . . 'It was such a *lovely* ending, Mum' [sniff] – you know, like that. She cries at things on TV, too, she sits there and you can watch her

trying to control herself, and then she'll look at me and she'll come and sit at the side of me and says 'Let's both have a cry, eh, ducks, shall we?' Yes – she's deeply touched at things like that.

Baker's wife:
    He wouldn't want to go. He just refuses to go, and then you have to talk him into it. Oh, now we went to see *Mary Poppins*, he did want to see that; he was quite thrilled about that, and that's the only thing I've known. He wants to see *Dr Who* – it's coming round, so . . .

Table 10 *Children who have been to a concert (other than at school) with their parents*

	social class					summary		
			III			I&II+	IIIman,	overall
	I&II	IIIwc	man	IV	V	IIIwc	IV, V	popn
	%	%	%	%	%	%	%	%
boys	9	3	7	1	9	6	6	6
girls	12	14	8	0	5	13	6	8
both	10	9	7	6	7	10	6	7

Significance: trend n.s.   m.class/w.class n.s.
                        between sexes   n.s.

Only a tiny proportion of children were said to attend concerts with their parents (Table 10), even though concerts were defined broadly enough to include pop, folk, brass band and classical music, as well as the variety concerts of light music which are often available at seaside resorts. Although there is a slight increase at the upper end of the class scale, this is entirely accounted for by middle-class girls. However, the conclusion must be that this is simply not a popular form of entertainment for children of this age in Nottingham.

By contrast with the last question, the overall percentage of children who have been to the theatre is remarkably high (Table 11); and we suspect that this is primarily due to the extended pantomime season which Nottingham enjoys each year at the Theatre Royal, rather than to the more widely known Nottingham Playhouse. Children are in fact very well provided for in Nottingham; both the Theatre Royal and the Playhouse present a number of programmes that are suitable for children during the year, as well as the special

Table 11   *Children who have been to a theatre with their parents*

	social class					summary		
		III				I&II+	IIIman,	overall
	I&II	IIIwc	man	IV	V	IIIwc	IV, V	popn
	%	%	%	%	%	%	%	%
boys	78	55	34	35	18	67	33	42
girls	75	63	48	36	36	70	45	51
both	77	59	41	35	27	68	39	47

Significance: trend ↘ ****   m.class/w.class ****
                        between sexes *

children's programmes at Christmas, and there are also several excellent amateur theatre companies who cater for children during the Christmas season. (The Playhouse also, more recently than this round of fieldwork, runs children's workshops on Saturday mornings and introduces children in schools to their mobile theatre.) Rather more girls than boys appear, which may reflect their interest in ballet and romantic musical shows. The strong social class gradient in the proportion of children who have been to the theatre no doubt again reflects an economic factor as well as the other consideration that we have mentioned in connection with cinema-going. Further factors are likely to operate in addition. 'Live theatre' as opposed to canned cinema has a parallel in natural, unprocessed food as opposed to canned food, and we have noted elsewhere[13] the special valuation that professional/managerial people tend to place on the 'fresh and natural'; many middle-class parents would feel that they had a duty to introduce children to the tradition of live theatre, however good the 'theatre' provided by television. This feeling of duty may well outweigh the anxiety frequently mentioned in connection with concerts and theatres: that these events, more formal than a cinema show, demand standards of behaviour that some children are not yet capable of maintaining.

Loco fireman's wife:
    Ooh no – she wouldn't sit still, I don't suppose, that long.

Chemical worker's wife:
    She likes going to open-air lidos – anywhere like that as long as she hasn't got to sort of sit and listen to anything. It wouldn't be

any good taking Hazel to a panto, where it would be a long thing, because she would be bored . . . she would be fidgety . . . she wouldn't sit down for anyone behind to see. She must be somewhere where she can have plenty of room to spread herself – sprawl. She's looking forward to going to the lido again, anywhere like that Hazel likes – where she can just let herself go, with no restrictions. It's no use taking Hazel where you can walk through lovely gardens to look at the pretty flowers and you've got to walk along the path . . . I mean, you know – anywhere where she's got to be quiet and hushed, that wouldn't suit Hazel.

Table 12 *Children who have been to a museum or art gallery with their parents*

	social class					summary		
			III			*I&II+*	*IIIman,*	*overall*
	I&II	*IIIwc*	*man*	*IV*	*V*	*IIIwc*	*IV, V*	*popn*
	%	%	%	%	%	%	%	%
boys	94	91	72	64	56	93	69	75
girls	85	84	65	76	49	84	65	70
both	89	88	69	70	52	88	67	73

Significance: trend ↘ ****   m.class/w.class ****
between sexes n.s.

Visits to museums and art galleries (Table 12) represent a very popular activity; and this is presumably because the Nottingham local authority itself maintains several establishments of historical interest which are open to the public free of charge. In particular, the two most mentioned were Wollaton Hall, an Elizabethan mansion which at the time of the survey was mainly a natural history museum, though it now also houses an industrial museum, and Nottingham Castle, known more for its appearance on Player's cigarette packets than for its beauty, which incorporates both a museum and an art gallery. There are several additional public and private galleries within the city boundary, and a number of stately homes which can be visited within easy access – but these, of course, involve expense.

Once again the social class gradient is clear and consistent, but here the sex difference disappears (is if anything reversed). Perhaps natural history and the weapons, armour and subterranean tunnels of the Castle are thought to be more manly interests.

Toolmaker's wife:
> She's been to quite a few museums. Um . . . the Castle . . . that's something we try to do at weekends, so she's got something to write about. And Wollaton Hall – she's been up there a time or two. She writes down anything – just a subject for her to think about and write about . . .

Labourer's wife:
> She went round Woburn Abbey, you know, last week and, er – she really enjoyed it. I didn't think she would, you know, because I wasn't very interested myself. It was nice and that, but it wouldn't be of interest . . . to myself. But she was looking at everything as though it was real. I was surprised really.

Lorry driver's wife:
> He doesn't like that. I tried taking him round. The only things he liked in the Castle Museum were the old stage-coaches, the swords, and the chains on the dungeon walls.

During the short period when a Conservative government imposed museum charges, it was frequently argued that families who were interested enough to visit museums would also be prepared to pay an entrance fee. These figures are of interest in comparison with those for theatre attendance, when one looks at the economically deprived end of the class scale. Half the Class v children have been to a museum with their parents, compared with only a quarter of this group who have been to the theatre. It is clear that many of these already educationally deprived children would be still further de-

Table 13   *Children whose parents have taken them to a zoo or circus*

	social class						summary		
			III				*I&II+*	*IIIman,*	*overall*
	I&II	*IIIwc*	*man*	*IV*	*V*		*IIIwc*	*IV, V*	*popn*
	%	%	%	%	%		%	%	%
boys	87	88	83	68	58		87	77	80
girls	91	88	81	67	69		89	76	80
both	89	88	81	67	64		88	76	80

Significance: trend ↘ ***   m.class/w.class ****
between sexes n.s.

prived by a charge on museums, which for a family in poverty may be the only family outing feasible. Four out of five of these children have been to zoo, circus or both (Table 13). The circus visits Nottingham every year, and usually includes a small travelling zoo; and there is a small permanent zoo on the outskirts of Nottingham. Families wanting to visit a 'real' zoo must travel further afield. The social class difference reflects the financial outlay which is involved in taking a family party on what will usually prove to be a rather expensive trip, either for circus tickets (with likely additional expenditure on programmes, ices and popcorn, and all the circus mementoes which are given the hard sell in and around the tent), or for travel and admission to the zoo and the subsidiary expenses incurred there. This form of entertainment is equally popular with both sexes.

Optician's wife:
  Well this year we didn't go to my parents' [for summer holiday], so they just sort of had a choice each of outings; but we landed up at the zoo when she had *her* choice. Twycross Zoo – that's where we always land when she has *her* way. She's not interested in the seaside.

Bleacher's wife:
  . . . I mean, all I think is what will keep them amused, because walking round gardens isn't amusing, and if *they're* not amused then *you're* not amused, and they get annoyed and it's a vicious circle; so I try to think what would amuse them best, even if it wouldn't suit me. I mean, like a circus – I've *no* interest in a circus at all, never have had; but I take them, and you know I clap as loud and laugh as loud as . . . and all the other daft stuff. Now my husband wouldn't do that – he'd say 'Well *you* go' . . . . . To my mind he doesn't – what's the word? – *enter into* the thing as a child. I'll act daft as the rest, where he'll *sit*, you know . . . . . if we've gone to a show, he'll sit there, and after all, all the turns *aren't* good, I don't suppose, but I clap 'em, I think 'Well, poor souls, they're doing their best', you know . . . . . he won't, and we argue about this.

The category of miscellaneous other exhibitions or shows (Table 14) was included to make sure that we had not inadvertently omitted any major category of family activity from our specified list, and in order to include those families who might indeed not be interested in the outings we had suggested, but who spent much time at some

Table 14   *Children who have been with their parents to other exhibitions or shows*

	social class					summary		
		III				I&II+	IIIman,	overall
	I&II	IIIwc	man	IV	V	IIIwc	IV, V	popn
	%	%	%	%	%	%	%	%
boys	32	38	14	21	12	35	15	21
girls	31	22	15	7	3	27	12	16
both	31	30	15	14	7	31	14	18

Significance: trend ↘   ****   m.class/w.class   ****
                                        between sexes   n.s.

---

of the specialist and sometimes esoteric 'shows' advertised in the *Nottingham Evening Post*: exhibitions of cacti, coins, antique dolls, foreign birds, veteran steam engines, model railways or tropical fish; cat shows, dog shows, horse and pony trials, flower shows, fetes and galas; night clubs and 'drag' shows, trade fairs, revivalist concerts and political or youth club rallies. All of these items figured at least once; none of them was popular enough to have merited a category of its own, and the fact that the overall percentage attending any of these miscellaneous events is only 18 per cent reassures us that we have not left out any major activity. Again there is evidence for a strong social class element; the child's sex is not a significant factor.

Dealer's wife:
> We went to the Children's Art exhibition at Nottingham University last year. [Did he like it?] Yes – he seemed to think he could do everything much better than they could!

It may seem surprising that far more children have been to theatres and to museums with their parents by this age, than to sporting events of any kind (Table 15). As perhaps might be expected, boys predominate in this activity, and it also tends to be fathers who escort them. What is perhaps more striking still is that the social class trend is in the same direction as was the case with the more conventionally 'educational' activities, and that it is equally pronounced. In other words, it appears that middle-class fathers are a good deal more likely than working-class fathers to take their young children along with them to sporting events, even though it may well be that

Table 15   *Children who have been to a sporting event with a parent*

	social class					summary		
		III				I&II+	IIIman,	overall
	I&II	IIIwc	man	IV	V	IIIwc	IV, V	popn
	%	%	%	%	%	%	%	%
boys	41	38	30	27	23	39	29	32
girls	34	24	20	13	5	29	17	20
both	37	31	25	20	14	34	23	26

Significance: trend ↘   ****   m.class/w.class   ***
                              between sexes   ***

working-class fathers are more likely themselves, on the whole, to attend such popular spectacles as football matches.

Builder's wife:
>   His Daddy runs a amateur football team – he manages one, so Rex always goes with him on a Sunday. There's not many he misses – he goes with him, and he's very interested in the team, and we've had to rig him out with shorts and all the rest of it: boots, you know. He's very keen there, and all the lads seem to make a lot of him as regards football, you know – I think they're as keen to make him a footballer as he is to be one!

Bricklayer's wife:
>   She's been once – both of them with their Daddy, but my husband said never again – they hadn't even kicked off when they both wanted to come home.

There is also a suggestion that middle-class fathers in particular may feel a sense of duty about encouraging the sporting interests of their sons (mothers certainly feel that it is their duty rather than a maternal one!) and that they therefore on occasion may drag themselves along to a sporting event in which they have no personal interest.

Because we are here basically concerned with the child's participation in company with its parents in the life of its culture beyond the home, attendance at a church or other religious service is included along with other more obviously recreational activities (Table 16).

Table 16 *Children who have attended a religious service with a parent*

| | social class | | | | | summary | | |
| | I&II | IIIwc | III man | IV | V | I&II+ IIIwc | IIIman, IV, V | overall popn |
	%	%	%	%	%	%	%	%
boys	51	29	23	14	19	40	21	26
girls	63	51	33	32	18	57	31	38
both	57	40	28	23	19	49	26	32

Significance: trend ↘ ****   m.class/w.class ****

between sexes ****

As with the other events discussed, we were not necessarily looking for *regular* attendance; our question was again in terms of 'does he *ever* go . . . ? In Catholic families in particular it was often emphasised by mothers that attendance at Mass was not by any means a question of 'does he ever?', but an unquestioned part of normal life.

Caretaker's wife:
> We all go to church regularly; and if there's anything special, very often we pop in, you know. I don't know whether you understand our religion really, but the point is . . . I mean, when we say our prayers we treat God as a person to talk to, you see; and therefore if you're passing a church and you want to, er, say anything, you know, you just go in and just say a prayer, or just wait for the service . . . you can just go in and ask for what you want, and if you're worried you can have a talk . . . . . But it's all brought in naturally, I mean . . . . . The Catholics don't thrust religion down, I mean it's not like that sort of thing, I mean it's the basis of life, sort of thing.

Accepting that public religious observance is a different activity in kind from the other cultural events we have looked at, it is also true that some families pursued some of the other activities with great energy and regularity; art, music, gardening, pet keeping or sport might all seem the 'basis of life' in certain families. It seems reasonable to discuss church attendance in this context, then, as one more outside aspect of the culture to which the child is given access through his parents, without reference to how intensively this aspect is presented to him.

Although our focus is upon child-plus-parent participation, the figures in the table are likely to reflect religious observance generally, which is well known to vary as a function of social class. There is thus, not unexpectedly, a clear and consistent class trend showing that fewer children attend church with a parent as we move down the social-class scale. It is also well documented that more women than men take part in church services; this may explain, at least in part, why more girls than boys go to church, since by a simple process of identification it may seem more appropriate for a girl to accompany her mother.

We can now proceed to derive from these individual questions an index of 'general cultural interests' to indicate the variety of extra-familial cultural contact which a child has received through his parents' efforts. The scores which contribute to this index consist of one point for each of the following activities: extra lessons; cinema; concert; theatre; museum/art gallery; zoo/circus; miscellaneous exhibitions/shows; sporting event; church service. This gives a possible maximum total of nine.

Table 17 gives an analysis of high and low scorers on this index in terms of sex and social class. It is clear that although boys and girls divide, as we have seen, on some of the *kinds* of cultural interests which they pursue with their parents (and although this may be partly a question of what is made available to them, it is certainly also partly a matter of what they see fit to accept), there is finally no significant difference between them in total variety of cultural opportunities. It is of interest that in this respect boys do not seem to be at a disadvantage, as they are in other educational areas.

The strength and consistency of the social-class trend, particularly steep in this case, is remarkable. When one reflects that the child only needs *one* experience of being taken to a museum, football match and so on in order to score in each of these contributory categories, the deprivation of the low-scoring children can be seen as very great indeed: and that this should be true for half the Class v population, and for a third of working-class children generally, is disquieting. It is particularly so because it cannot adequately be compensated for by direct educational provision; that is to say, while the school can provide the actual cultural experiences as part of its curriculum, it cannot so easily make good the parental involvement which conveys to the child the family's identification with cultural and educational aims. In the light of these findings, an active effort to involve parents, not just as visitors to the school, but as contributive members with their own funds of skills and expertise to offer, must be recognised as an essential factor in any compensatory programme.

Table 17   *An index of 'General Cultural Interests': high- and low-scoring children as a function of sex and social class*

	I&II %	IIIwc %	social class III man %	IV %	V %	summary I&II+ IIIwc %	IIIman, IV, V %	overall popn %
High scorers								
(5 or more)								
boys	62	45	25	17	9	54	21	30
girls	69	51	30	12	8	60	24	34
both	66	48	28	15	8	57	23	32

Significance: trend ↘ ****   m.class/w.class ****
between sexes   n.s.

	I&II %	IIIwc %	III man %	IV %	V %	I&II+ IIIwc %	IIIman, IV, V %	overall popn %
Low scorers								
(2 or less)								
boys	3	10	26	36	53	6	31	24
girls	5	8	29	37	49	6	33	26
both	4	9	28	37	51	6	32	25

Significance: trend ↗ ****   m.class/w.class ****
between sexes   n.s.

In discussing individual items on this scale, we have suggested that lack of opportunity often stems from the financial expense of some of these 'outings'; and this is confirmed when we examine the factor of family size, which is significantly related to cultural interest scores. Children from small families (containing three or less children) are more likely to score highly on the GCI index than are those from larger families (four or more children). On an overall analysis of factors contributing to the GCI index, the child's sex is not significant, but both social class and family size are significant at the 0·001 level.

Of course there are outings other than to museums and religious services which do not cost money; although for really poor families even the bus fares to the other side of town or the nearest countryside may be prohibitive. We asked: 'Is there any outing that N particularly enjoys? . . . If you were planning a treat specially for N, what do you think he would choose to do?' Most of the answers came into one of the categories already discussed, but a number showed children with inexpensive tastes who could be easily pleased just by the sense that it *was* an outing. Some examples of non-categorised answers are given below: what is rather evident from these, and from those we do not have space to quote, is that outings where less money is spent also tend on the whole to have less function in bringing the child into direct social contact with his culture as opposed to his environment.

Cycle worker's wife:
She likes to go down on the Arboretum and all over, and see all the birds, and take bags of bread for the ducks and swans.

Lorry driver's wife:
He likes walking beside the Trent – throwing stones in the Trent.

Cycle worker's wife:
Do you know what his best treat is? A trip to the woodyard; it is, and he'll go all the way from here right down to Lenton, and he thinks it's marvellous. He likes going there better than if you took him for a day to the seaside, cause he can ferret . . .

Guillotine cutter's wife:
She likes to go out with her Dad on the park, and she loves to go to the bluebell wood when the bluebells are out.

Assistant production manager's wife:
Oh, she's delighted if she can visit a graveyard! She thinks it's marvellous to visit a grave! She's picked hers out many a time, her headstone – can we afford one for her?

Student (father speaking):
He likes just to go out. If you put him in the back of the car . . . if I was going to the South Pole, I'd have to put James in the back of the car, and I know just before we got there he'd say 'Isn't it time we got there?' In between, he'd sit in the back, taking in everything. He gets a tremendous kick out of this.

Builder labourer's wife:
She likes going to town and going in the café for an orangeade and a cake. I get that every time I go to town – 'Ooh look, there's a café, Mummy!'

Wife of craftsman in own business:

. . . We stay in a hotel, and he glories in it – it's lovely – he likes his best bib and tucker on, and he has wine with his dinner – he thinks it's glorious, he does really, it's his height of delight, it is. Each night will be the highlight.

Lorry driver's wife:

Oh, I don't know what he'd like, he's never been on one, you see. [Do you ever take him to the Arboretum? (local)] No, I don't have time really.

We must also, for completeness, include a few children who had no wish for contact with the culture and on the whole resisted their parents' efforts to introduce them to it.

Milkman's wife:

We never know what Alex would like. We often sit and think. It's got to be something really outstanding to catch his interest, you know. Now Tim [sib] would be pleased to go anywhere, he gets thrilled about anything, but Alex . . . [Father:] I took him to see some lambs, a fortnight ago, wasn't it? Cause they got about fifty lambs, this family, I know the man personally, so I took them to see them. Our Tim was dead pleased, like, and he's nearly thirteen, but our Alex . . . [Mother:] He sat there watching these lambs – 'When are we going? When are we going home?' He couldn't really care less. [Father:] And he took his ball with him, he said 'I don't really mind going, but can I take my ball with me?', and we had to take him down by the embankment after, with his ball. Well, we *took* him to see the lambs, but he weren't bothered.

Driver-representative's wife:

She wouldn't be bothered, she's not bothered. As I said, you couldn't excite her. No, if you said 'We're taking you to the seaside', she'd say 'Do I *have* to go?' [When she gets there, does she like it?] No, no. She'd sooner be at home, yes, I'm afraid you'd be right there.

Manager's wife:

Staying at home, that's the best outing he can suggest, isn't it awful! You can't spend money on him, he just prefers to be at home, he loves . . . but if you *happen* to take him out, he would probably enjoy it. If I made him go somewhere that he didn't enjoy, he wouldn't sulk or anything like that, he'll be perfectly well behaved, but he'll resent the fact that . . . he's so busy at home. I can't really give him a treat as such, to take him out. If I took him to town and let him wander round a toyshop and said that he could choose anything he wanted, I think that would be his greatest pleasure. It's a bit deadly, isn't it, but it's true.

The rationale for including this chapter at all in a book concerned with parents' perspective on school has been that mothers and fathers are faced with both choices and constraints in relation to the wider culture. Living willy-nilly within a cultural web, they may none the less choose either to exploit it, or partially to isolate their children from it by not becoming involved as a family with any of the cultural events that are offered; though this choice may, of course, be somewhat determined by the difficulties of lack of money and lack of energy experienced by parents of large families. On the other hand, parents are very heavily constrained to hand over their children to the culture-bound institution of school; this is a powerful repository of cultural values which it is made extremely difficult to opt out of. In so far as school is concerned with cultural activities generally, as well as with literacy and numeracy in particular, the child will, in truth, feel more 'at home' at school if his parents make it clear that they regard such activities as relevant to themselves as well as to him. For this reason alone it has been apposite to consider in this context parent/child involvement in general cultural events.

But parents also exert choices within the home, in that they can choose to build a nurturant environment for their child's interests simply by taking his questions and activities seriously and making him a present of some part of their time and attention, without going further afield than their own neighbourhood. This too backs up the child's school experience, even before we consider ways in which parents directly try to involve themselves in any formal teaching of the 'three Rs'. The next chapter explores more closely the concordance between school and the child's home-based environment.

NOTES

1 Essay in J. S. Bruner, *The Relevance of Education* (London, George Allen & Unwin, 1972).
2 At this point we may seem to be using the word 'culture' in a different way: 'improvement or refinement of mind, manners etc. by education and training', as the *Oxford Illustrated Dictionary* has it. However, the dictionary itself combines these two uses under one head – 'particular form or type of intellectual development or civilization' – and we would regard them as so closely interwoven in origin that we deliberately choose to confuse them

here. We certainly have no intention of entering on value-judgements as to what activities are 'cultural' in the sense of refinement or intellectualism.

3   For instance, see J. Kagan, *Change and Continuity in Infancy* (New York, Wiley, 1971).

4   J. W. B. Douglas, *The Home and the School* (London, MacGibbon & Kee, 1964).

5   Central Advisory Council for Education, *Children and their Primary Schools* (Plowden Report) (London, HMSO, 1967).

6   R. Davie, N. Butler and H. Goldstein, *From Birth to Seven* (London, Longman, 1972).

7   Michael Young and Patrick McGeeney, *Learning Begins at Home* (London, Routledge & Kegan Paul, 1968).

8   B. Bernstein, 'Language and social class', *Br. Journ. Sociol.*, XI (1960).

9   J. and E. Newson, op. cit. (1968), pp. 430–59 (George Allen & Unwin), pp. 457–86 (Pelican).

10   J. and E. Newson, op. cit. (1976b), pp. 286–92.

11   P. M. Greenfield, 'Goal as environmental variable in the development of intelligence' (conference on 'Contributions to Intelligence', University of Illinois, 1969); quoted in Bruner, 'Poverty and childhood', essay in op. cit. (1972).

12   J. and E. Newson, op. cit. (1963), pp. 211–13 (George Allen & Unwin), pp. 224–5 (Pelican).

13   J. and E. Newson, op. cit. (1963), p. 166 (George Allen & Unwin), pp. 173–4 (Pelican).

Chapter 4

Both Intermediary and Beneficiary

Long ago there lived a live leaf. But one day some water came
and then mud then water then mud. Then at last it stopped and
the leaf was changed and it was a stone leaf. It was a grey stone
with the leaf in it. My dad found it in the pit. He brought it
home. Then I brought it to school. Some have animals and
some have a leaf all rocks are made in earth some are little and
some are not. We have got a fossil Miss B brought it some
rocks are shot up from a volcanoes.

Six-year-old girl quoted by David Ayerst,
Understanding Schools[1]

'Did Miss B (the teacher) or the father get in first with the fossil?'
asks David Ayerst: 'It does not matter: either way, home and school
play into each other's hands; the interested child is both intermediary
and beneficiary. Her world is one.'

The integration of the child's two worlds of home and school
through the bringing together of contributions from teacher and
father, moreover, has a third dimension here: the world of work,
which is not in fact the child's world at all, but from which her father
can bring his own special knowledge. A stone leaf, carried up in a
father's hand from the deep mystery of 'the pit' where it had rested
undisturbed from 'long ago' until now, makes accessible and vivid
to the children notions of hardly imaginable time-perspectives, with
an immediacy which any teacher might find hard to achieve, however
well supplied with specimens from the Schools Museum Service.
Some of our own children echo this child's experience.

Miner's wife:
He's got two fossils that he's very proud of, which his Daddy

brought them up out of the pit. And he's *very* fond of taking them
to show his teacher. They've got leaves, branches of leaves. And
he's got a very very old newspaper, about eighteen-ninety-some-
thing, which he likes to take. I'll tell you what he's very interested
in – museums, castles – anything old he really likes. He will take
an interest.

Yet fathers and mothers from far less remote workplaces than the
pit have resources of experience which could enrich schools: both
extending school horizons, and making explicit the points of contact
and overlap between the too-separated domains of home, school and
work.

From this point of view, what is striking when we look at the ways
in which the home backs up the school's educative role is not so much
what the school gains from the home as what it does not even try to
gain. As we shall see, there were dozens of examples of parents
helping with writing at home, 'hearing' a child's reading, overseeing
spelling, setting sums; and schools themselves were often reported as
taking the initiative in sending home reading books, asking for stage
costumes to be made, inviting mothers to help escort a school trip,
requesting jellies and cakes for the Christmas party, or goods for a
stall at the summer fete, and generally using parents as a resource for
old cartons, tins, toilet roll cores, egg-boxes, bottle-tops and other
necessities of primary school life: but we did not have one example
of either father's or mother's work experience being deliberately
made use of. Considering that junior schools do think it relevant to
have in their libraries rather pallid accounts of 'The Nurse', 'The
Merchant Seaman', 'The Miner' and so on, it seems strange that they
do not attempt to tap the real-life experience of the coalface workers,
lathe operators, lorry drivers and bricklayers who are their children's
own fathers, many of whom work shifts which would allow them
to bring their knowledge into school. How many children really know
what it's like to mind a textile machine?

Watching the cones, checking the fabric, attending the machines
which constantly break down, you're on the go all the time. If a
machine stops, it must be started, and when it is going the cones
are running out and have to be replaced. Hour after hour without
break, from one machine to another and back, putting up ends,
changing cones, starting the machines and trying to watch the
fabric. The machines aren't designed for the operator. You bend
low to see the fabric, and climb up on the machine to reach the
arms holding the thread. To see all the cones you have to walk

twenty-five feet round. Usually an operative has three machines with a total of 150 cones – many of which you can't see immediately because they're on the other side of the machines; you have to memorize which cones are going to run out. With bad yarn the machines snag constantly; it's gruelling keeping everything running . . . . .
Hey, the machine's stopped. A top red light? Find a stick, disentangle the thread – break off the balled-up yarn, put the end up, check the thread is not caught, press the button, throw the handle. Peer at the fabric – needles? lines from tight yarn? Feel the yarn as it runs, alter the tension; we're not supposed to, it's the supervisor's job but he's too busy. Change a tight cone. A red light above droppers – cone run out? press-off? A yellow light – the stop motion has come up, maybe something is out of position on the needles, a build-up of thread or a broken needle. Clear the build-up, change the needle, start the machine again. And the other machines, are they all right? One of them stops every other minute on average. Can't spend more than thirty seconds looking at one, leave it for the two others, make sure they're all right, come back to the first. May take five or ten minutes to clear. By the time the trouble's clear, another one's stopped. Break off the bad yarn, disentangle the cone, re-start the machine – a few seconds later do the same again . . . Repetitive little tasks too expensive for any machine to do, but cheap enough for underpaid labour. Machine minding goes with semi-automation.[2]

In this and the following chapter, then, we shall be looking at how school interests are taken up, supported and supplemented at home, rather than the other way round, and will try to explore how parents see their home-based role as educative forces in the child's life. We shall be particularly concerned with the overlap between parent and teacher roles: how far do parents chiefly see themselves as providers of emotional and material support, or do they feel that they too may appropriately 'teach' in the formal sense? and what do they think that teachers think about overlapping roles?

An index of 'home–school concordance' was devised in an attempt to quantify these factors which seemed to us to have significance for the child's subjective experience of education. As usual, the meaning of the index is defined by the questions which contribute to it. These are as follows: the reader will note that they do not appear in direct sequence.

110. Does he often take things to school to show his teacher?

112. Does he ever come home and start doing something he's been shown at school?
113. Does he ever ask you questions about something he's heard of in class?
     What sort of things?
115. Can you always answer his questions?
     What do you do if you can't? [What would you do if you couldn't?]
128. Do you or his Daddy ever help him with other things [than reading], like sums or writing or any other school work?
134. Does he do any drawing or painting at home?

As with the previous index of general cultural interests, we will present analyses of the data from each of these questions in turn, and will then consider the index as a whole.

'I encourage her to take things because he's a good little teacher, and I think it gives them more heart if somebody's interested . . .'
There are a number of ways in which 'taking things to school to show the teacher' can be interpreted; and how the mother perceives the intention of the act will inevitably influence whether she approves of and encourages it. She may simply regard it as a way of contributing to and enhancing the interest of the topic under discussion at school.

Caretaker's wife:
　Well, he takes books; he's taken a bird's nest; ships, they had a display on ships and he took quite a few. [Do you encourage him in that – would you suggest that he should take something to school if he didn't think of it?] Oh yes, yes, I do. If they have a project or anything, you know, he'll take a book with the subject in, and he'll perhaps learn it at school or praps write something out from the book.

Electrician's wife:
　Oh yes, oh yes, I mean if we find things, say at the seaside – if we found shells I'd say 'Oh, you ought to take these to school'; but he's not very bothered, he doesn't do, and yet I'd like him to – I think it's interesting, you know.

On the other hand, she may see the child's contribution as a hindrance to getting on with the proper business of school life – something which might cause an unnecessary distraction.

Foreman's wife:
Not a lot, because I haven't encouraged that, I don't believe in it, because while they're playing they can't be learning, can they? But he's got a guitar, you see, well it *is* a nice one, and Sir played – I don't know what the names are, you know, it's always 'Sir'! – played some tunes on it, and he said 'Sir said could I bring it again on another day'; so I said 'Yes', I said, 'but you tell Sir to tell you *what* day to take it, and whether it's morning or afternoon . . . Well, he took that; and his Action Man – they'd been talking about them in class or something, so he took it two days. Well he wanted to keep taking it, but I persuaded him out of it. But he don't take books and his birthday things, he doesn't take all that. Some of them do, you know, they come with quite a parcel.

Representative's wife:
Oh no! I think they go to school to learn, not to play with things.

'Sir' is clearly a positive influence here; other teachers are not, and mothers are bound to be inhibited by the thought of their child being seen as a nuisance.

Van salesman's wife:
Sometimes, but not often, because it's not encouraged there. She took this Koala bear when she had it. She would like to take things to show her teacher, but it isn't encouraged there at all, they get cross with them. [How do you feel about it?] Well, I think it forms a communion with the teacher. I would have thought it was perfectly all right.

Company director's wife:
If she wants to I don't stop her, but I don't think the teachers want to be bothered too much with that sort of thing – I wouldn't suggest it.

The 'apple for the teacher' tradition is at the back of some mothers' minds: they worry that the child's offering might be seen as propitiatory, either by the teacher herself or by his peers.

Policeman's wife:
I would discourage that really, it draws too much attention to themselves. It gives the atmosphere to the other children that he's the teacher's pet.

Cable former's wife:
Well, I don't like her to take them to show the teacher. I should
hate to think she was being the teacher's favourite, you know.

Electrical engineer's wife:
[Would you suggest she should take something to school if she
didn't think of it?] No. Sometimes if we'd got some roses in bloom,
and she said could she take them, I'd let her take them. [You
wouldn't yourself say 'Why don't you take them?'] No – cause I
think she praps thinks we're getting round the teacher, you know.

These mothers find the 'giving and showing' relationship suspect,
or are wary lest others might find it so; others again regard it as a
natural and happy way in which a 'communion with the teacher' may
be established, fostered and maintained.

Boiler cleaner's wife:
Yes, I like him to take things, because it does really help that little
bit in getting used to the teachers, doesn't it?

Printer's wife:
Oh yes, she took three roses this morning, two white and one red;
if she likes the teacher, she really likes to take her flowers on a
Monday, and if I've any flowers in the garden I have to cut them
for her.

University teacher's wife:
Anything new she has. She had a pair of plaits for dressing-up,
which I made her. In this particular case, she had to go round all
the forms in the school, showing them. This is in fact a sort of
principle of the school, that all the forms are accessible – the
headmistress likes the children to know the teachers of the other
forms, and so she tries to get them sent on errands and to show
things and so on; and I like this very much, and Polly absolutely
loves it.

Doctor's wife:
Yes, I think that's the beauty of it today – taking the little presents,
and they're just like mother and daughter. Cause we were quite
afraid of ours.

One further reason why mothers may be not altogether willing for
things to be taken to school is that neither children nor teachers are

always clear as to which contributions are for giving and which only for showing. Even fossils or seashells may be personally valued by the mother, so that she can be a little ambivalent about their removal to school; other articles have monetary value.

Hosiery presser's wife:
> Last week she wanted her father's football cups to show the teacher, she took them. Um . . . we had a pot of bulbs, she took those to show the teacher, but they didn't come back. [The teacher thought they were for her?] I suppose so.

Advertising manager's wife:
> Well no, I tend to try and discourage him; he's at the swapping stage, and he's lost several good books that have been swapped.

Table 18 shows the children who take things to show their teacher 'often' or 'never'; the middle category 'sometimes' is residual. It can be seen that nearly half the children take things 'often', with a detectable class trend but not a very marked one. More well-defined

Table 18   *Children who take things to show their teacher*

	social class					summary		
		III				*I&II+*	*IIIman,*	*overall*
	I&II	*IIIwc*	*man*	*IV*	*V*	*IIIwc*	*IV, V*	*popn*
	%	%	%	%	%	%	%	%
'Often'								
boys	49	47	41	43	35	48	41	43
girls	65	57	52	57	44	61	52	54
both	57	52	46	50	39	55	46	49

Significance: trend ↘   **
                             between sexes   ***   m.class/w.class   *

	I&II	*IIIwc*	*man*	*IV*	*V*	*IIIwc*	*IV, V*	*popn*
'Never'								
boys	12	12	19	12	14	12	17	16
girls	3	6	10	7	21	5	11	9
both	7	9	15	10	17	8	14	12

Significance: trend ↗   *
                             between sexes   ***   m.class/w.class   *

is the sex difference, girls being significantly more likely than boys in every class to take things 'often'.

Considering that only 12 per cent of children 'never' take things to school in this way, it is interesting to find that when the mothers were asked whether they actively encouraged the child to do so, only 21 per cent took a totally positive line. The majority (69 per cent) had some reservations of the kinds illustrated above, though only 10 per cent were definitely and actively discouraging. Class and sex differences are not significant in these terms, and it thus looks as if the class trend is a matter of *degree* of encouragement by the mother, rather than on an all-or-none basis. This presumably is also true of the sex divergence; in this case, it is likely to be contributed to by mothers' perception of boys as more heedless and careless of their property, and possibly also by a closer identity with school and teacher on the part of girls, which might make girls more highly motivated to insist on taking things to school.

'They come home from school and expect you to know everything about everything . . .'

We were interested in how far school activities were transferred bodily into the home setting, whether lines of inquiry initiated at school continued to be followed up at home by the child, and whether this was fostered by parental attitudes. The question 'Does he ever come home and start doing something he's been shown at school' was answered affirmatively by 83 per cent of mothers. Class differences were insignificant; a small sex difference in favour of girls was entirely attributable to skilled and semi-skilled class boys, 24 per cent of whom did *not* do this (compared with 12 per cent of middle-class boys). Among the children who did not transfer school activities to home there was very much the feeling that the school was dusted off their feet as they left the school gate: 'As I say, when he's been to school, that's it. In the summer when he's had his tea, he's out – he's a real outdoor child. He forgets school.'

Furnisher's wife:
> I don't really know what he enjoys. We can find out very little about school from Sam at all – very little. In fact I was shattered to hear from [another boy] yesterday that Sam is the best reader in the class! Now the impression he gives *me* is that he's, you know, pretty average – almost sort of bordering on the bottom of the class – but he said oh no, that without any doubt he's the best reader in the class; which annoyed me! And he said 'The teacher really does like him'. I said 'Why's that?' – 'Oh', he said, 'he's

always so lively and happy'. Now I wouldn't have been able to give that impression of my own child – so obviously he must be responding at school, though we can't get anything out of *him* about it. He can never remember – that's the big phrase – 'I just can't remember, Mum'. He can't remember what he does.

A point made by the mother quoted next is apposite, remembering that both middle-class children generally and working-class girls are more likely to be collected from school by their mothers than working-class boys:

Administrative assistant's wife:
> If he's been writing at school and got interested, he may come in and get a book and copy writing . . . it depends on his train of thought – if he comes straight home with me, he comes home quicker, and he has that train of thought and carries on with it. If he comes home with schoolchildren, he may have lost that train of thought and carries on with something new.

The activities inspired by school are very various, even excluding for the moment reading and writing help given formally by parents. The following examples refer, as do the percentages given, solely to activities voluntarily followed up by the child, although some may have been deliberately suggested by the school.

Lorry driver's wife:
> Oh yes – in, um, well we used to call it art – I don't know what they call it now. They get all pieces of material now, and cut it into bits, and stick it on things. Ooh, she's always doing that, and she's got a vivid imagination as well for making things on her own, you know, at home – things you'd never think of, you know – she'll get the toilet-roll cardboard, I couldn't do it myself, you know, and she made a beautiful rocket; the way she decorates things up, you know, oh yes, she's got a vivid imagination for making things.

Nylon winder's wife:
> Yes, he showed my daughter of ten how to make a windmill – they'd been cutting them out at school. I said, 'Oh, you'll be able to do a trade down the road, sell them at sixpence each!'

Cook's wife:
> When she learns something new at school, different types of sums and so forth: she comes straight home and asks me to write her some of these particular sums she's been doing.

Milk roundsman's wife:

She's always got a book and pencil. Well often it's something they've wrote at school, you know; they have these names what they call the news at school – she'll often write some news. Perhaps not what they've *done* at school, but perhaps something she would have liked to have wrote at school but doesn't get chance.

Miner's wife:

Well, such as – they'd been doing sewing, and the teacher must have showed them, like, and Karen said to me '*You* show me how to do it, and I'll tell you if it's the same'. So I said all right – but no, apparently I don't do it right. And then she wanted to know why have you got to put stitches in things – *why* have you? – can't you just stick it together? There's only one thing, when she starts with that, you must hide all your needles and cotton, cause she's sewing everything she can get her hands on – and there's nothing worse when you're trying to lift a towel off a chair, than it's sewn on to your back cover!

Tobacco worker's wife:

Oh yes, you know, painting – he sort of – I think they experiment with colours, you know, mixing things and colours.

A specific example of overlap of home and school experience is in fact in the area of drawing and painting, and we wanted to know what proportion of children were involved in this kind of activity at home as well as at school. In practice, school is likely to provide a wider range of art materials; and from the transcripts it was clear that much home drawing was done either in small drawing books or notepads, or using commercially-produced painting or crayoning books, which rely rather heavily on tracing, copying and 'colouring-in', and thus give rather limited scope to children's creative and imaginative ability. We wondered afterwards whether we should not have been more restrictive in our question and its coding. Forty per cent of children were said to draw or paint 'most days', and differences were not significant in this group. However, a class difference did appear among the children who hardly ever drew or painted, where the proportions ranged from 5 per cent of middle-class children, through 10 per cent of the skilled and semi-skilled groups, to 15 per cent in Class v.

Of greater interest, perhaps, is whether the child follows up school topics in the form of questions to his mother (Table 19); and we were interested both in the child's behaviour and in the mother's response

Table 19   *Children who ask mother questions about school topics*

	social class					summary		
			III			I&II+	IIIman,	overall
	I&II	IIIwc	man	IV	V	IIIwc	IV, V	popn
	%	%	%	%	%	%	%	%
boys	71	73	52	58	53	72	53	58
girls	75	54	62	61	46	65	60	61
both	73	64	57	59	49	69	56	60

Significance: trend ↘ ****   m.class/w.class ***
                        between sexes   n.s.

to it. To some extent this is a circular matter: the child is likely to ask questions about what he perceives as relevant, and his mother's encouraging response not only rewards this question and stimulates additional ones, but also confirms his perception of the relevance of investigation generally; conversely, a mother who fobs off questions not only negatively reinforces the act of questioning but also devalues the spirit of inquiry that prompted the act. Thus we must expect, and we do in fact find, some correlation between child's and mother's behaviour.

Insurance inspector's wife:
Oh yes, always. This teacher – I think all primary teachers are marvellous! – she gets their interest. Wollaton Park, for instance, was a topic, they were drawing it and painting it. And he has to know all the details you know yourself, if you know any. We do eventually hear about all the topics they've been discussing, and if he hasn't heard enough or heard correctly, we have to tell him.

Administrative assistant's wife:
He does, usually because he doesn't quite know what the teacher's said; and then I've had to try and work out what she's thinking and what he's heard from his tale, and go on from there! Because he'll come out and ask a direct question, what do you know, do you believe so-and-so Mummy? And I'll say either yes or no, according to what . . . 'Well, my teacher says . . .' – the opposite, as a rule. And then I have to put her in the right as well, and I have to get a bit further just to see what she *has* said, and work it from there! [Would he tend to trust you rather than the teacher, or the teacher rather than you?] Well, when it was Mrs Lester, his first,

it was the teacher all the time, I just didn't stand a chance! But now it's often fifty-fifty, according to what he thinks I'm capable of knowing!

Lorry driver's wife:
Oh yes, he likes to know the ins and outs of everything. He came home one day and said, 'Mam, you know that man that had his head cut off when he . . . this woman was dancing with him . . . he lost his head . . . there was a chapter in the Bible all about it . . . there's a very sad ending in the chapter, do you know it?' – he was going on in a garbled way. I said 'Do you mean John the Baptist who had his head cut off?' – 'But Mr Field said there's a very sad ending to it – the chapter – do you know it?' So I read through this chapter and I thought, well, *I* can't find a sad ending to it, and the doves came down from Heaven and everything; and I thought, oh well, I can't go through the whole Bible, it'll take weeks. So in the end he nagged me about this, he wanted to know the sad ending; and I put my coat on and I went down to see the headmaster, and apparently it was just that he'd had his head cut off; well I *knew* that, but I was looking for the sad ending. But they come home from school and expect you to know everything about everything.

Jointer's wife:
I'm too busy really – I don't always listen. She jabbers on – I don't always know *what* she's on about.

We collected examples of questions that the child asked, both as a result of 'something he's heard of in class' and in general; and we went on to ask whether the mother could always answer the child's questions, and what she would do if she couldn't.

As we saw when the children were four,[3] there is a difference between *can* answer and *wants* to answer; at this point we were looking for mothers' strategies if they simply did not know the answer to the child's questions. It was not uncommon, however, for a mother to begin in terms of questions she did not wish to pursue with the child, usually involving sex information.

Maintenance worker's wife:
Well, I don't really know . . . I'd have to try and get out of it . . . take her mind off it. There's quite a few things that other children tell her and really they never ought to know theirselves, and she asks us these questions, and we've got to get her on to something else.

Labourer's wife:
Not all the time . . . I wouldn't like him to know the things he asks me [meaning look]. I make up something.

A rather more subtle interpretation of 'can't answer' involved meeting children's questions in terms of belief or faith rather than fact.

Teachers:
The questions that I can't answer are about God and Heaven, you know – I'm just flummoxed. [Father:] Now that *is* difficult to cope with. [Mother:] I always say ask Daddy! [Father:] Now this is difficult, because I don't want to, er, make her mind up *for* her either way. In some respects I don't want her to just accept blindly that there is a God; but on the other hand I wouldn't like to sort of say to her, now look, this is superstitious nonsense or something, that would be the opposite extreme. When she's sort of telling me something which is sort of blind acceptance of what *she's* been told, I'm hedging; because – um – I don't want to sort of chop her down on what she's been told, but at the same time I can't go along with her and agree with it. But I think as time goes along I shall help her to sort of . . . well, to make up her own mind about it. [Mother:] Well, you usually say 'Well that's what some people say'. [Father:] Yes, but it's a sort of feeblish . . . sort of . . . [Mother:] I can't answer that.

Postal worker's wife:
It is difficult on religion; because I don't always understand it myself . . . . . I mean – when you hear of these things happening to children – like it happened when all those children got killed [Aberfan disaster]. Well, that was an instance when he came in and he said 'Why did Jesus let it happen?' Well: I couldn't answer that. Well, I said 'He does these things to test us all – and he doesn't *mean* for this to happen to little children, you see'. But they do come out with things like that, don't they?

Having reiterated if necessary that we were interested in what happened when mothers merely did not have enough information to answer, we found that we could divide their responses into four categories: Mother consults books or newspaper, etc.; she asks someone else; she does nothing, but admits her ignorance; she attempts to conceal her ignorance from the child. These categories were regarded as an hierarchy in the sense that a mixed answer in the

first two categories ('If we couldn't find it in the encyclopaedia, my
neighbour might be able to tell us') would be counted as 'consults
books'. Examples of responses in the four categories follow.

Consults books, newspapers, etc.

Teacher's wife:
> We've got an encyclopaedia and we'd look it up in that, or in a
> book in the library. But usually between us we've got the book or
> the knowledge. We go on to the end to satisfy him – if only because
> *we* become interested! He might perhaps have lost interest, you
> know, on the way, but we still go on!

Departmental manager's wife:
> I *try* to answer them all. I don't think there's many I can't, because
> when you've had three other children, you get used to *every* kind
> of question. [What do you do if you can't?] Well, it's no use
> avoiding questions, because if you avoid them they'll still come
> back with them. If I can't, I have to think of the rest of the family,
> Jennifer, Bruce, their Daddy, and if there's one of those can
> answer it, then I pass it along to them. He's quite interested in the
> astronauts going up into space; and there's a lot of questions I
> can't answer about space! But he does want to *know* the answers;
> so we have to go through the papers, newspapers and that; and if
> not, as a rule Steven [eleven] will take him to the library and they'll
> look it up in one of the books. Very good at that, Steven is. And
> of course Bruce [fourteen] can often answer a few of them. But
> they don't *settle* at one question, do they?

Tobacco worker's wife:
> I would tell him I didn't know about it and we'll try and find out,
> and a lot of things he does want to know . . . my sister's got a
> terrible lot of encyclopaedias. I don't tell him that *he* should ask
> his Aunty. I tell him that *we* will find out.

University teacher's wife:
> Very often his father can provide information, unless it's one of
> the biological sciences, in which case we have to make do with
> what I can manage. I haven't had to look something up so far;
> the exception to this is geology. He's very interested in these
> stones, and I've bought some books and I've read something, and
> have started to flog the subject for myself. It's difficult, this sort of

thing, because it's really a bit advanced, and I don't want to make it boring by too much fact.

Student teacher's wife (herself a teacher):
We can't always, but we know where to go to find the answers. [And do you do that?] Yes we do, the other day she was asking about music and we'd no idea, and I'd got an old book there which has one or two things, and we looked and found what we wanted. [Father:] Yes, that was another thing – we were informed only a few weeks after they went back to school that we were not as clever as Miss Machin, *she* knew the answers to everything – *we* kept having to have a look in a book! [Mother:] So much for the first year at —— Training College!

Asks someone else

Lorry driver's wife:
Oh no, if I'm really stumped I usually ask somebody else. I mean, if I was *really* stumped I should go down and see the headmaster or his teacher to find out, cause they set the tests in school and they're bound to know the answers [laughs] – at least I hope they do!

Machine operator's wife:
Well, the parents round here are pretty good; what we don't know they do. The boy next door comes here for certain things – English and maths – and Edgar goes down the street to a chap who's a Jehovah's witness for religion, and we sort of . . . I mean, this chap down the street, what he doesn't know about the Bible isn't worth knowing, and it's very handy. And the lady next door, she's very good as well, she'll answer pretty well everything that we can't, and we do the same for her children.

Representative's wife:
Well, I try and remember to get him to ask his Daddy while I'm there, so we both know about it.

Miner's wife:
Sometimes I can, other times I don't know how to word it, sort of; sometimes I manage quite well. [What do you do if you can't?] Say 'Tell you what, darling – I'll ask somebody, and tell you tomorrow'. [And do you?] Yes, quite often – maybe have a word with one of the teachers at her school.

Does nothing, but admits ignorance

Driver's wife:
I've always said 'When I find out the answer, I'll let you know' –
and they've been satisfied with that. [Do you find out?] No.

Miner's wife:
I mostly find out how to [answer], I have to think it over carefully
first. I say 'Oh well, wait a minute, Barbara, I'll tell you in a
minute when I've done this', and I'll think about it first, which
way I'm going to answer. [What do you do if you *don't* know the
answer?] I say 'Well, I don't know the answer, Barbara'.

Display manager's wife:
Well, I try very hard to give *some* sort of answer; I don't like to say
I don't know. [And if you really didn't know?] Oh well, I'd say
'I'm sorry, I don't know'.

Tries to conceal ignorance

Metal polisher's wife:
I put him off. It's a funny thing, that . . . you try to put 'em off,
don't you?

Railwayman's wife:
I pretend I haven't heard her then. Say if she asks me if I can spell
such-and-such a word, and I can't; then I say 'Oh, ask me a bit
later, I'm busy'. I'll put her off if I can.

Electrician's wife:
Pass it off, or make a mild excuse.

Structural cleaner's wife:
I tell him his brain isn't big enough now to hold it all.

Depot manager's wife:
Well, I'm afraid I'd try to answer it in one way or another; I
wouldn't exactly slide out of it, but try and pacify him . . . he gets
a little bit annoyed because he's not got a proper answer.

Mothers' strategies when they are unable to answer their children's
questions are summarised in Table 20.

Table 20   *Mothers' strategies when unable to answer their children's questions*

	social class					summary		overall
	I&II	*IIIwc*	*III man*	*IV*	*V*	*I&II+ IIIwc*	*IIIman, IV, V*	*popn*
	%	%	%	%	%	%	%	%
Consults books								
boys	37	16	8	9	2	27	8	13
girls	39	25	14	9	3	32	12	17
both	38	21	11	9	3	30	10	15

Significance: trend ↘ ****   m.class/w.class ****
                        between sexes   n.s,

Asks someone								
boys	39	38	42	36	19	38	38	38
girls	27	40	30	26	21	33	28	30
both	33	39	36	31	20	35	33	34

Significance: trend ↘ *   m.class/w.class n.s.
                        between sexes   *

Nothing: admits ignorance								
boys	21	35	34	35	61	28	37	35
girls	25	25	41	45	63	25	44	39
both	23	29	37	40	62	27	41	37

Significance: trend ↗ ****   m.class/w.class ****
                        between sexes   n.s.

Conceals ignorance								
boys	3	11	16	20	18	7	17	14
girls	9	10	15	20	13	10	16	14
both	6	11	16	20	15	8	16	14

Significance: trend ↗ ***   m.class/w.class ***
                        between sexes   n.s.

Middle-class mothers, by virtue of their own educational advantages, are better equipped to answer their children's questions; this is likely to encourage their children to turn to them with questions more frequently, and no doubt contributes to the class difference in the actual asking of questions arising out of school which we have already seen in Table 19. The mother's attitude when her knowledge is not enough for the child takes the situation a step further, however. It can be assumed that the first two categories given are educationally supportive, since an effort is made to acquire the information asked for; that the third is neither supportive nor especially discouraging; and that the fourth, concealing ignorance, is frankly unsupportive, since the child is usually deliberately discouraged from persisting with these questions which diminish the mother's self-image.

Consulting books obviously comes more easily to middle-class mothers: more likely to have books at hand, to know their way around a library, to be able to pursue a topic through an index and cope with formal and elaborated prose, their whole white-collar or professional life-style imbues them with the expectation that the most authoritative information is obtainable from this source, and, moreover, that it is there to be used. The mother who consults books with her child, however, does more than induct him into an important subcultural expectation; she also immediately involves herself in the inquiring role in a particularly active way. This is much more marked in consulting books than in asking other people; although a mother may 'get him to ask his Daddy while I'm there, so we both know about it', her role tends to be active only in the initial stages, soon becoming passive as the informant takes over. The use of books, on the other hand, is likely to remain a co-operative effort throughout, since seven-year-olds are not yet very skilled at winkling the knowledge they need from a book without help in both scanning and actual reading. Additionally, because of this personal involvement, she thereby identifies his questions as being of interest to *her*, and worth giving *her* time and trouble to answer; whereas if she refers him on to some other person, she may not continue to be involved in any way at all. Thus, while we can hardly be surprised at the very clear class differences in turning to books to satisfy children's questions, the most significant feature of the act is its *implication*: that it defines to the child *the pursuit of knowledge via reading* as relevant for mothers as well as schoolchildren.

Looking at the second half of Table 20, we find ourselves with a rather large group (57 per cent) of mothers in the working class who are not educationally supportive of their children when they do not know the answers to the child's questions. Of some interest among these, although a small group, are those mothers who attempt to conceal their ignorance from the child by various 'fobbing-off' methods: twice as many in the working class as in the middle class. We can understand this class difference by looking at other attitudes which make up class styles. For instance the more authoritarian stance adopted further down the social scale depends upon the premise that mother knows best by virtue of her status: a demonstration of her ignorance is more difficult for her to tolerate and incorporate into that image than it would be for the more democratically-oriented mother, who has already conceded to the child that she can be wrong (a parallel to this is the class difference in mothers' willingness to apologise to the child).[4] If middle-class mothers do feel that they have lost face by not knowing the answer to a question, they can easily regain it by showing their expertise in using resources; this course is less open to the lower-working-class mother, who may indeed feel it safer not to embark on a search which may still end in failure. Further up the social scale, educationally-oriented mothers may even welcome a situation which gives them the excuse to introduce the child to the use of dictionaries and encyclopaedias; further down the scale, mothers are less well equipped with such aids. Finally, we have indeed used mothers' attempts to conceal their ignorance from the child as one item in our index of 'bamboozlement',[5] seeing it as one way in which the mother may try to maintain her authority at the expense of truthful dealing with the child; this index, like the index of 'evasion or distortion of truth' at age four,[6] shows major class differences.

The (minor) sex difference in the category 'Asks someone else' needs some comment, particularly as it unusually favours boys rather than girls. Reading the transcripts, it seems to be mainly due to the fact that many of the boys' questions are unanswerable by the mother but easily answerable by the father because they relate to conventional male interests – mechanical things, football, war and battles, space exploration, for example. In situations like this, where mother knows that her husband has the information needed, the obvious course is to 'ask Daddy when he comes in'.

For clarity, it is worth combining the first two sections of Table 20, in order to present in one scale the two categories judged to be educationally supportive. Table 21 makes it very plain that the whole issue of taking responsibility for extending children's information sources beyond the confines of the mother's own knowledge is closely class-linked; the child's sex is not a factor.

So far, we have considered items which we might expect to contribute to the concordance between home and school in ways which

Table 21 *Mothers who take responsibility for finding out the answers to children's questions if they cannot themselves provide them*

	social class					summary		
			III			I&II+	IIIman,	overall
	I&II	IIIwc	man	IV	V	IIIwc	IV, V	popn
	%	%	%	%	%	%	%	%
boys	76	54	50	44	23	65	46	51
girls	66	66	44	35	23	65	40	47
both	71	60	47	40	23	65	48	49

Significance: trend ↘ ****   m.class/w.class ****
between sexes   n.s.

are somewhat peripheral to what parents see as the core purpose of school: to turn out a literate and numerate child. The most direct way in which they might back up this purpose (leaving aside for the moment whether either parents or teachers think them competent to do so) is by helping the child with reading and other school work at home. The question of help with reading is very dependent upon the child's actual reading competence, and raises many problems of how to measure the quantity and quality of such help; this is discussed more fully in the next chapter, which deals with literacy and reading competence *per se*. Help with other school work tends to be of the more generally encouraging kind that the concordance index is concerned with: an environment is provided which is hospitable to ideas, inquiry, the following-through of initiatives, the sustaining and completion of projects. Sometimes parents will set and mark sums for the child; but this is usually at the child's request ('Do me some sums, Dad, dead hard ones!'), rather than stemming from the parents' anxiety that the child is not yet numerate; parents are wary of tangling with the mysterious processes of 'new maths', and all too often their doubts are reinforced by a scornful '*That's* not how we do it at school!' Help with writing is most often described in terms of spelling, but may also be largely a matter of taking thought to create a conducive environment – '. . . set the table out and a nice sheet of paper and sharp pencils – everything to invite him to write'.

Lorry driver's wife:
They'd been talking about London [at school]; and I've got a set

of encyclopedias which are for him when he's old enough, but of course I fetched them down. When was the Tower Bridge built, and who lives at Buckingham Palace, and all sorts like that. I filled a great sheet of paper.

Showroom foreman's wife:
He's doing a brief on water, and we've bought him a junior dictionary, and I've taught him to look words up – I have to help him to find out where the word is, but he knows it's water in the 'w's, you see. He's also got an encyclopedia, and he looks at the pictures, you see; so if he wants to look at the boats of other years, I get him to look at that.

Foreman's wife:
Well, he brought some home about a fortnight ago, and we sat and went through it with him, you know how you do. Well it was adding up. Now – here's where you're up against it really, because we told him – like he says he's got to count. He says 'I can't just add the two numbers'. So I says, 'Well, always *think* . . .' – it was a 6 and a 4 – '. . . always think of the biggest one, you see, the 6; then you've only got to add 4, you see'. So I said: 'Say 6 in your mind, and then get your fingers, and then go from there, that's 7, 8, 9, 10'. He says, 'We don't do it that road at school' – you see! So I says 'What *do* you do?' So he says, 'Well we get six blocks and we put them one side, and four blocks this side, then add 'em all together'. So you kinda – you think you're teaching them what you think is an easy way, but it's completely different to that, so . . . . . [And you haven't always *got* blocks, have you?] No – I says we shall finish up with blocks all round the house before we've done, when he gets on tens, units and hundreds!

Lorry driver's wife:
I've tried helping with sums, but they do them so differently in schools now to what I did them. Michelle brought some sums home the other day, and I *couldn't* understand – now I got the *answers* quick, but she said 'You're doing them wrong, Mum, we don't do them like that'. They add up backwards from right to left, well we were always taught the other way. Well, I couldn't explain it because I can't even understand it.

Departmental manager's wife:
We help him with this arithmetic; and now, though the school doesn't approve, we're teaching him his tables. *They* say at school

they're not *allowed* to teach them their tables. [Who doesn't allow?] The Education, so they say. I happened to be talking to his teacher about how we taught Steven and Jennifer their tables – because Jennifer found that more help than anything when she got to Mundella [grammar school]. And I says 'Why don't you teach them here?' And she said 'We're not allowed to teach them tables. If the school inspector came and found us teaching tables, we'd be in trouble'. Well, I can't understand that. So we've taught them all, and Keith got interested when we were teaching Steven [eleven]; so I said well, if he is interested, we'll start him now. He thinks it's fun, you see; because one of us has Steven and the other has Keith, and he's *hoping* to get better than Steven at it!

Cotton winder's wife:
> When the weather's been bad, I've been learning him to play cards; I thought to myself, well, this'll help him with his numbers, it'll learn him them, it'll help him know how to exchange money, you know. And apart from that, it'll learn him *not* to gamble later on – they both start off with sixpence, and when he loses, like, when they've lost, they've lost – they can praps borrow, but they have got to pay it back when they win again . . . . . When we first started to play, he knew some of the numbers but he didn't know 'em all. Well, now he knows, and he knows which not to put down, and he can change his money. So we're helping him there on that. He thinks it's a game, but it's an education really.

Table 22 shows proportions of parents who have regularly or often tried to help with school work other than reading, compared with those who have not attempted this at all; there is a residual middle category of parents who sometimes try to help. Class differences are similar to those found in other items of this index. Sex differences are not consistent: girls are favoured in the managerial/professional class in that only an eighth of them have *no* help, compared with twice as many boys, but equal numbers of boys and girls are given frequent help. Girls are favoured with frequent help in Class IV, but equal numbers are not helped at all. Once again Class V boys have the least favourable environment from an educational point of view.

The scoring of the home–school concordance index is shown in Table 23; as usual, we have then divided the sample into groups as nearly as possible equal in size, on the basis of their scores, and in Table 24 the low scorers and high scorers are shown in terms of social class and sex.

Table 22   *Parents' help with school work other than reading*

	I&II %	IIIwc %	social class III man %	IV %	V %	summary I&II+ IIIwc %	IIIman, IV, V %	overall popn %
Frequent help								
boys	35	23	19	7	12	29	16	19
girls	32	29	23	27	10	31	23	25
both	34	26	21	17	11	30	19	22

Significance: trend ↘ ****
                 between sexes   n.s.

m.class/w.class ***

	I&II	IIIwc	III man	IV	V	I&II+ IIIwc	IIIman, IV, V	overall popn
No help								
boys	25	12	20	21	35	19	22	21
girls	12	14	18	23	21	13	19	18
both	18	13	19	22	28	16	21	19

Significance: trend ↗ *
                 between sexes   n.s.

m.class/w.class n.s.

Table 23   *An index of home–school concordance*

Based on		Response	Score
Q.110	Child takes things to school to show his teacher	Often	2
		Occasionally	1
		Never	0
Q.112	Child continues school activities at home	Yes	1
		No	0
Q.134	Child draws/paints at home	Most days	2
		Sometimes	1
		Rarely	0
Q.113	Child asks about things he's heard of in class	Yes	1
		No	0
Q.115	Mother takes responsibility for finding answers she doesn't know	Yes	1
		No	0
Q.128	Parents try to help with school work	Regularly	2
		Occasionally	1
		Not at all	0

Possible score range 0–9, max. 9

Table 24   *High and low scorers on the home–school concordance index*

	social class					summary		
			III			I&II+	IIIman,	overall
	I&II	IIIwc	man	IV	V	IIIwc	IV, V	popn
	%	%	%	%	%	%	%	%
High scorers								
(7–9)								
boys	39	31	28	17	16	35	24	27
girls	55	43	37	37	10	49	34	38
both	47	37	32	27	13	42	29	33

Significance: trend ↘ ****   m.class/w.class ****
                                between sexes ***

Low scorers								
(0–4)								
boys	13	10	34	41	42	12	36	30
girls	11	14	24	21	31	12	24	21
both	12	12	29	31	36	12	30	25

Significance: trend ↗ ****   m.class/w.class ****
                between sexes **   interaction class/sex p = 0·08

The results given in Table 24 very clearly confirm marked social class trends in terms of both low scorers and high scorers on home–school concordance. In the working-class group as a whole, families are rather evenly spread across the score range, with just under a third appearing in each of the high and low categories and just over a third in the middle category; the unskilled group, however, is notably unlikely to score high (13 per cent) and unskilled-class boys in particular score low (42 per cent). In the middle class, families are not at all evenly spread through the score range: only 12 per cent show a low degree of concordance. Professional-class girls stand out as especially likely to score high (55 per cent).

The clear-cut sex difference deserves comment: it might not have been expected, since only one of the individual items (taking things to school) produced a sex difference of a similar magnitude. Of the other two results which showed sex differences of lesser significance, one favoured the girls, but the other the boys. This is an example of

how an overall index measure of this kind can in fact tell us something over and above what we can learn from the individual items
that make up the scale. In other words, the index allows us to draw
conclusions about the *degree* of home–school concordance which is
experienced by boys and girls; whereas the individual items strictly
only allow us to make statements about the proportions of girls, as
compared with boys, who behave in a certain way. The sex/class
interaction found among the low scorers, though marginal, is of
interest because it underlines an interaction effect to which we have
previously drawn attention; in its clearest terms, lower-working-class
boys are disadvantaged and upper-middle-class girls advantaged by
virtue of both their class affiliation and the sex to which they belong.

An analysis of variance based on the index scores both confirms
and extends these conclusions. Occupational class is the most important factor, followed by sex, and both these are significant at the
0·001 level. A less salient result, significant at the 0·02 level, is that
children from small families have higher scores on home–school
concordance than those from larger families. Over the full range of
scores, however, the sex/class interaction fades and no longer reaches
borderline significance.

We can bring together the two groups of findings which we have
discussed here and in the previous chapter, and which we have presented as indices of 'general cultural interests' and 'home/school
concordance'. In both cases, we can see striking differences between
social-class groups. These can be summarised in terms of a number
of tendencies: as we move down the social scale,

(1) The range of cultural interests experienced by children as mem-
    bers of their family group becomes more narrow and restricted.
(2) Although children in all classes sometimes carry over school
    activities into the home, further down the scale they are less
    inquiring at home on school-inspired topics.
(3) Parents become less inclined to take up and expand children's
    questions, of whatever source, by whatever means.
(4) Parents are, in particular, less likely to use books or newspapers
    to further the child's knowledge, and are more likely to attempt
    to conceal their own ignorance.
(5) Children are less likely to receive help, direct or in the form of
    the encouragement of a 'hospitable environment', with school
    work other than reading.

The range of cultural interests, as expressed in the GCI index, is not
apparently affected by the child's sex, whereas the concordance index

scores are significantly higher for girls. This makes sense in terms of the mainly family-based nature of the first index compared with the child-based nature of the second: that is to say (leaving aside extra-curricular lessons), the trips and excursions of the GCI index will tend to be organised for the whole family, and therefore available to both sexes equally, whereas in the HSC index we are looking at parents' interactions with one particular child.

The factor of family size, on the other hand, is more consistently at work through both indices: families with four or more children are less likely to be taken out into the community by their parents and less likely to score high on the items which indicate a good concordance between home and school. Thus children from large families tend to be disadvantaged on both these counts. This is understandable in terms of a shortage of money, space, time, patience, energy; that it is understandable does not make it any less real as a disadvantage.

To sum up, when we consider circumstances of home background which fall broadly within the scope of the child's general education outside school, once again it is working-class boys, and in particular unskilled working-class boys, who seem most seriously disadvantaged; if they also come from large families with low incomes, the odds will be correspondingly more heavily weighted against them. In a variety of ways the interests of girls at this age tend to be home-centred, as we have seen,[7] which also means that they tend naturally to be relevant to the educational process as it is conceived in school; boys' interests are less obviously relevant, and are often at loggerheads with school demands. Furthermore, there are a number of sex–class interactions in the data analysis which always point in the same direction, even when they do not reach significance level; taken together, they indicate an attempt by middle-class parents of boys to ensure home–school concordance as well as to introduce them to wider cultural events. In this respect, as well as in others which we have already mentioned, the difference between the sexes in their experience of socialisation becomes markedly greater as we move down the social-class scale.

'School doesn't like you to help him – their ways are different'
In this chapter and the previous one, we have been exploring the ways in which the school is or is not backed up at home by the parents' willingness to enlarge the child's cultural horizons and to provide an environment stimulating of and responsive to his ideas. It is, of course, also the concern of the school itself to provide such an environment. In a sense, however, the voluntary nature of home

educational activities compared with the compulsory nature of school is paralleled by the voluntary nature of the school's cultural activities compared with the compulsory nature of its efforts towards literacy and numeracy: that is to say, parents, teachers and children all tend to subscribe to the belief that it is the business of junior schools to teach the three Rs, whatever else they may or may not teach. No parents are totally unconcerned as to whether their child will learn to read. At the same time, to say that literacy is important to all parents for their children does not imply that it is personally *relevant* to all parents' own lives. To what extent do parents regard it as their own ultimate responsibility to ensure the attainment of reading competence in their child, and how far are their attitudes in this respect defined by the relevance of literacy to their own life-styles? Certainly what parents seem to have in common (and this includes parents who are teachers by profession) is doubt and uncertainty as to whether their role in helping the child should overlap with the teacher's.

We have suggested already[8] that the roles of teachers and of parents are fundamentally different. Parents have a clear duty to do their best for their own children; and that best includes a partiality for their own which has no 'reasonable' limits. Teachers, on the other hand, must be both reasonable and impartial; for although parents might be only too glad to see their own children preferred at school, they also realise that they would find it intolerable were other children given preferential treatment at the expense of theirs. 'Having favourites' is regarded as a major criticism by parents, teachers and children; fairness and impartiality is an important part of the 'good teacher's' role. To sustain this notion, a corollary is invoked: that teachers must be given a reasonably free hand to educate (and discipline) children without too much parental pressure and 'interference' in the classroom. In an era of educational thought which is more and more concerned to involve parents in their children's education, including classroom involvement, it was interesting to find how few parents were demanding any such thing: the prevailing attitude was that teachers have a difficult enough job, and could well need to be protected from particular parents who might have an overactive interest in the welfare of their own children. In this climate of thought, being a parent who was not 'always up and down to the school' was most often seen as a positive virtue. Even when children were clearly making rather poor progress, parents seemed to be leaning over backwards in an effort not to criticise the school and teachers directly – perhaps because they were acutely aware of the possibility of being branded as 'overprotective' or 'difficult' parents.

The parental dilemma is, in fact, that intervention – even when it seems necessary and reasonable – might all too easily upset a delicate relationship, and in the longer run make matters worse for the child rather than better.

When children fail to make good progress, teachers also naturally feel concerned; but again their feelings are complex. They know that their classroom is not unobserved. Although parents still do not often spend time in classrooms during the working day, they are strongly motivated to discover what goes on there, and are fairly well placed to fill out the details of the picture they are given on Open Day: after all, their children and those of neighbours do talk at home about what they have been doing in school, and although some children are more reticent than others, and accounts given are not always very accurate, mothers are not socially isolated from one another; in talking among themselves, they can if they wish rapidly piece together a more-or-less consistent picture. A good deal of information is exchanged through the gossip chain around the school gates among parents waiting for their children, and (just as the conversation in the waiting-room of a group practice surgery endlessly compares the doctors' personalities and talents) much of this concerns the relative merits of different teachers. The teachers themselves can hardly fail to be aware that parents compare and evaluate them; they also know that, particularly with children of this age, the onus is very much upon them to ensure that their pupils acquire the basic skills of reading, writing and elementary mathematics.

At the same time, teachers are conscious that there is a certain amount of disagreement in the teaching profession about the best methods for teaching the three Rs or the most effective organisational framework in which to do so; it is also a matter for open professional debate whether teachers in training are adequately prepared in techniques for teaching these basic skills. There may be understandable reluctance to admit these professional uncertainties to parents. What often happens in practice, therefore, is that schools let it be known to parents that they use up-to-date educational methods, without being too explicit about the exact nature of these methods or their implications. Rather rarely, and usually where there is an active middle-class parent–teacher association, a school will put on a special workshop meeting to explain an innovation such as new maths; still more rarely does a school take parents into its confidence concerning techniques of teaching reading, let alone enlist direct parental help (other than 'hearing him read') in putting such techniques into practice. It is hardly surprising if to parents it seems that the teaching profession is closing its ranks behind the somewhat doubtful proposition that parents are not competent to help because the whole educational approach has changed too much since they themselves went to school – with the corollary that they cannot *learn* to help, either, because of the weight of expertise now required.

It is an advantage of a study such as this one that it provides an opportunity for parents to express their feelings about these problems more freely than they might to the teachers of their own children, who are likely to receive a muted version of any alarm parents may feel, if only for courtesy's sake. In the next chapter, parents' views on reading, and on their own role in its teaching, are (we hope) given depth and meaning by being presented in a framework of other indications of home literacy and the child's own competence.

NOTES

1 David Ayerst, *Understanding Schools* (Harmondsworth, Penguin Books, 1967).
2 Mike Taylor, 'The machine-minder', in Ronald Fraser (ed.), *Work 2: Twenty personal accounts* (Harmondsworth, Penguin Books, 1969).
3 J. and E. Newson, op. cit. (1968), ch. 12, 'Who told thee that thou wast naked?'
4 J. and E. Newson, op. cit. (1968 and 1976*b*).
5 J. and E. Newson, op. cit. (1976*b*).
6 J. and E. Newson, op. cit. (1968).
7 J. and E. Newson, op. cit. (1976*b*), chs 3 and 4.
8 Chapter 1, pp. 43–4. See also J. and E. Newson, op. cit. (1976*b*), ch. 2.

Chapter 5

A Necessary Condition of Liberty

... though I have the uttermost contempt for a teacher so ill-
mannered and incompetent as to be unable to make a child
learn to read and write without also making it cry, still I am
prepared to admit that I had rather have been compelled to
learn to read and write with tears ... than left in ignorance.
Reading, writing, and enough arithmetic to use money honestly
and accurately ... become necessary conditions of a child's
liberty before it can appreciate the importance of its liberty, or
foresee that these accomplishments are worth acquiring.

George Bernard Shaw, Preface to *Misalliance*

Parents may not describe reading quite in Shaw's terms; but it is
clear that most of them would agree with him, in the sense that in
talking about the child's school progress they return again and again
to reading as the *essential* skill, the prerequisite for further progress,
the first key to the locks that shut off future choice for the child.
Whatever else is or is not expected of the school, children must be
taught to read.

Yet the teaching of reading is a mysterious business, not least to
teachers. Few of us can remember precisely the processes by which
we came to the degree of reading competence required for the reading and understanding of this page of symbols arranged in complex
patterns and sub-patterns. As Plowden points out, 'the most successful infant teachers have refused to follow the wind of fashion and to
commit themselves to any one method'.

Probably most teachers believe that a group of children will learn
most effectively in a rich reading environment which encompasses a
multi-angle approach to reading skills; the richer the environment,
the more hope that one of its ingredients will make reading 'click' for

the child. On the other hand, like someone who takes six remedies at once for a cold in the hope that one of them will help, although teachers can describe what they do and explain why they do it, few could say with any certainty which ingredient had been the most efficacious for any individual child, or whether it was the combination or the sequencing which was the decisive factor.

The ambiguity of the situation is the greater because of the variability of children's ease of learning even within a relatively homogeneous group under the same teacher. Why do some children make such heavy weather over learning to read, while others, like Shaw, 'have no recollection of being taught to read or write' and feel as if they were 'born with both faculties'?[1] Like most skills in which material which at one stage was meaningless eventually comes to make sense for the learner, for a few children sense will be made from the first time symbol and meaning are explicitly presented side by side; for many more, there will be periods (perhaps to be counted in minutes) of very rapid and crucial learning, which to the child and the observer appears as a 'penny-dropping' experience. Every teacher knows the moment when suddenly a child appears to have 'got the hang of it'; parents, teachers and authors of reading-schemes recognise this characteristic in their use of phrases like 'at last she's away', 'just on the edge of reading', *Breakthrough to Literacy.* 'Yes, she's just got to that stage [of reading well enough to enjoy a book for its story]', says a doctor's wife, 'and how delighted I am. Isn't it marvellous!' Yet the sense of a lucky moment of fusion between something in the teaching and something in the learner increases the ambiguity which surrounds the process of the teaching of reading.

None the less, a child's proficiency in reading is one of the most tangible ways in which parents can assess progress in the primary school, and it is also an area in which many parents feel not quite incompetent to participate as instructors. Compared, say, with mathematics, where ideas, teaching methods, and the sorts of things the child is expected to know have changed markedly in the past twenty or so years since these parents were at school, the end result of being able to read remains fairly constant over the years. Changes have of course occurred in how reading is taught, and schools have followed these trends to greater or lesser degrees;[2] but parents retain subjective yardsticks of what they expect their children to be capable of reading.

With the subjectivity of this yardstick very much in mind, we asked the mothers about their children's reading ability: 'How good is N's reading? Can he read well enough to enjoy a book for its story? When he's reading a book to himself, does he say the words

aloud or read silently?' From the mothers' answers we made an
initial distinction between those children who couldn't read a book
for its story and those who could, and this second group was further
divided according to whether they read aloud, mouthed the words,
or read silently. Table 25 shows the proportions falling into these
categories; the residual category comprises those who read aloud.

Table 25   *Children's competence in reading*

	social class					summary		overall
	I&II	IIIwc	III man	IV	V	I&II+ IIIwc	IIIman, IV, V	popn
	%	%	%	%	%	%	%	%
Cannot read								
boys	19	35	45	46	54	27	46	41
girls	5	24	30	31	41	14	31	27
both	12	30	38	38	48	20	39	34

Significance: trend ↗   ****   m.class/w.class   ****
                            between sexes   ****

	I&II	IIIwc	III man	IV	V	I&II+ IIIwc	IIIman, IV, V	popn
Reads silently or mouths								
boys	55	35	17	16	16	45	17	24
girls	60	37	21	16	21	49	20	28
both	58	36	19	16	18	47	18	26

Significance: trend ↘   ****   m.class/w.class   ****
                            between sexes   n.s.

These figures indicate a very clear association between reading and
social class. The child of an unskilled manual worker is four times
more likely to be a poor reader than the child of a professional father.
Conversely, three times as many children from professional homes
as compared with unskilled working class homes can read silently.
These results bear a close resemblance to those for seven-year-olds
obtained by the National Child Development Study[3] using a test of
word recognition: 13 per cent of their children in social Class I & II
fell into the category of poor readers, rising to 48 per cent of Class
V. The clear predominance of our boys (41 per cent) over girls (27
per cent) among the ranks of the poor readers is another finding that
is confirmed by a number of surveys of primary-age children.[4]

We have no independent assessment of the children's reading ability at the age of seven, but as part of a related study[5] the reading age of just over a quarter of the sample was ascertained, using the Neale Analysis of Reading Ability,[6] when they were at the transition point between primary and secondary education. Some measure of the accuracy of the mother's assessment at seven can be gauged by relating it to these test scores obtained three years later. Using a straightforward distinction between those who cannot read a book for its story and those who read silently or merely mouth the words, and, subsequently, between those who read at a level below the average for children of their own age and those with reading ages above their chronological age, in 76 per cent of the cases there is a correspondence between the mother's judgement and later test score. It is not surprising that this correspondence is not perfect; mothers are not equally aware of how well their child can read, nor are they all basing their judgements on the same standard book – much depends on the level of difficulty of the books they expect a seven-year-old to be able to read. Furthermore, despite criticisms of the competence of junior schools in teaching basic reading skills,[7] children's reading can be accelerated after the age of seven; lack of correspondence does not necessarily imply that the original judgement was inaccurate.

In this chapter we will be looking at the various ways in which the home can give specific rather than background support to the child who is learning to read; and will as far as possible relate the presence or absence of such support to the child's reading ability as judged by the mother. Where it seems relevant, we will also refer to the results of the smaller study employing standardised measures.

The previous two chapters have explored different aspects of the relationship between home and school with particular emphasis on the part played (or not played) by parents in backing up the work of the school. The acquisition of reading skills is a key area in which parents generally feel that they have a part to play, though, as we will show, there are important differences in how this is manifested and with what effect.

In our conversations with these mothers about their seven-year-olds, our questions about help with reading and other school work were aimed at the here-and-now. But help with reading is not something that begins at seven; its roots can be seen in the child's experiences before his earliest days in the infant school. We did not inquire systematically about pre-school help, but because of the longitudinal perspective of this study we were able to look back to relevant material from the four-year-old stage.[8] Few parents, it would seem, set out to teach their four-year-olds to read in a systematic way, but many do read *to* the child. Reading to a child implies several things – that reading material is available, whether owned or borrowed, in the home; that the parents themselves can read[9] and that the child's eventual acquisition of reading skill will be set within a 'meaningful environment'. As John Downing has put it, 'The best way for a non-reader to learn the true purpose of reading is to share in a purposeful reading activity with a reader'.[10] All this could loosely be labelled 'motivation to read', but it seems likely that more than this is involved; one current theory about how children learn to read effectively holds that what is important is to be able to predict what is coming next from a knowledge of the language structure.[11] The print on the page enables the reader to reduce to one the number of alternatives available. Being read to by an adult (or, for that matter, another child) familiarises the young child with the structure of written English, and it is plausible that this will be of value to him in his own early efforts to read.

In practice there are, of course, differences in what people mean by 'reading to' children: whether it is systematic and regular, whether the child's attention is drawn to the content and meaning of the story, and perhaps to the letters and words themselves, whether it is deliberately intended to widen the child's horizons or whether it is seen as a device for rounding off the day, quietening the child down, or just keeping him amused – or all of these things. Jean Jones[12] found that only 19 per cent of working-class mothers read to their pre-school children according to some regular pattern, compared with 71 per cent of middle-class mothers. The latter were also more likely to stress the educational value of reading rather than its value in keeping the child amused or quiet.

The questions that we asked our mothers at four years do not allow these sorts of fine distinctions to be made, but two questions do give us some idea of whether or not the child had some experience of being read to. The mothers were asked to describe a typical bedtime for their child, and any reference to stories being told or read to the child was noted (although no specific questions were asked about this). Mention of reading to the child can thus be taken to imply that this was a regular part of his experience. As we reported then,[13] 27 per cent of children overall were read to in this way, and this was strongly class-related: the proportion increased to 56 per cent of the professional and managerial group, and reduced to 14 per cent in the unskilled group.

What relationship is there between being read to in this way and reading proficiency at age seven? Forty-four per cent of the children who were good readers at the age of seven had been read to at four, compared with only 22 per cent of the non-readers. This is a significant relationship: which is not to imply a directly causal one. However, when this same relationship is investigated class by class, there is a marked and puzzling divergence between Classes I & II, III wc and III manual taken together, where the difference between readers and non-readers is substantial (in the order of 20 per cent) and in the expected direction; Class IV, where the relationship goes in the opposite direction (i.e. being read to at four is *negatively* related to reading performance at seven); and Class V, where there is no difference between the two groups. It may be that the sort of reading engaged in by parents in these latter two groups is qualitatively different from that in the other families (Jones's distinction may well be relevant here), with differing long-term outcomes.

We also asked at four about the ways in which the child's father participated in his daily life, and in this context we noted whether or not he was described as reading to the child. Overall, 42 per cent of fathers read to their children 'often'; again, this was class-related, the most noticeable difference being between Class I & II (64 per cent) and the rest (43 per cent in III wc down to 35 per cent in Class V).

When we look at the relationship between father reading at four and the child's reading ability at seven we find, as before, that there is a significant link. Overall, 35 per cent of those children who cannot read at seven were read to 'often' by their fathers at four, compared with 52 per cent of those who are by this time proficient readers.

So the experience of reading, even vicarious reading, that children have received before starting school appears to have benefited them after two or more years of schooling. However, this is far from being the complete story since this sort of reading experience does not occur in isolation: parents who are helping their children in this way are also likely to be providing an educationally supportive environment in other ways; and, of course, help with reading itself does not cease when the child starts school – indeed, for many this is when it really begins.

'I've got an idea of what they do, but I mean it's not my way; I mean she can write her name, but she can't tell you the letters in her name . . .'
When we asked the mothers about this when the children were seven, we did indeed find that the large majority – 81 per cent – were helping the child with his reading, or had done so in the past (Table 26). Of particular interest in these figures is the complete absence of any sex or social class differences; although the help may well differ in quantity and quality, four-fifths of parents in the working class, as

Table 26   *Children whose parents help them with reading*

	social class					summary		
		III				I&II+	IIIman,	overall
	I&II	IIIwc	man	IV	V	IIIwc	IV, V	popn.
	%	%	%	%	%	%	%	%
boys	78	81	85	74	67	79	81	80
girls	75	88	84	81	82	81	83	83
both	77	84	84	78	74	80	82	81

No significant differences

well as in the middle class, are prepared to participate in the task of teaching reading to their child.

The initial part of this question was deliberately worded rather broadly, so that mothers could feel free to include any positive steps they might have taken to help the child with his reading. The second part required them to be more specific as to how they helped, and it soon became clear that a wide range of activities was being subsumed under the heading of 'help'.

A handful of parents had begun to teach their children in a systematic way before they ever attended school; Mrs Lord, a primary teacher whose husband was himself doing teacher training as a mature student, had continued to exercise her professional skills at home:

> When she was three I looked after a little boy of four, and I thought, right, I'll just see what pre-reading I can do with a pre-school child. And I did flash cards; and things like that, which he just turned his nose up at, Antonia, at three, just took, and said 'This says so-and-so', and she just went. She wasn't pushed. She just did it.

A secondary teacher's wife, while protesting that she didn't set out to teach her son to read, nevertheless illustrates the literacy-oriented mother's near-compulsion to provide an environment that stimulates reading:

> I can hardly remember a time – this sounds ridiculous – when he couldn't read. You know what I mean? Right from two or three he could read packet names and street names, and so it went on.

I used to name everything in the room – have tickets up with 'door' written on, and things like that. I never *consciously* taught him. And then when he got further on, he started the Ladybird series; about two books, and it was all there by then. It's just a thing he grew up with; when they see everybody picking up books, I suppose they want to be reading themselves.

It is not without significance that in both of these examples the families have strong links with the educational profession. Not only does this give them knowledge of the value of having a head-start in such an important skill, but they also have access to appropriate materials and techniques (simple though those may be) and, perhaps more importantly, a confident base from which to defend themselves from critics – particularly from those with whom they might find themselves in competition, the teachers in the infant school. It is one thing for a teacher to level a charge of interference at a mother who has no formal education beyond the age of fourteen; it is quite another to make that accusation to someone who has inside knowledge of schools and teaching.

Some indication of the nature of the help that parents gave was obtained from the transcripts. The question did not ask precisely when this help was given: whether mainly in the pre-school period or once the child had started school. The books that the child is using at school frequently act as a focus for regular help or more casual 'hearing him read'; a minority of parents buy additional copies of these books, but most rely on their child bringing the book home.

Merchandise supervisor's wife:
> We would go to Sisson and Parker's and buy her the book she was reading at school so she had one at school and her own at home; then I'd help her every night. If you're not *afraid* of the lessons, I think that's half the battle.

Shop manager's wife:
> When she first started school, I bought the reading-books she was doing at school, and I used to give her an hour every evening – even when I was in the shop busy, I did. I used to get her reading books, and we used to read through her reading-books, and I used to encourage her to read. If she stuck over a word, I used to say 'Now, break it up', and I used to put my finger over part of it and say 'Now what's that, and that? Now, what's that *together?*' I've always encouraged her to read.

Professional engineer's wife:
> Yes, well, the school books that they had . . . um, Janet and John, you know . . . we've got them all; and we read with them each night, and she just sort of twigged on to it.

Although these three mothers seem well in control of the situation, others find their attempts thwarted: either by the child's reluctance to co-operate or by fears of incompatibility between the school's approach to teaching reading and the parents' own method, based usually upon how they were themselves taught.

For some children – and from the transcripts there seems to be a preponderance of boys – there is a marked disinclination to sit down with a book and be helped, though whether this is a matter of their own temperament or the approach taken by their parents we are unable to say. In the subsample rather more of the poor readers were also described as 'outdoor' children[14] (significant at the 0·05 level) at the age of seven. Though it is impossible to distinguish between cause and effect, there is a case for suggesting that since 'outdoor' children are less likely to spend time in sedentary pursuits such as reading with a parent, their overall reading development is adversely affected. On the other hand, perhaps children become 'outdoor children' because they have a basic antipathy to sedentary activities.

Clerk's wife:
> The teacher says she's got to practise, but she's never in. I don't like to fetch them in and push them.

Cabinet maker's wife:
> I'm beginning to sit with him in the lunch hour and help him with his reading. We just go through this book . . . he couldn't care tuppence; he looks at the ceiling, he looks at everything but the actual subject in hand.

Children's enthusiasm fluctuates in this area as in any other, and an awareness of this fact by the mother can help her to accommodate her efforts to the peaks of the child's interest; the act of helping cannot be divorced from the atmosphere in which it takes place.

Unemployed car repairer's wife:
> Well, I don't like to interfere. If he comes and asks me, all well and good, but I wouldn't push myself on to him – I wouldn't get hold of a book and say 'Well, let's hear you do this, and let's hear you do that. See what you can read'. If a child comes up and asks

you to listen to him, yes, take interest; but I don't think it's a good idea to force your attention on to him, because they're inclined to . . . they don't want to know – it's not the right time for them to read. They'll perhaps have a reading book in their hand, or perhaps they're looking at it, and you go up to them and say 'Come on, let's hear you read'. Down! – the book's shut up; they don't want to know. Whereas if a child comes and *asks* you, I think that's the time when they really are interested in what you're going to do for him.

By far the greatest source of conflict perceived by parents who tried to help with reading at home was the clash, real or imagined, between the methods of teaching that they considered appropriate – derived from common sense and their own school experience – and the current practices of the primary school. Some persevered with help, despite a nagging anxiety that what they were doing might be in conflict with what the child was learning at school.

Window cleaner's wife:
> I read to him, and I let him tell me the words and that sort of thing; but I don't think the teachers like you to help, you know, in case you teach them the wrong way.

Company director's wife:
> When I knew what books they were reading at school, I went out and got a book to try and help him; but then again, it's a different proposition – they read by the visual method here and not the phonetic method, so it's very different, and you can do an awful lot of harm trying to do one if the other's not quite right, can't you?

Others see this clash as a good reason (or possibly excuse) for not giving help at home:

Storeman's wife:
> I haven't helped, because I think the school has one way of teaching them and we have another. It's no good sort of interfering.

Works manager's wife:
> Not since going to the school and talking to his teacher. I found out that we were doing the wrong thing, teaching him a different way, you see, so it's best to leave it alone.

As well as illustrating these different reactions, the transcripts serve to underline two points: firstly, that the confusion about teaching methods is not restricted to working-class parents whose own education may have been limited; and secondly, that there seems to have been very little effort on the part of teachers to harness the good intentions of the parents so that school and home might work effectively together in the child's best interests.

The possibility of confusing the child is indeed often stressed by teachers to discourage parents; another argument is that parents are too emotionally involved to behave as effective teachers towards their own children, with the implication that children may be over-pressurised to the point where they might lose all spontaneous desire to learn. As a working assumption, many teachers also seem to believe that if parents try to teach they will inevitably resort to rather formal and old-fashioned methods of instruction because these are the methods which will have been remembered from their own childhood. Formal instruction based partly upon rote learning had not at the time of interviewing received the public rehabilitation that subsequent studies provided.[15]

It can be argued that sooner or later a certain amount of rote learning is almost indispensable for the child if he is to use a dictionary or telephone directory, or be freed from using his ten fingers to count with. Thus if teachers fear that parents will revert to old-fashioned techniques, they may be right, in the sense that the decline of formal teaching is often equated by parents with a decline in standards. Parents frequently argue that it may be wiser not to allow children to think that all learning is necessarily fun, and many of them feel rather strongly that this needs to be brought home to children fairly early in life, because they will otherwise be ill-prepared for the demands which they will have to face if they are to achieve even limited success in their later school careers. Thus the concept of learning through play – the fun morality of the classroom – is still regarded with alarm by many parents who feel that it may too easily be used as an excuse for allowing children to neglect certain basic skills which may require some real effort to learn.

Although most parents can appreciate the value of praising success and of making a game out of work, most also suspect that there comes a point when children have to be made to do certain things despite the fact that they regard them as a chore and a bore. As a result of experience in their working lives, parents generally assume that some persistent effort and a certain amount of unpleasantly hard work are often necessary in order to make any real headway in our contemporary competitive society and they see a need to teach this value to their children. For teachers this is less of a problem because they tend to see academic success as something which it is in the child's own best interest to strive for: if the child chooses not to make sufficient effort through lack of motivation, the teachers will not necessarily regard this as a failing in themselves; instead they will be strongly tempted to give their time and attention to other children who are intrinsically more rewarding to teach because they do make an effort. It is this aspect of the permissive atmosphere in schools today which clearly worries many parents. They believe that their children could achieve more if the teachers were prepared to be stricter and to push the children harder, and they do not think that their children should be continually cushioned from the idea that learning is sometimes difficult and arduous. Thus 'help' from the parent may be in the form of the 'push' that they feel is lacking. Often parents suggest that their children would probably enjoy the challenge of a stricter and more formal teaching situation. One mother described her son's move from a permissive to a formal school:

He came home absolutely thrilled because he'd got his own desk and chair. You see it's such an entirely different method of education. I did worry terribly because the City school where he was, it was *no* education in my opinion, and a lot of other people . . . they played all day. In one class they had the same group of children right through to the juniors, which if he could have stayed was over three years. Quite honestly they never did a thing, not one sum – he didn't know what a sum was, *or* reading. Unless they went to the teacher and asked her, the teacher never made them do anything, they did just as they liked. It's supposed to be this new education, which I personally think is terrible, because if your child is lazy, that means if they can't be bothered, they just don't learn anything. They've got to be pushing to know things; well naturally, my boy, if they play with sand and water and clay he'd do it rather than learn a sum. Well he started *this* school – ooh, it's so different. They have set lessons, they sit in a chair and desk all day, and they're really made to graft, and course the other children were *way* ahead of him. They could do sums, and he didn't know what one was. He's catching up, and my husband's started with him, and had a word with the headmistress about how far behind he was. We *tried* to educate him to a point, but it's very difficult and you're frightened to teach him one thing and then if they teach him something at school – we didn't know what the method of reading was. But you can make a mistake like that;

because we, on the whole, left it to the *school* to educate him, and
I'll be honest, until he came here he hardly knew anything. It was
two years just down the drain. He's a lot of catching up to do.

Many mothers gave the impression that they expected the school
to be critical of the help they were giving, and some had actually
been told not to interfere:

Representative's wife:
　　When I went to the school and asked why he wasn't reading very
　　well, and said should I help him, the teacher said 'Oh no, it won't
　　be necessary'.

Administrative assistant's wife:
　　No – because when he was a bit slow I went to one of those
　　parents' . . . you know . . . days. I was a bit worried about his
　　reading, I thought he wasn't getting on very well, and I asked if I
　　should help him; and she discouraged it. I'll often *listen* to him,
　　but I don't actively help – if you understand what I mean? I just
　　help him with the words, that's all; because she so adamantly
　　discouraged it, you see, that I just didn't, I thought it was best not
　　to . . . [Do you or his Daddy ever help him with . . . . . other school
　　work?] No, because we were so totally discouraged about it. [They
　　discourage you from doing anything at all to help them, do they?]
　　Yes, they do. I suppose they work on the principle, the two differ-
　　ent trains of thought – obviously we're not trained for it – would
　　confuse them.

Unemployed labourer's wife:
　　Mrs Donington's always said 'Don't teach your children. Don't
　　learn 'em to write, cause we learn 'em to write different to what
　　you do'.

Clearly there are two sides to this question. In particular instances,
a teacher may have good reasons for believing that a parent may be
incapable of giving any useful help or may try to put too much
pressure on the child. None the less, there is a danger that these
specific reservations may become generalised into an attitude that
parents as such have no role to play, and that any help they could
give is bound to confuse. Reference to active encouragement on the
part of the school were few. Sometimes an attempt to involve reflected a school's general approach, or that of a particular teacher:

Headmaster's wife:
The headmaster at her school thinks parents can help with the
reading a lot by going over reading with them at home.

Labourer's wife:
They tell her they want so many words with 't' on you know; I
don't know these things she calls them . . . 'double something'
they call them at school – so we dig out all the papers we can find,
all those that start with a 't' or, you know . . . sometimes it's a
difficult job!

But even in these examples the link is either vague or apparently detached from anything else. We found almost no instances of a school
going out of its way to introduce parents to the means by which the
teaching of reading was approached, in order to enlist their informed
help. This mother (see another example of her concern on page 127)
felt that real encouragement had come far too late.

Departmental manager's wife:
Reading – now we *are* helping him at home with that; because he
couldn't read when he came down to the juniors. In fact I had an
argument with his teacher up at the infants; he stayed with one
teacher from starting at five till he came down here at seven
[vertical streaming]; and I went up one or two times, because it
was obvious, we knew he wasn't reading; and I asked her if she
would let us help him at home; but she refused, she said 'You'll
teach him differently' – to what they were teaching him there. She
said 'Leave him, and *we'll* do it'. Well, he *still* couldn't read; so
about a month or six weeks before he came down to the juniors, I
went up to see her again; and she *still* wouldn't. I said 'Well, you
tell me how you're teaching him, and I'll do it the same way'. But
she *still* wouldn't let us do it; and of course I was undecided, I
didn't want to start in a different way and mix him up all the more.
So she says 'We'll leave him, and I'll have him every day reading';
but he *still* couldn't. So when he came down here [to the junior
school] I left him a while to see what was happening, and then I
went to see his teacher in the juniors, and she was very pleased to
have help; and she told me the way that she was doing it, and I've
been having him for about quarter of an hour, no longer, at night;
I think that's long enough; and he's coming on very well now.
[Does he bring books home from school?] No, we get them from
the library. It's been hard, really, because he's *wanted* to read.
[It's a problem, isn't it, to know what do . . .?] Oh dear! It is!

You see, there're so many different ways that they teach them now. I *still* say they should teach them reading and arithmetic when they start school. [You think they leave it too long?] I *do*! I think they play *far* too much – up there he was doing nothing but play – water and – oh, I don't know, he used to come home filthy, covered in paint and wet. I mean, let them *have* a playing period, yes, but I think they're ready for school work. [Did he not have *any* reading work at five, that you could see?] Well, he never seemed to. I think he could read more when he *started* school than what he could when he'd been up there a while – you see when he started school we left off teaching him because I didn't want to mix him up; you see all his brothers could read, he knew the school work they were doing, well he wanted to do the same thing; but after he started that school, he got so he knew *we* would read to him, *they* would read to him, and so he got out of it! Oh, but it did annoy us! Because he is the sort of kiddy that *wants* to do it – he'll sit hours with a comic . . . . . Well, it is a worry; because it's bound to pull them back from going to grammar school or into a grammar stream.

That over 80 per cent of our sample claimed in fact to have given help with reading would suggest that, in their varying ways, most parents see themselves as having some part to play in this basic aspect of their children's education, and yet this willingness is too often mis-channelled for lack of advice, encouragement and appreciation from those best qualified to give it.

Those parents who do not give help fall into four groups. Some might have helped in the past, but once their child was reading independently no further help was required:

Grocer's wife:

It was something she picked up without any trouble. I don't remember her ever learning. She used to bring her book home from school and you wouldn't say 'Well, let's practise your reading' – the minute she came home she'd have a book open and she'd be reading and reading and reading all the pages she'd learned. She's loved reading, right from the start.

There was a tendency for mothers giving this sort of answer to come from the professional/managerial group, and this early competence perhaps accounts for the slightly lower proportion (77 per cent) giving help in what would otherwise have been expected to be a particularly supportive group.

Other mothers, as we have seen, were reluctant to help in case they cut across the school's approach. A further small group were unable to help because of their own lack of skill, and in a number of these cases the role of helper was taken on by an older sibling:

Porter's wife:
She's never asked me [for help]. With Janet [eleven] being a big girl, she asks her. I'm not a scholar, you see.

Storeman's wife:
I can't read. If he ever does [want help] he asks his Dad or the girl [eleven].

The final group was one who gave no help because of their own lack of interest and concern.

Presser's wife:
No, that's something I don't do, cause I don't like reading myself. I only pick the paper up about once every other week.

Cleaner's wife:
No – she's never asked.

When we looked at the relationship between help given and the child's reading ability we found, perhaps suprisingly at first sight, that those children judged to be unable to read were as likely to have received help as those who could read (76 per cent in both instances). However, this finding conceals qualitative differences between the two groups; it seems that the parents of poor readers are more likely to intervene when it becomes apparent that the child is experiencing difficulties,[16] whereas the parents of the good readers have helped from an earlier age, and, by the time the child is seven, feel that their assistance is no longer required.

'Oh yes, he's got books. I bet there's four upstairs'
Direct help of the kind that we have been discussing is only one of the ways in which the home can support and encourage the child throughout the process of becoming literate. The skills required in learning to read are of comparatively little value if they remain isolated from what is being read and the experiences that the written word can provide. We therefore went on to ask a series of questions aimed at building up a picture of the 'literary climate' of the home. Although a quarter of all our children were able to read fairly

competently for themselves, the reading ability of the average seven-year-old does place limitations upon the complexity of the vocabulary that he can cope with. Typically he will fail to read accurately the majority of the following words taken from a reading test:[17] blocked, centre, frightened, horse, milkman, quickly, returned, safety, school, stopped, traffic, wandered. And even when he can read, the halting rhythm caused by indecision over certain words tends to detract from the enjoyment of the story as a story. Although such limitations are borne in mind by children's authors when they select the vocabulary for their stories, there continues to be a place for the reading aloud of stories by adults.

It was therefore meaningful to ask the mothers of readers and non-readers alike whether they read to their children, and, if they did so, how often. Table 27 shows the proportions of children who are never read to at home and those who are read to 'often'. The residual category is of those who are sometimes read to.

The figures show a strong relationship between social class and reading to children: twice as many children from lower-working-class homes as from professional homes are never read to by their

Table 27   *Reading to children by parents*

	social class					summary		
			III			I&II+	IIIman,	overall
	I&II	IIIwc	man	IV	V	IIIwc	IV, V	popn
	%	%	%	%	%	%	%	%
Never								
boys	17	36	27	48	46	26	33	31
girls	23	27	29	29	41	25	31	29
both	20	31	28	39	43	25	32	30

Significance: trend ↗   ****   m.class/w.class   n.s.
                                    between sexes   n.s.

Often								
boys	45	36	22	17	18	40	20	26
girls	46	24	28	21	20	36	26	29
both	46	30	25	19	19	38	23	27

Significance: trend ↘   ****   m.class/w.class   ****
                                    between sexes   n.s.

parents; conversely, more than twice as many children from professional homes compared with lower-working-class homes are read to often. In a sense the force of this difference is greater still since more of the children from professional homes are likely to be good readers and therefore capable of reading for themselves. This is borne out by the finding that only 20 per cent of the good readers are read to 'often', as compared with 30 per cent of those who cannot read (significant at 0·05).

The reasons for the class difference are varied. The time taken up by looking after the physical needs of the larger working-class family may lead to relegation of story-time, as may the mother's own lack of facility with reading, like the presser's wife who 'picks the paper up about once every other week'. But, as we found at the age of four,[18] the more fundamental difference seems to be in terms of middle-class (and particularly professional) parents regarding reading to the child as part of their parental role and duty rather than as a way of keeping the child amused when there is nothing else to do or when he demands attention. To let story-time be swallowed up by household pressures, these parents see as a failure on their part.

Administrative officer's wife:
> I'm ashamed to say, not very much. Um . . . I always feel a little bit guilty about this; but quite frankly, by the time I've got the pair of them into bed, evening meal out of the way, I just collapse, you know. [Does his Daddy read to him at all?] Sometimes – once again, not very often. Once again, you see, it's a pretty busy time, round about tea-time . . .

As in the case of more direct help with reading, there are no sex differences in the proportions of children who are read to – an unexpected finding, perhaps, when viewed in the light of the boys' comparative lack of skill and the girls' increased opportunity to be read to as a result of spending more time within the home; perhaps these two factors tend to cancel one another out.

Having established whether or not the child was read to, we went on to explore the type of reading material concerned. We tried to make a distinction between long books which would have required an interest maintained over a number of sessions, and short pieces such as fairy tales and the short stories specifically written for children of this age. In practice the distinction was difficult to make; do the stories of Winnie-the-Pooh or Paddington Bear rate as short because of their individual length, or long because they make up a sizeable book with a sustained theme? However, the imposition of a fairly crude rule-of-thumb on the books that were mentioned did show that children from professional/managerial families were far more likely to have long books read to them than children from other class groups. Thirty-six per cent of Class I & II mothers referred to long books as against 14 per cent from Class III wc and 10 per cent of the working class taken as a whole (significance: $p < 0.001$ between I & II and the rest).

In the main, the books that the mothers mentioned were the classic children's books: *Winnie-the-Pooh, Black Beauty, Alice in Wonderland, Peter Pan* and the Uncle Remus stories. Fairy stories also figured large, as did Bible stories and the works of Enid Blyton. Little mention was made of contemporary children's fiction, but this may have been because the mothers' comparative lack of familiarity with these titles led to the traditional stories coming to mind first when the question was asked.

This difference in the type of reading material that children of different social classes encounter is further reflected in the actual ownership of books. We attempted to establish how many books the

Table 28   *Books owned by, or permanently available and appropriate to, the child*

	social class					summary		
		III				I&II+	IIIman,	overall
	I&II	IIIwc	man	IV	V	IIIwc	IV, V	popn
	%	%	%	%	%	%	%	%
0–2 books								
boys	0	7	20	26	44	3	24	18
girls	0	8	17	19	36	4	20	15
both	0	8	18	22	40	4	22	17
Significance:	trend ↗	****				m.class/w.class		****
			between sexes	n.s.				
26+ books								
boys	62	33	13	14	10	48	13	22
girls	62	33	21	20	3	48	19	27
both	62	33	17	17	7	48	16	25
Significance:	trend ↘	****				m.class/w.class		****
			between sexes	n.s.				

children had of their own, or, in the case of there being more than one child of similar age, how many books there were of probable interest to the seven-year-old. Table 28 shows the proportions for the two extreme categories.[19]

Middle-class children – once again, particularly those from professional homes – are more likely to have sizeable collections of books. Such children have constant access to stories and information, and the larger the collection the more varied and more detailed are the worlds of fact and fantasy that are potentially at their fingertips. Since at this age the buying of books is mainly under the parents' control, a collection of books can usually be taken as an indication of their wish to inculcate the habit of reading from an early age. The child is shown that the book is taken by his parents to be a valued and useful possession. One of the implications of this for school is that some children already assume a positive evaluation of books as a key source of information and pleasure ready to be exploited, while others have to be inducted at school into the world of books and taught more formally how to use them.

The mere possession of books does not necessarily mean that they are read, or even looked at; but one would expect to find a relationship between the provision of books and other positive attitudes towards learning on the part of the parents. We found, for example, that there was a link between the number of books the child owned and whether or not the mother consulted books (her own or the child's) in answering his questions (page 123). In 37 per cent of those families who consult books in order to answer questions, the child has twenty-six books or more; whereas only 22 per cent of those who don't consult books in this way have children with that number of books (significant at the 0·001 level).

One factor which may go a part of the way towards explaining the massive class difference in book ownership is an economic one; children's books take a low priority when there are other calls upon a limited income. (None the less, compare pocket money rates, which increase as one descends the class scale.)[20] But the home is not the only source of out-of-school reading material for seven-year-olds. By this age they have long been eligible for membership of the local public library, where books can be borrowed without charge. Nottingham is well provided with such libraries, all of which have special junior sections with carefully selected books and staff on hand to advise on book choice. We asked whether the child belonged to such a library (Table 29).

Overall 42 per cent of the children were said to use a public library, and there was a highly significant social-class effect, with

Table 29   *Children who belong to a public library*

		social class III				summary	overall popn
	I&II %	*IIIwc* %	*man* %	*IV* %	*V* %	*I&II+ IIIwc* %	*IIIman, IV, V* %	%
boys	68	54	38	26	18	62	33	41
girls	75	57	37	36	23	67	35	44
both	72	56	37	31	20	64	34	42

Significance: trend ↘   ****   m.class/w.class ****
between sexes   n.s.

nearly twice as many middle-class children attending as working-class.[21] Given that encouragement to make use of the library comes in the main from parents, these figures suggest that even when the consideration of cost is removed, the working-class child remains at a disadvantage.

Where mothers saw the need to justify why the child did not belong to the library, it was sometimes in terms of problems over returning books on time and in good condition.

Factory worker's wife:
He did join the library, but it gets to the fact where he'd forget to take them back again, and perhaps I'd forget to remind him, and of course we kept getting cards through the door, so I had to make him pack it in.

Sometimes either the mother or the child himself decided he was not yet ready.

Lorry driver's wife:
I've got the tickets under the cow [sic] there now. He used to go every week, then he dropped off, and so I told him to finish until he wanted books out again.

Foreman's wife:
We've told him when he can *read*, then he can join.

There was a relationship between library membership and the child's judged reading ability. Fifty-two per cent of the silent readers were members, compared with only 31 per cent of those who couldn't read; this difference held for each of the five social class groups. There was a similar difference in the tested sub-sample, where 65 per cent of the good readers were library members compared with 26 per cent of the poor readers (significant at the 0·001 level). From the evidence it is impossible to say more about the causal direction of this relationship; certainly some mothers, like the foreman's wife quoted above, see library borrowing as something that *follows on* from being able to read, whereas others see regular library use as a part of the general orientation towards books which in turn *leads to* successful mastery of reading skills.

'He likes you to read comics to him, you know – you have to read "Pow! Pow!" in the balloons'
So far we have been talking about children's reading experiences solely in terms of books; but, of course, there is another major source of reading material produced and marketed particularly for children, namely, comics. The status of comics as suitable reading for children has been variable,[22] but despite falling circulation (generally attributed to television), and the critical onslaught of writers[23] and educationalists,[24] they still survive to provide an often substantial part of the reading diet of children of all ages.

Lorry driver's wife:
> They have one comic a week each, and they usually read these between them. They share them – that's what he's more interested in, because . . . I think myself . . . once you've read a book, you've read it, you don't read it again.

Labourer's wife:
> I buy the comics for myself – I like to read the *Diane*, the *Bunty* and the *Judy*, and she's always reading them; and especially them thriller comics, she likes to read them and all.

Scientist's wife:
> He has a comic which we've stopped now – we think it's a bit babyish, so we're just wondering what else to get in its place.

Seven-year-olds are indeed at somewhat of a transition point where comics are concerned, having outgrown the so-called infant comics, the lives of whose characters Tucker has described as 'blandly trivial', and being ready to embark on the next stage of juvenile comics with their wider horizons, greater range of themes, and more exciting stories, some of them romantic, some with war interest. It is just these features, together with the language and the sentiments expressed in the stories, which makes some parents chary about what their children might get hold of. While they are buying the comics themselves, parents can exercise a substantial influence over what the child does or does not look at; but the increasing environmental independence of the seven-year-old[25] means that he is quite capable of buying his own comics at the newsagent's. Left to himself, he may well not choose in accordance with educational considerations, but rather on the promise of thrills and belly-laughs, crowned, perhaps, by a free gift.

We asked whether the child had a regular comic or magazine. As Table 30 shows, just over half the seven-year-olds had at least one comic on a regular basis. Clearly, many more saw comics that were bought by older siblings or passed on by friends, and others bought comics with pocket money on a more sporadic basis, but they do not appear in these figures.

Table 30   *Children who are bought a regular comic*

	social class					summary		
		III				*I&II+*	*IIIman,*	*overall*
	I&II	*IIIwc*	*man*	*IV*	*V*	*IIIwc*	*IV, V*	*popn*
	%	%	%	%	%	%	%	%
boys	68	58	54	58	56	63	55	57
girls	59	59	51	51	36	59	50	52
both	64	58	53	54	46	61	52	55

Significance: trend ↘ ***   m.class/w.class ***
                         between sexes n.s.

Perhaps surprisingly, there is a higher level of comic buying in the middle-class families (61 per cent) than in the working class (52 per cent). This may well reflect the emphasis in the question on the regularity of purchase – a number of working-class mothers said that which comic was bought depended on the free gift being offered that week. Also, with larger families and closer spacing of children in working-class families, the likelihood of comics being shared increases. The class difference may also reflect a tendency on the part of middle-class parents to control the child's reading matter; an 'ordered' comic is chosen by advance decision, and delivered through the door with the evening paper. As we have already observed, the working-class child enjoys greater freedom to buy what he fancies from the local newsagent, not only because of his greater geographical freedom but also because he has more money in his pocket and less pressure to account for how it is spent.

There is a wide range of comics available, and the market is continually changing as some titles disappear, only to be replaced by a revitalised concoction of similar ingredients. A few, notably the *Beano* (first published in 1938) and the *Dandy* (first published in 1937), have remained essentially unaltered for years. When we looked at the actual comics mentioned, these two topped the list, the *Beano* being bought regularly for one in seven of the children, and the *Dandy* for one in ten.[26] In all, fifty-two different comics were mentioned; among the other more popular ones were *TV21*, *Bimbo*, *Topper*, *Sparky*, *Lady Penelope*, *Jack and Jill* and *Beezer*.

Generally speaking, numbers were too small for meaningful statistical analysis; but there were tendencies for some comics to be mentioned more frequently by one social group than another. Both *Dandy* and *Beano* were found significantly more often further down the social-class scale; *Robin*, *Playhour* and *Jack and Jill*, on the other hand, notably 'childish' comics, had a predominantly middle-class readership.

Comics have enjoyed a varied relationship with the teaching profession and those concerned with children's literature. Some argue that reading comics can act as a spur to reading more 'desirable' literature, particularly in those homes where other reading material is absent. In some instances they have been deliberately employed as part of a remedial reading programme in school.[27] On the other hand critics have inveighed against the paucity of the language used,[28] the image of childhood portrayed in the stories[29] and the perpetuation of racial stereotypes.[30]

Whereas the juvenile comics may aptly be described as 'licensed letters-off of steam',[31] those aimed at the younger child do have a more obvious didactic function. The stories have spelled-out morals, and there is usually a page of puzzles somewhat akin to activities used in school to stimulate language and perceptual-motor skills. For those parents who see comics as playing a positive part in their child's development rather than being just a time-filler, there is something of a dilemma in filling the gap once the child has outgrown the infant stage.

Insurance manager's wife:
    Teddy Bear's the comic – we've had that for a long time, and we

have that every week. That's a sort of regular comic. There doesn't seem to be anything suitable for her alone, you know, for *her* age, really.

One solution is to turn to those comics which have an avowed aim to educate through special features, puzzles and suggestions for projects. Of those then available, only one, *Treasure*, was mentioned by a sizeable number of parents, and even then it only came eleventh in the league table of popularity. Where it was mentioned, this was mainly by middle-class mothers (6 per cent) as opposed to working-class (less than 1 per cent). However, these educational comics are not free from the criticism of educationalists. Peter Bensley[32] claims that one of the saddest things about them is their 'facility for turning all the gold that they touch into dross', and Sidney Robins[33] attacks their 'misdirected factual bittiness'. The publishers, it seems, cannot win.

In our sample of children, taking a comic did not have a deleterious effect on reading ability; in fact, just the opposite. Overall, 61 per cent of those children said to be silent readers had a regular comic, as compared with 50 per cent of those who couldn't read; but in fact this difference was restricted to the working-class families, where 61 per cent of the good readers had a comic compared with 46 per cent of the poor readers (the figures in the middle-class are 62 per cent and 62 per cent). In the sub-sample, too, rather more good than poor readers had had a comic, though here the difference just failed to reach statistical significance.

However, once again disentangling cause from effect is the problem; was the child's poor reading attributable in part to the absence of reading matter at home, or were comics not bought because, being unable to read, the child couldn't enjoy them to the full? Unfortunately the verbatim transcripts give few clues as to why parents and/or children refrain from comic buying, although a headmaster's wife, whose daughter *can* read, undoubtedly typifies one outlook:

> I've told her, quite honestly, not to waste her money. I would much rather go and buy her puzzle books or things like that. The comics, I think, are horrible – there's no *story* in them.

Joyce Morris[34] found that, with ten-year-olds, the reasons given were different depending on whether the child was a good reader or a poor reader. Many good readers had decided, chiefly of their own accord, that they were too old for comics and preferred books, whereas many poor readers wished that their parents could afford to buy comics for them.

Clearly, some parents are happy for their children to read comics because they see no harm in them, and feel they may even be of mild educational value. A bricklayer's wife turns her son's difficulty with some words in his comics into a mini reading lesson:

> As regards comics he gets puzzled, and he'll ask me, and I always say 'You read – you read it out to me and tell me the letters, and I'll explain them'

– and a cycle assembler's wife sees her child's lack of interest in comics as part of his lack of interest in reading generally:

> No – although his brother has comics regularly. He's just the opposite for reading. It never occurs to him to slip through a comic.

Table 31   *An index of home literacy*

Based on	Situation	Criterion	Score
Q.115	Mother consults books to answer	Yes	1
	child's questions[35]	No	0
Q.123	Child belongs to library	Yes	1
		No	0
Q.124	Child owns books	26+	3
		11–25	2
		3–10	1
		2 or less	0
Q.125	Child has regular comic or maga-	Yes	1
	zine	No	0
Q.126	Mother reads to child	Regularly	2
		Sometimes	1
		Never	0
Q.127	Types of material read to child	Long books	2
		Short pieces	1
		Comics only	0
		or nothing	
			—
			—

Score range 0–10   Mean score = 4·5

'A child's mind is open in my opinion'
As all of these questions have illustrated individually, there are large and consistent differences in the degree to which children are exposed to reading material of various sorts, and are encouraged to engage in activities which might be considered supportive of reading. Not only is the amount of contact different, but so are the underlying attitudes of the parents – the mother who ensures that the child has a good selection of books is also more likely to read them to him or positively encourage him to read them for himself. In this situation, many children are caught in a spiral which includes the element of home–school concordance.

Table 31 shows how our index of home literacy was derived. Whilst there are certainly some anomalies – those parents who don't buy comics because they consider them trashy, or who no longer read to the child because he can read for himself whatever he wants to – the combined scores give a reasonable indication of the active encouragement of reading and the availability of reading materials in the home.

Table 32   *Children scoring high or low on the index of home literacy*

	social class					summary		
			III			I&II+	IIIman,	overall
	I&II	IIIwc	man	IV	V	IIIwc	IV, V	popn
	%	%	%	%	%	%	%	%
High scorers								
(7–10)								
boys	54	29	7	11	5	42	7	17
girls	55	27	16	20	3	41	15	22
both	54	28	11	16	4	42	11	20

Significance: trend ↘   ****   m.class/w.class   ****
                         between sexes   n.s.

Low scorers								
(0–3)								
boys	9	34	30	54	61	21	39	34
girls	9	22	35	35	62	16	38	32
both	9	28	33	44	61	18	38	33

Significance: trend ↗   ****   m.class/w.class   ****
                         between sexes   n.s.

Table 32 shows the distribution of low and high scores on this index. In both instances, the size of the social-class trend is very striking and this serves to underline the link between the environment of the middle-class home and the aims and priorities of the primary school; each acts in support of the other.

It would be naive to expect that the disparities in such a situation can easily be remedied. None the less, there is perhaps some room for optimism in the very large numbers of parents who have tried to give their children *some* help with reading, often in the face of lack of interest or downright discouragement from the formal educational system.

Here we have to return once again to a point we have made both earlier in this book and previously: that there is a fundamental difference in role between the parents of a child and those who are *professionally* concerned with children, in terms of partiality and fairness. It is an intrinsic part of the parental role to seek the best that is possible, whatever that may be seen to mean, for their own child: and because this function belongs to parents in respect of their own children only, it is not incumbent on them to take responsibility for the progress of other children. Teachers, on the other hand, have the role of being fair and impartial in helping to the best of their ability *all* the children in their care; to an extent this may mean giving special help to a particular child in need, but there are limits as to how far they can go in giving extra help to individuals for fear of being seen to favour one child *at the expense* of others.

We have elsewhere suggested, however, that a successfully integrated personality structure requires that a sense of personal worth be dovetailed with a sense of the needs of others; and further, that the harmonious development of these two understandings is best served by the children experiencing both that normal special partiality which parents offer their children *and* the fairness and even-handedness which is the role of other adults to children with whom they are professionally involved.

If both these roles are seen as necessary and complementary, is there any reason why parents and teachers should clash? Whether parents try to help the child in order to give him a head-start, or to attempt to make up for some deficit, this does indicate a readiness to take some sort of action which teachers could welcome as appropriate to the parental role and ancillary to their own. The help parents give now may be ill-informed or ill-directed; it may be too tentative to be effective, out of fear of what 'the school' may say; it may be too little, too late, or too fragmented. But if eighty-one in every hundred parents are trying to help their children with reading and most of them don't know how to, schools are surely not only failing dismally in their educative role, but wasting the most valuable resource they have. A revolution in literacy could be sparked off and fuelled by parents and teachers in determined co-operation.

NOTES

1 George Bernard Shaw, 'Parents and children', Preface to *Misalliance*.
2 Trends in the methods of teaching reading in this country have been described by H. Diack in *In Spite of the Alphabet* (London, Chatto and Windus, 1965). One notable method, the use of the initial teaching alphabet (i.t.a.) as a medium for the early stages of learning to read, has not been adopted in Nottingham.
3 R. Davie et al., *From Birth to Seven* (London, Longman, 1972).
4 J. Morris, *Standards and Progress in Reading* (Slough, National Foundation for Educational Research, 1966); M. M. Clark, *Reading Difficulties in Schools* (Harmondsworth, Penguin, 1970); R. Davie et al., op. cit. The complicated relationship between sex and reading attainment is summarised in G. B. Thompson, 'Sex differences in reading attainments', *Educational Research*, 18 (1975).
5 Peter Barnes, 'Some factors associated with reading ability', M.Phil. thesis, University of Nottingham, 1974.
6 M. D. Neale, *Analysis of Reading Ability* (London, Macmillan, 1966).
7 J. Morris, op. cit. (1966); F. McBride, 'The professional preparation of students in colleges of education for the teaching of reading', *Reading*, 1 (1967).
8 J. and E. Newson, op. cit. (1968).
9 Not a trivial point when one considers that there are an estimated 2 million illiterate adults in England and Wales (*Guardian*, March 1974).
10 J. Downing, 'Relevance versus ritual in reading', *Reading*, 4 (1970).
11 J. Reid, *Reading: Problems and Practices* (London, Ward Lock Educational, 1972).
12 J. Jones, 'Social class and the under-fives', *New Society*, 8, no. 221 (1966).
13 J. and E. Newson, op. cit. (1968), p. 259 (Pelican edn, p. 274).
14 For a more detailed discussion of the differences between 'indoor' and 'outdoor' children, see J. and E. Newson, op. cit. (1976b), ch. 3.
15 For instance N. Bennett, *Teaching Styles and Pupil Progress* (London, Open Books, 1976).
16 Young and McGeeney, in their study of one London junior school, showed that parents tended to read to their children more when they were *not* doing well at school (op. cit., 1968).
17 M. D. Neale, op. cit. (1966).
18 J. and E. Newson, op. cit. (1968).
19 There is a close correspondence between the social class distribution of this data and the number of books, *other* than children's books, found in the homes of the families who were surveyed on behalf of the Plowden Committee. Overall, 18 per cent of those families had *no* books, ranging from 6 per cent of Class ɪ & ɪɪ families to 42 per cent of Class ᴠ; Central Advisory Council for Education, op. cit. (1967).
20 J. and E. Newson, op. cit. (1976b), pp. 234–44.

21 The range here is much larger than the comparable figures from the Plowden survey, where 73 per cent of Class I & II children were found to borrow from libraries, compared with as many as 54 per cent of Class V children: Central Advisory Council for Education, op. cit. (1967).
22 See G. Perry and A. Aldridge, *The Penguin Book of Comics* (Harmondsworth, Penguin, 1971), for an illustrated guide; and P. M. Pickard, *I Could a Tale Unfold* (London, Tavistock, 1961), for a history of children's comics.
23 George Orwell, 'Boys' weeklies' (originally published in 1939), in *Critical Essays* (London, Secker & Warburg, 1946).
24 For example, N. Tucker, 'Kiddies' cosy corner', *New Society*, 13, no. 335 (1969).
25 J. and E. Newson, op. cit. (1976b), ch. 3.
26 G. H. Pumphrey found that 60 per cent of a sample of eight-year-old boys listed *Beano* as among their favourite comics, and 50 per cent listed *Dandy*. The corresponding figures for girls were 35 per cent and 31 per cent. The popularity of these comics is in part attributable to their cheapness compared with their rivals; as value for money they have always been remarkable. *What Children Think of their Comics* (London, Epworth Press, 1964).
27 Kay Haugaard, 'Comic books: conduits to culture?', *The Reading Teacher*, 27 (1973).
28 J. J. Taylor, 'The reading of comics by secondary school pupils', *Use of English*, 24 (1972).
29 N. Tucker, op. cit. (1969).
30 N. Johnson, 'What do children learn from war comics?', *New Society*, 8, no. 197 (1966).
31 S. Robins, 'Comics: the funnies and the weepies', *Where*, Advisory Centre for Education, 48 (1970).
32 P. Bensley, 'Educational comics', *Where*, 49 (1970).
33 S. Robins, op. cit. (1970).
34 J. Morris, op. cit. (1966).
35 This question and the implications of possible answers are discussed in full in Chapter 4.

Chapter 6

The Tender Leaves of Hope

The child's image of himself as a person related to society, and similarly the mother's image of her child, can be in part defined by the kinds of future work-roles which they expect or hope for. By the time the adolescent reaches school-leaving age, this will, of course, have become formalised: both parental ambitions, and those of the child himself, while reflecting their perception of his skills, interests and personality traits, will also be constrained by the reality of 'how well he has done' so far in school, the most obvious measuring-rule for success. Over the period of secondary education, whether or not this started (as it has for our 700 children) with the judgemental act of 'eleven-plus selection', both child and parent will have had many opportunities for casual or more formal testing-out of their hopes against the reflected appraisals of other people; for ambitions are seldom expressed without some kind of feedback from the listener as to their appropriateness as perceived by that listener. Similarly, the remarks initiated by other people to a child about his future role inevitably must be absorbed into his own self-image as judgements of what might be deemed suitable to his intelligence, personality and sex. Many studies have drawn attention to the differential job expectations expressed as appropriate to different sexes in books written for young children (such as the 'Ladybird' series), and reflected in young children's play; but comments like 'she's really artistic – make a good hairdresser', 'I wonder whether they'll still be long-haired when *you're* a student' or 'if she puts all this argumentativeness to good use, she'll end up a lawyer or a politician' have their own equally powerful implications for the child. Casual remarks, particularly when they build up into a consistent structure, can crystallise and define both the child's place in relation to his peers and his family's place in relation to society. A fourteen-year-old girl in an extended family of high-achieving professionals, told 'you'd make a good nurse' in an intended compliment to her nurturant/organisational talents, was deeply insulted: 'Thinks I'm too dim to be a doctor, obviously'.

We have already suggested, in this and in the two preceding reports on our sample at seven and at four, the many ways in which being born low on the social-class scale can disadvantage a child for school achievement, both before he even arrives in school and during his early years there. In this our findings support and extend those of Douglas et al., Pringle et al. and Bernstein et al. Although educationalists generally are concerned that a good educational system should include the flexibility to retrieve children after disadvantaging periods, Douglas has shown the cumulative effect on school performance where disadvantage at school entry has all the weight of inertia to make it a self-fulfilling prophecy. None the less, in theory the situation is still open at seven: while the child's mother may be becoming anxious lest he should be falling behind in his reading progress, she might at the same time reasonably feel that the world was still his oyster. To this extent, seven seemed to us an interesting age at which to discuss with parents their hopes and expectations about the child's future, both in terms of his education and as to the kinds of job they visualised for him.

The questions we asked (following the whole discussion of his school progress and how the school suited the child personally) were:

130. If he showed the ability, how far would you like him to go with his education?
131. Have you any ideas now about what you would like him to do when he's grown up?
132. Has N any ideas about that?

These questions are deliberately open-ended: it would not have seemed appropriate to require clear-cut replies about matters which were hypothetical, a long way in the future and which also might be very dependent upon the child's wishes, not just his ability. The resultant data is inevitably confused by such considerations: some mothers, for instance, felt that they very definitely had no right to pre-empt the child's decision, even so far as to express an opinion on it, and many emphasised the importance to them that the child should choose for himself.

Student psychologist's wife (herself in similar training):
I would like him to go as far as he could get anything out of it and

wasn't frustrated by it, I think this is the only thing that matters –
the moment people cease to get anything out of it, life is miserable.
I think, on principle this is, that I try to keep a completely open
mind about this. I don't really think parents are entitled to have
preconceived ideas about what their children are going to do; and
if they have, I think they have a chance of cramping their style
quite seriously.

Labourer's wife:
No, I think that's up to the child, if the child wants to do a thing
. . . if he wants a certain job, I mean to say – going in the army –
if they really want to go, when it came to the time of his age, I
shouldn't stop him, I should let him go. Mind you, I should explain that he'd be away from home and all this, you know, to him,
before he did decide, and then I should leave it to him. I mean, it's
no good stopping a boy from – or a girl if it comes to that – if
they wanted to do a certain job and if they'd be happy doing it –
well it's up to them, isn't it? Well, I think so, anyway.

Electrician's wife:
Well, it's no good me having any ideas what he wants to do, it's
not what *I* want him to do, it's what *he* wants to do, isn't it? –
cause he's got to do it. I can't say really I've got anything special
in mind. We could think we'd like him to do all kinds of fancy
things. Just what he could. I really think he'll do something with
his hands. At the moment he seems to be more that way. But in a
year or two he might branch out in other ways.

HP collector:
[Father speaking:] No, that's up to me, not to the wife, duck [i.e.
the question is not appropriately put to his wife]; and I believe a
man should go into any trade he wants. I wouldn't push him – my
Dad pushed me, and I've never liked pushing – I don't believe in
it. My Dad pushed me into engineering, which I've never liked. I
done it and I'm out of it. It's up to him – if he said he wanted to
be a road sweeper and was happy at it, I'd prefer him to be that
way. There's no point in doing something you don't want, cause
you're going to do it the rest of your life.

Some mothers, while emphasising that the choice was basically
the child's, also made it clear that they were not advocating un-
qualified freedom, and that some pressure would if necessary be
exerted to make sure that the child did not throw his chances away.

Greengrocer's wife:

No, I would like him to be able to choose for himself; but I do want him to have something which, er, he's very *interested in*; er – something which is obviously going to bring him a good income, but not that to be the main point. Because often you can get a good income to what I'd call a dead-end job, with no particular interest but there's a lot of money in it. To me that isn't good enough – there's got to be a lot of interest, even if it means a slight drop in the wage. The interest is the main point, because after all you're there a long time, aren't you? So we don't want them to be in the shop – we'd prefer them to study hard; in fact we're hoping that, if they can get through, we would be prepared to pay for them to go to a decent school – we want them to get the best type of education rather than go into business. A business is all right for us, but we know the ties. If they can get a good education, they can get a good job with a certain amount of free time, which is the one thing which *we* don't get. And that's the one thing we want them to have – everything as good as we've got *and* the time, actually.

Student teacher [wife herself a teacher]:

[Father:] Only that we feel – I do anyway, I think Gill's the same – that we should like to see her trained for something. [Mother:] To have something behind her at the end. [Father:] To have some qualification for something, rather than just . . . [Mother:] Too many people just waffle. I think we shall encourage her all along the line to get some qualifications, you see, if it's only a commercial qualification – something that she's got behind her.

University teacher's wife:

Well, I would like her to do what *she* wants to do. This isn't in fact completely without reservations, in that – um – although I want her to do what she wants to do, if what she wanted to do was to go and serve in a coffee-bar or something like that, I would be dead against this, if this was *all* she was doing; and, er, I would put pressure on to make her get qualified for something, in some sort of way. I don't particularly mind what, although obviously some things give me more pleasure than others: I mean, I would like to think it was a *worthwhile* thing she was doing . . . um . . . but what she does, within reason, is her own affair, I wouldn't try and put any pressure on her there, but I would certainly be very keen that she should get qualified. I mean, in a way I think this is a *moral* duty – to qualify to do something or other useful in society.

Um . . . if she wanted to do something tremendously interesting, like just going round the world, I would be very sympathetic to this; but at the same time I would feel that one must think about getting qualified somehow, and try and get her to qualify first, rather than miss the boat in some awful way.

Sweetshop owner's wife:
I'm sort of changing. I thought I'd let the children please themselves. Now I think they've got to be pushed a bit – encouraged. I really want her to . . . I don't know. I'm in two minds at the moment. I'd like her to go to college, but I wouldn't like her to go to college and struggle all the while. But I think she's one that needs pushing – she's got the ability but she's lazy. She won't push herself, somehow. [Have you any ideas now about what you'd like her to do when she's grown up?] I'd like her to be a teacher or a nurse. [Has Elizabeth any ideas about that?] No – I'm madly brainwashing!

This last quotation raises issues which recurred many times in different forms, but which really boiled down to the question, 'How far should one push children for their own good?' Parents have to balance in their minds considerations of the child's ability (present and prospective), his happiness (present, short-term future and long-term future), how far they see happiness as dependent upon money, security, choice or intrinsic job satisfaction (or combinations of these), how far their own experience leads them to value education as such or security as such, and how far negative experiences determine them to avoid similar problems for their children. Mothers were clear about one thing: they did not believe in pushing children beyond their ability, and the dangers of expectations that were too high for the child were constantly stressed.

Policeman's wife:
Well, as far as he possibly could, but not to *scrape* through his eleven-plus; I would rather him not pass than *scrape* through.

Teacher's wife (herself trained as a telephonist):
As far as it comes easy . . . . . I wouldn't like her to go to the High School, for example, and be bottom of the class. I'd rather her go to the grammar school and be middle than have to strive all the time to make any headway at all and feel inferior. I wouldn't like her to go to university and end up in an office, and I wouldn't like her to stay two extra years at grammar school and

then do nothing. I think they ought to know what they want to do and make the best of their education.

Assistant sales manager's wife (herself a shorthand typist):
Not the vaguest idea, but I'll tell you one thing – I'd rather a happy-go-lucky long-distance lorry-driver than an unhappy screwed-up little barrister.

Unemployed labourer's wife:
Well, if they've got it in them, I say let 'em go on, but if they haven't got it in 'em, what's the use of them staying? I shouldn't stop them staying at school if they wanted to stay on.

Foreman's wife:
Well, as far as possible. I mean, I've always said I won't make myself poor to push it in, but if it's there I'll do everything in my power for 'em. I mean – same as me going to work, you know – some folks says about going to work. Well I've said you don't really know what's going to happen till they're eleven. I says, 'Well, by the time they're eleven, if it's necessary I'll go to work full time'. [To send him to grammar school – to keep him there till he was eighteen?] Yes – *if it's there*; but I'm not going to push him through it. [And if he wanted to go on after grammar school, say to training college or university . . .?] Yes, definitely, yes, yes.

One difficulty, which arose from our unwillingness to press mothers too hard to be definite at this stage in the child's life, was that rather a large number (between a third and more than half in any one class) said, like the foreman's wife above, that they would like their child to go 'as far as possible' or 'all the way' – 'no limits'. Because some of them, but not by any means all, then went on to suggest what 'all the way' meant to them, it became clear that we could not assume that this necessarily meant that they had professional or managerial ambitions for their children. For instance, in a random group of fifty mothers of skilled-manual-class girls, twenty-one wanted them to go 'as far as possible', but of the five who then specified further, only one had a professional ambition; three hoped for office jobs and one wanted her daughter to do a hairdressing apprenticeship. Similarly, in a group of fifty mothers of semi-skilled-class boys, twenty-nine wanted them to go 'as far as possible'; of the sixteen who went on to specify, five hoped for professional careers, two for office work and nine had in mind a skilled trade. This contrasts with mothers in the professional/managerial class: in a further group of fifty mothers of boys in this class, thirty-six said 'as far as possible', twenty-nine of these going on to specify professional careers and the rest remaining non-specific.

Thus in interpreting Table 33, where we show mothers' stated professional/managerial ambitions for children in different social classes, it must be assumed that these numbers are underestimated in every social class because we have not included 'as far as possible' ambitions unless the mother has gone on to be specific that this means professional qualifications; and we also have to assume that they are more heavily underestimated in Class I & II.

Table 33   *Mothers stating specifically professional/managerial ambitions for their seven-year-olds*

	social class					summary		
		III				I&II+	IIIman,	overall
	I&II	IIIwc	man	IV	V	IIIwc	IV, V	popn
	%	%	%	%	%	%	%	%
boys	68	39	6	22	11	54	10	22
girls	60	41	24	30	34	51	26	33
both	64	40	15	26	22	52	18	27

Significance: trend ↘ ****   m.class/w.class ****
                         between sexes ****
(*Table based on a detailed analysis of a random sub-sample of 476 children*)

It can be seen that, even without allowing for these differential underestimations, middle-class mothers have higher hopes than working-class mothers, and professional-class mothers are more ambitious than white-collar mothers. Examining the transcripts, another difference emerges: professional ambitions tend more often to be expressed as *expectations* in Class I & II than elsewhere, whereas in the working class they are more likely to be expressed as *hopes*. In addition, there is below the professional-class level the hope that the child will do well 'if he has it in him', 'if it's there' – i.e. ability, especially intellectual ability – whereas Class I & II mothers tend more to assume that the child could if he would, so that the question is more 'would he want to?'

Manager and wife:
[Speaking together:] University! [Father:] This is our ambition, *of course.*

Doctor's wife (herself professional):
  Oh, the best, whatever that would be – university *anyhow*.

Doctor's wife (herself SRN):
  Well, we'd like her to go to university. That's what I have in mind,
  and that's what I'm going to encourage. That's all you *can* do –
  you can't say 'you must go' – but we *expect* her to get her exams
  and we *expect* her to go.

Businessman's wife (herself a teacher):
  . . . he wouldn't, for example, make a doctor . . . he couldn't
  face . . . he hasn't enough thought for other people; but I think he
  could go quite far in, say, research – or planning: something on
  those lines.

Gardener's wife:
  Well, if she passed everything I'd like her to go all the way. She's
  always on about she'd like to be either a nurse or an air hostess,
  you know. [Would you be quite keen for her to do that?] Yes, I
  would. You see, the lad's not as forward as what the girl is, and
  he's twelve; you see she's got it up there, where he hasn't.

Car sprayer's wife:
  Well, I don't think I can say till he's older, but I can say more
  from the other child – I want *him* to go to a grammar school. If
  he showed ability in a certain way . . . if I felt they were worth it
  . . . if they've got it in them . . .

Unemployed car repairer's wife:
  Well, if, er, he's bright; now there's not much you can say while
  he's in infant and junior school, you've got to wait for that coming
  when he's in his senior school, or say when he gets to the age of
  ten, I think you've got an idea whether he's going to be bright or
  dull. Well, I've found that out with the elder ones. Now all my
  kids have got brains if they'll use them, but they won't, they're
  lazy. Well, if they're not going to help themselves to give themselves a push, I don't see why *I* should be the one to get behind
  'em and push 'em, and I don't see why I should waste teacher's
  time putting them through the eleven-plus if they're going to fail
  it . . . . . If he turned out to be bright . . . if I thought – and I know
  every parent should know whether a child's bright or not – if I
  thought he was going to turn out like the girl, now: the things
  she's come to me and told me that I've never dreamt of, and if he

come the same when he got to her age, all well and good – if he
was going to make something of it . . .

*'Well, I think you always like them to go a bit further than what
their Dad had . . .'*
Where working-class mothers did feel that their children 'had it in
them', there was no shortage of determination to seize the benefits
of education for them with both hands – sometimes backed by their
husbands, sometimes not. With both husbands and wives, there was
often a sense of opportunities lost to themselves, or never presented,
which they were not going to miss for their children.

Lorry driver's wife:
> Well, I'd like him to go as far as he possibly could: grammar
> school, ooh yes, definitely, and even university if he could get
> there. Now we . . . my husband reckons it's just nosiness in me,
> but even now I still like watching those children's programmes on
> television, you know, the education ones; because you can learn
> a lot from them. And he laughs at me, because I've always said
> to him, 'When the children are old enough, Dave, I'm going back
> to night school, I'm going to take up languages' – and he says to
> me, 'Oh, it's just nosiness'. But it *isn't* – I *am* a big believer in
> education, specially for girls . . . . . But I would like Julian – well,
> I'd like *all* of them – to have a good education; but I don't think
> they're going to get it here, I'm hoping it'll be different in Canada,
> in fact that's one of the main reasons we're going, to be truthful.
> I don't think there's a very good education here; considering it's
> a university town, I don't think so. They just don't seem sufficiently
> interested in them in the juniors. Now at my school in Wales, the
> teachers were big believers in *learning*, you had to *learn*; and I
> think that's what does it. But up here they concentrate on making
> models out of soapboxes – they do, honestly! That's what annoys
> me.

Labourer's wife:
> As far as possible, I think, really – I never had that chance. I think
> I'd let her go as far as she *can* go. [What about when she finishes
> school – college or university?] Yes. We haven't much money, but
> if they can get by, we'll help them all we can.

Engineer's wife:
> Oh, I would like her go a *long* way. They say you educate the
> mother and you educate the family. I wish I'd have had the
> education.

Bricklayer's wife:
As far as she could, because I think education is a very important thing, both to males and females. I had the opportunity when I was fifteen, but I'm afraid all I was interested in was going out and earning money; but by heavens, that's not important really, because if you've got a good education you take the opportunities that are given you – you can get a job at any time of life.

Nylon knitter's wife (herself a trained shorthand-typist):
Oh, I'd like him to go to the top – all of them, boys *and* girls – but Hugh I *would*, I'd scrub and clean to see that he got there, you know. I mean I would, I mean even if they threw it back in my face it's worth it; I think that if they've got it in them it's their *right*, in a way they're entitled to it and it shouldn't be denied them.

Chemical worker:
[Father:] As far as she can ever possibly go. I'd push her as far as I could ever push her.

As one might expect, it was among working-class families that ambitions were specifically expressed in terms not just of seizing opportunities which the parents had not had, but of deliberately avoiding a negative model offered by the parents' own experience. Among approximately fifty children of each sex in each class whose parents' ambitions we analysed in detail, comments of 'not like me . . . not like his Dad' occurred several times in each of the three working classes, but only once for the middle-class groups (green-grocer in his own business, see page 169).

Tobacco worker's wife:
I would like to think that he's not sort of got to work like his . . . Nigel's father sort of has to work long hours, you know, for a decent wage – which is his own fault, he was sort of training for an apprentice and he didn't do it. So I would like to see Nigel . . . a job that he can use his *skill*, and not sort of having to, you know, work and *work* at things. I mean if he did anything sort of . . . joinery, which for his age I think he's fairly good at . . . I should be pleased.

Baker's wife:
As long as he, um, gets a decent job and doesn't have to work as hard as his Daddy, sixty-eight hours or something like that for the

money. It's all right, the wage, but the hours kill me sometimes, you know – it's very hard going. I should like him to have more of a *mental* job, if you know what I mean. I don't know – it's probably just the way I am, but I don't think really you need to slave your guts out to get your money. I don't want to put it into their heads that they don't have to work, but it *is* a lot really, all that time out of the house. [Father:] I feel the same about it. I should be very pleased if they could get a bit of a job where their mental capacity was used on the job.

Miner's wife:
> *He* wants to be an engineer. I don't care *what* he does as long he don't do same as his Dad – I wouldn't like him to go into Pit.

Window cleaner's wife:
> I've never really given it any thought, not just yet . . . I would like them to go in an office, where they mek summat of theyself; something that I've never been able to do myself.

Unemployed plasterer's wife:
> If I'd got the money I'd let . . . I'd like her to go right to the top. I wouldn't like them to be like I am, can't even write a letter to anybody.

It is interesting, in view of the number of parents who are thinking about social mobility for their children, that anxiety about the distancing from the family that this might bring is rarely expressed at this stage. Perhaps ambitions for seven-year-olds are too rosy and unreal for the less happy implications of mobility to cast shadows at this stage. This mother is, unusually, strongly aware of her own emotional reservations, and of how they are likely to limit her encouragement of the child.

Bricklayer's mate's wife:
> Well of course we want our child to be better than anyone else's; but, er . . . it's something that does worry me in a way, because, er . . . we aren't very well off. I should never want to hold him back; but I should feel a bit more easy in my mind if he hadn't got the ability to go too far. Do you know what I mean? I should love him to be, er . . . capable; but I don't know whether I'd be happy about it, you know. I should hate him to be condescending to us – to be, um, contemptuous of us – to be ashamed of us. But there again, it happens to other families these days, but . . . er . . . I'd

never hold him back, but there again I'd never go out to work more than I do now to help him. I shouldn't make any more sacrifices.

'I think it's more essential *for a boy to be better educated and have a better job – I know it's very* handy *for a girl . . .'*
The reader may have noticed that several of the mothers already quoted have spontaneously implied that a difference might by some people be considered appropriate between parents' ambitions for boys and for girls. It has been clear that all these mothers have been reacting against an understood notion that boys' education is more important than that of girls: either by their need to specify equality ('all of them, boys *and* girls'; 'both to males and females'; ' – or a girl, if it comes to that'), or by their presentation of a special feminist case ('they say you educate the mother and you educate the family'; 'I *am* a big believer in education, specially for girls'). This last mother, a lorry driver's wife brought up in South Wales, went on:

I mean, a lot of people round here – I land in more arguments than anyone! – they seem to think that because a girl's going to get married, she's got to leave school at fifteen. Now *I* don't see why a housewife should be illiterate. And that's the truth – because when they come home from school, the first person they ask if they want to know anything is their mother, isn't it?[1]

Milkman's wife:
Well, I've often said that I wouldn't mind if she was a doctor or a dentist; but *he's* education-mad! [father]. I mean . . . I don't think he'd ever ram it down her throat that she'd got to study, study and never have any fun out of life; but he thinks she's got quite a quick brain, and with the chances there are now – more than we had at school – he wants her to . . . he doesn't believe in this tale that education's wasted on a girl, he says that's ridiculous – because a lot carry on after they're married, or come back to it.

Once again, in assessing how typical these feelings are, we are hampered by the fact that they are spontaneously expressed: we did not ask a direct question in terms of whether parents did feel that boys had prior claims on education. Many volunteered that they did: before looking at the data we have more closely, let us hear this point of view. The almost exclusively working-class representation in the discussion of sex differences, on either side, reflects the fact that it barely came up among middle-class mothers as a live issue;

and this itself reflects the diminished differential between men's work and women's work as one moves up the social scale.

Stoker's wife:
Well, for a boy: as far as possible; because I think a boy's more important than a girl, on education. Cause in years to come they've more or less got a family to keep, where a little girl is more probably housework and children – a boy is more education than a girl.

Driver's wife:
Well, I would really like him to pass the scholarship – the boys more so than Margaret. Nowadays – I mean it's as well for a girl to pass the scholarship, but I *really* would the boys.

Building worker's wife:
Of course, Tom [elder sib] is quite clever, and we've said if he did want to go on, we'd let him; but I think with a girl, a lot of it is wasted, you know. They get married and they leave; if you sent them to a university, even, they'd leave and get married. [. . . if she wanted to stay on till sixteen, or beyond sixteen . . .?] I *think* I'd say no – it depends what she wants to do. I think if it was something she could take up, perhaps, you know, if she got married and had kiddies and then wanted to go back to work – well – perhaps. But we haven't really got round to discussing the girls yet, Tom is the one we have to think about at the moment. And I think with a boy it's far more important than with girls. I don't think girls appreciate it . . . *some* do, but . . . I know *I* didn't. Mind you, I didn't go on, sort of thing; but I know I *wouldn't* have done.

Cook's wife:
Well, for myself personally, I'm not bothered with a girl; I mean, if she gets on – she can go as far she can go, I mean I wouldn't hold her back at all, but as far as I'm concerned, if she stays at the ordinary school and leaves at fifteen, it wouldn't worry me at all, not with a girl . . . probably I'm wrong. [Would you be pleased if she *did* go on?] Ooh, I'd be pleased to *know* that she was so brainy, you know, but it wouldn't bother me at all if she wasn't. [And you'd feel differently about Harry (sib), would you?] Well, I like a boy . . . I think if a boy gets on it's nice.

Looking again at Table 33, we can see, however, that in terms of professional ambitions for them held by their parents, girls are in fact *favoured* over boys consistently throughout the working class. In the majority of the working class this difference is very considerable: it will be seen that a quarter of skilled manual workers' wives and a third of unskilled workers' wives would like to see their daughters in professional occupations – four times as many as boys' mothers in the skilled group, and three times as many as boys' mothers in the unskilled group.

Most people would find these figures rather surprising. To understand how they come about, we have to look more closely at the specific occupations actually mentioned by mothers.

As we have indicated, the detailed analysis of ambitions was carried out on a random sub-sample consisting as far as possible of the first fifty boys and fifty girls (alphabetically) in each social class. In Class III wc there were only forty-nine girls, so we compared them with the first forty-nine boys in that class; similarly, Class v only provided thirty-nine girls, who were compared with the first thirty-nine boys. The sub-sample thus consists of 476 cases. Because of the variation in number in these classes, it is convenient to give within-class figures as percentages for comparative purposes: in interpretation, the usual caution should be exercised, bearing the size of each class/sex group in mind.

We have seen that many mothers are unwilling to specify any particular profession or other job, but prefer to answer in terms of 'as far as he can' or, more precisely, 'get a professional qualification' or 'into a skilled trade'. However, where the job *is* tentatively mentioned, different patterns begin to appear between ambitions for boys and for girls. In the professional/managerial class, in the first place, boys' parents are less inclined than girls' parents to mention specific jobs at all, a difference obtaining in no other class. Of jobs actually mentioned in this class group, the *range* of suggestions is equal (twelve jobs offered for each sex); but the *pattern* is different, in that for boys no specified job attracts more than two (4 per cent) parental choices, whereas for girls 20 per cent of mothers suggest teaching and 10 per cent nursing.

Going on to other class/sex groups, the range of jobs specified is surprisingly stable: nine or ten in each of the eight groups except one, where there is a notable exception – mothers of boys in Class IV have seventeen different jobs to suggest. We have many times pointed out that Class IV as defined by the Registrar-General is a particularly anomalous and heterogeneous class, including as it does semi-skilled heavy workers such as loaders, stokers, hod-carriers and tradesmen's mates, together with much more white-collar type workers such as bus conductors, ticket collectors and hotel porters. It is perhaps this anomalous composition which produces so many possibilities; probably if one looked at the two kinds of Class IV worker separately, this illusion of wider choice would disappear.

It is worth looking in a more detailed way at the actual jobs mentioned when these are made explicit; it must be remembered that some mothers specify more than one preferred job. In Class I & II, taking boys' mothers first, doctors, teachers, 'something in electronics', 'research workers' and scientists receive two mentions each, while engineering, accountancy, weather forecasting, social work, army and fire service are each mentioned once. For Class I & II girls' mothers, teachers receive ten choices, nurses five, doctors one, with one each for research, animal technician, 'hairdresser or typist', shop assistant, industrial chemist, social worker, ballet, domestic science and actress. In Class III white collar, boys attract four choices for teaching, three for medicine, two as draughtsmen and one each for bank clerk, traffic clerk, civil engineer, electrical engineer, dispensing chemist and lawyer; girls' mothers mention nursing six times, teaching five times, secretarial work three times, entertainment twice, and policeman, cook, tailoress, hairdresser and journalist are each mentioned once.

Mothers' specified ambitions for boys in the skilled manual group comprise two choices for police and one each for bricklayer, butcher, joiner, electrician, miner, RAF, clerk and architect; for girls in this class group, the choices are eight for nursing, six for typing, four for teaching, three for hairdressing, two each for skilled machining and 'fashion', and one each for kennel maid, dancer and policewoman. In the semi-skilled group, boys attract three choices for engineering, two each for doctor, draughtsman, mechanic, office worker, and army, and one each for actor, policeman, teacher, scientist, fireman, electrician, shopkeeper, joiner, sportsman and lorry driver; girls' mothers give eight choices to nursing, five to teaching, four to secretarial work, two each to machining and dressmaking, and one each to doctor, 'something with children', 'something with animals', artist and nun. Finally, in the unskilled manual group, boys' mothers make one mention each of tailor, wrestler, entertainer, electrician, fireman, mechanic, driver, doctor, policeman and engineer; while girls' mothers choose nursing six times, teaching three times, typing and tailoring twice each, and one choice each for doctor, scientist, hairdresser, artist and factory worker.

The briefest inspection of the actual jobs specified now makes it clear why girls in the working class are more favoured than boys in terms of the professional status of their parents' ambitions for them:

and, ironically enough, it is the direct result of what the Women's Movement would deplore as sex-role stereotyping. Nursing and teaching are seen as highly desirable occupations for girls in *every* class: only in the skilled manual group does typing move into the 'top two' ambitions. Thirty-three girls' mothers overall specify nursing, and twenty-seven teaching, compared with sixteen who mention the next most popular ambition for girls, secretarial work. In contrast, although 'doctor' is the most popular parental ambition for boys, it only actually attracts eight choices; teaching is mentioned for seven boys, and nursing not at all.

When mothers' ambitions for their children are compared with children's ambitions for themselves (so far as their mothers know about them), this same tendency is consolidated: that is to say, nursing and teaching are very much favoured by girls (still more than by their mothers), while only one boy in the sub-sample wanted to be a teacher, and not one to be a nurse. Seventy-six girls altogether had specified nursing, fairly evenly spread through the class scale with a slight rise in the skilled and semi-skilled group; twenty-nine girls had mentioned teaching as a preference, slightly more at the upper end of the scale. The favourite ambition for boys themselves was policeman (thirty-four overall), which was the top choice in all classes except Class v (where it was also favoured, but equally with soldier and driver).

This question of correspondence between mother's and child's ambitions is an interesting point. In general, correspondence between mother and child (in the the sense of having the same ambition: teacher/teacher, army/army – or a closely compatible one: scientist/geologist, actress/model)[2] is much higher among girls and their mothers than among boys and theirs. The *smallest* sex difference in correspondence is in Class I & II, where we found four corresponding ambitions among boys and eight among girls. In the other classes, the ratios were: III white collar, three boys, ten girls; III manual, four boys, thirteen girls; Class IV, three boys, twelve girls; Class V, three boys, nine girls. Obviously much of this correspondence between girls and their mothers derives from the acceptability of nursing and teaching to both; in contrast, only four mothers held 'police' ambitions for their sons.

The congruence here between mother and daughter as opposed to between mother and son must be seen as one more way in which girls are more closely in conformation with adult influence. The fact that this involves their conforming also to a sex-role stereotype may or may not be seen as a destructive factor. If mothers and daughters both tended to believe that going into service as a kitchen maid was the most appropriate ambition for girls, we might indeed regard such sex-typing as destructive. In so far as mother and daughter are at this stage mutually supportive in *professional* ambitions, however, one might see girls as advantaged over the boys by virtue of this stereotype. This is likely to be more true of working-class girls, for whom teaching or nursing qualifications will be a step up, than for middle-class girls, for whom such a stereotyping may remove choices that they might otherwise have considered. And all of this begs the question as to whether ambitions at seven, in either parent or child, bear any relationship at all to later achievement. This we shall eventually be in a position to comment upon.

Taking simply the here-and-now, however, if girls are expressing ambitions which seem desirable and realistic to their mothers, they are likely to be taken more seriously as people with sensible grown-up opinions; whereas boys who suggest romantic or otherwise unrealistic or unacceptable ambitions are more like to receive a response which, while indulgent of their fancies, regards these as just that and no more. Whether little girls' conversation is taken more seriously because it is more mature, or whether they mature more quickly because they are taken more seriously is another moot point which we merely offer for consideration. We are not suggesting here that boys tend to be more romantic than girls, but more that girls' idea of a romantic occupation comes closer to what their parents can regard as possible and desirable: nursing happens to be a particularly common example of this happy combination. Idiosyncratically, boys too may nourish ambitions which carry credibility for their parents.

Nylon operative's wife:
> Well, I think he wants to be . . . branch out on his own. I mean, he comes back with pieces of lead and, er – what else is it? Oh yes, lead and scrap. And he's sawed it off, you know, and he likes to take it down there to the, er, scrapyard nearby, and he comes back with all the money. I think he'll perhaps be something like that. Mind you, they alter so much, don't they? [General dealer, that sort of thing?] Yes. Anything for nothing, he'll get something for it!

Foreman's wife:
> Well, do you know, since he was very tiny he's always wanted to be a doctor. Now he's never done any of that steth . . . – you know how kiddies do, he's never played at it; but it's always stuck with him. Now same as I've said, he'll move away when anything's on there [TV] that's frightening, and my husband'll say 'Well, he'll never make one, you know!' But it's *there*, you know, when you're

talking – he isn't always on about it. But he'll sit there and he'll say 'Do you have to do a really lot of studying for a doctor, Mummy?' And I say 'Yes, Barry, but there's other doctors besides them sort, there's people who, er, when a doctor finds a thing, then people know of a cure, and they call that research'. You know, and things like that. But he doesn't turn round and say 'I'm going to be a doctor – I want to be a doctor'. Nothing like that, but always in conversation it'll come up every so often. It's in the back of his mind this is what he'd like to do. [And would you like to see him in that sort of work?] I would, yes. I mean, it would be a marvellous thing really. But as I say, whether anything . . .

It is in fact difficult to categorise children's ambitions in terms of whether they are romantic or realistic: for one thing, being a doctor might be a realistic ambition to one child and romantic, in terms of being unattainable, to another; similarly, 'spraying the weeds on the side of the road', the ambition of a teacher's child, is romantic in the sense of catching the imagination *now* as a lovely thing to do, but being entirely unlikely as an ambition to survive the course of time – though perfectly attainable. In Class I & II, fourteen boys in fact had specified ambitions which were below their family's social class – twice as many as girls; in the white-collar group, ten boys specified manual occupations, and nine girls did likewise, but seven of the latter were in hairdressing which tends to be considered by ordinary people (as opposed to the Registrar-General) a white-collar type of occupation.

It may be suggested that nursing should not count as a professional occupation in that mothers may be thinking in terms of sub-professional grades of nursing, or may not be distinguishing between grades. However, *if we simply omit all nursing choices* from all the working-class groups, which is to delete the largest group of choices, both girls and their mothers remain more ambitious in professional terms than boys and their mothers in the skilled and unskilled groups, and equally ambitious in the semi-skilled group. There is clearly more here than can be accounted for by the romance of the nursing profession.

'A child of his age, you don't know what his outlook in life's going to be in schooling . . .'
Parents, faced with a question about what they would like their seven-year-old to do when he's grown-up, tend to shy away a little

and to emphasise that 'it's early days yet'; none the less, to consider such a matter is consonant with their long-term intentions. That is to say, parents act and talk on the assumption that the child is indeed father of the man; we particularly saw this to be true when we were looking at problems of discipline, where mothers are continually exercised by the problem 'If I let this go now, what will be the effect in time to come?' Similarly, parents' anxiety about the child's progress at school at this age is entirely derived from the belief that it has both prognostic and causative significance: if they felt that time lost now could be easily retrieved, nothing would matter beyond the child's happiness. Parents on the whole work on a Kellyan basis: 'There is a continuing movement toward the anticipation of events, rather than a series of barters for temporal satisfactions, and this movement is the essence of life itself'; at the same time they find it difficult to accept his reassurance that 'No one needs to be the victim of his biography'.[3] It is precisely because they fear that their children will become victims of their biographies that they try to write the early chapters to a pattern which they hope will build up to a successful dénouement.

We ourselves as developmental psychologists must also admit to a long-term orientation: indeed, it is hardly likely that we would have undertaken longitudinal research, with all its logistic inconveniences, had we not had a rather certain notion of a developmental pattern which would make it important to look at the same children throughout their childhoods rather than take discrete groups at different points in childhood. We suspect, too, that both we and the reader would be astonished if we did not eventually find some consistent and cumulative pattern in individual children's progress towards adulthood, or if our data forced us to talk entirely in terms of 'a series of barters for temporal satisfactions' rather than (as we think it does) compelling us to include a teleological dimension. With this in mind, it does not seem inappropriate to end this book on a forward-looking note, even though, in a sense, we may seem to anticipate the next stage of this study.

It was decided at a fairly early stage in the study that during the long period of interviewing the children's mothers (ages one to sixteen years) we would avoid any feeling that we were 'checking up on' the children or on what their mothers had said by resisting singling out the children at school for any direct study. Thus, although a group of seventy-nine children were investigated at age five for their their adjustment to school,[4] after that time, apart from the reading test of a sub-sample of 124 discussed in Chapter 5, the only direct contact in school was with 150 of the children who, together with

1,080 of their classmates, were the subjects of an investigation of literacy skills in relation to personality and environment.[5] However, as we have already mentioned, all our sample were to reach the age of eleven, the age of transfer from the junior school into secondary education, at a time when the 'eleven-plus' selection procedure was still being used to decide the child's educational future. In the Nottingham area, there was one single-sex (boys) comprehensive school, on a large council estate, so that the selection between grammar school on the one hand and secondary modern school (later known as bilateral school) on the other was a very real dichotomy. The Catholic schools were divided in a similar way, and the two single-sex 'High Schools' adopted a creaming procedure from the grammar school entry. There was also a Church of England school of some status, but which had the reputation of taking children who might not in fact have reached the grammar school, provided that their parents could show suitable evidence of religious observance. Additionally, there were a number of small private schools together with a minor boys' public school within commuting distance.

The eleven-plus selection procedure consisted of two 'verbal reasoning' tests; those used for the majority of the children were tests issued by the National Foundation for Educational Research. Some children now resident outside the City of Nottingham boundary were given similar tests from the Moray House list. We were fortunate enough to be given access to the results of these tests for research purposes. Head teachers' ratings were also collected by the Education Authorities for these children, but they did not form a major part of the selection procedure and we did not seek access to these. The verbal reasoning tests were administered on separate days, and this was intended as a fail-safe for the child who was unwell or nervous on one of the days. The results of the two tests do in fact show a high correlation (0·95), and in the discussion that follows we have therefore taken as the child's verbal reasoning score the average of his scores in the two tests. We are indebted to Alison Kiln for the analyses of scores and the factors associated with them which we now present.[6]

Table 34 shows higher-scoring and lower-scoring children in terms of sex and social class. The mean score for girls overall was 98·7 and for boys was 93·6. This difference is significant at the 0·001 level of significance.

The sex difference shown between the means is not at all unexpected in view of the fact that we are dealing with scores in verbal reasoning: it reflects what has many times been confirmed, that girls

Table 34   *Children who score high and low on verbal reasoning at eleven years*

	social class					summary		
			III			I&II+	IIIman,	overall
	I&II	IIIwc	man	IV	V	IIIwc	IV, V	popn
	%	%	%	%	%	%	%	%
High scores (110+)								
boys	48	29	9	7	0	39	8	16
girls	67	39	10	6	3	54	8	21
						—	—	—
both	58	34	10	6	2	46	8	18

Significance: trend ↘ ****   m.class/w.class ****
                        between sexes n.s.

Low scores (under 85)								
boys	2	8	32	36	56	5	34	26
girls	2	16	17	22	55	9	22	19
						—	—	—
both	2	12	24	29	56	7	28	23

Significance: trend ↗ ****   m.class/w.class ****
                        between sexes n.s.

are more linguistically competent at this age than boys, and it is well known that boys' scores have to be weighted in educational selection if they are to be equally represented with girls in selective schools. We have discussed in previous volumes the patterns of behaviour in children and their parents which support girls' linguistic superiority over boys: girls are encouraged to bring their friends home more than boys and in other ways are more closely chaperoned by adults; girls are smacked less, which is likely to bring them more into verbal social relationship with their mothers; boys are more likely to be considered 'outdoor children' than girls, and outdoor play tends to be less verbal as well as less subject to the special verbal contribution of adults; girls show more preference for imaginative, role-playing games, which demand verbal interaction of a comparatively high level, while boys show more preferences for rough-and-tumble play, which does not. We have also pointed out more speculatively that a basic genetic sex difference such as Erikson suggests, in terms of 'person-oriented' girls and 'thing-oriented' boys, would be sufficient to explain all these findings and others; that such an initial difference would be

. . . quickly built upon, sustained and perpetuated by cultural forces. It is suggested that the chain goes thus: girls, orienting to persons, are rewarded by conversation and chat, which moves them on to the escalator of verbal precocity on which they will remain until after puberty. Their person-oriented games demand verbal fluency to sustain them, and this they have, so they continue to find such games satisfying and thus to practise their verbal fluency. Boys meanwhile, attracted by things, confine their conversation more to information exchange, and are less rewarded by chat for the sake of it. Their games are played out at the pre-school stage (and after) in less close proximity to people, and greater physical activity implies more fleeting social contact; verbal fluency is depressed compared with that of the well-practised girls.[7]

The differences in terms of social class are extraordinarily dramatic, particularly as between middle class and working class: how many educationalists would have predicted such a difference between manual and non-manual within Class III, for instance? Once again, the blunt instrument that we originally assumed the Registrar-General's classification must be has turned out to be surprisingly well honed.

None the less, to say that 'verbal reasoning scores are associated with social class' and leave it at that will hardly do; although we may have started out by defining social class, for simplicity and ease of replication, in terms of the Registrar-General's classification, we have seen that the life-styles which characterise different social classes, of which father's occupation is only one part, are far more complex, even where we only look at them from the vantage-point of child-rearing. In the end, the life-style defines the social class: father's occupation is merely a shorthand index to it which happens to be more reliable than most other indices that one might choose.

With this in mind, it seemed useful to analyse the verbal reasoning scores in terms of other factors, some of which are also associated with social class. For instance, Table 35 shows mean scores in terms of sex, social class and family size; it will be seen that previous research[8] is supported in the finding that the child from a small family is likely to do rather better in an 'intelligence' test than the child from a larger family. Nisbet suggests that this is due to an enriched

Table 35   *Mean verbal reasoning scores at eleven years and family size*

	social class					summary		
	I&II	IIIwc	III man	IV	V	I&II+ IIIwc	IIIman, IV, V	overall popn
				MEAN SCORES				
Boys' scores small family								
(1–3 chn)	112	106	93	96	84	109	93	97
large family								
(4+ chn)	96	92	88	83	85	94	87	89

Significance: trend ↘ ****   m.class/w.class ****
family size: large/small ****

Girls' scores small family								
(1–3 chn)	115	107	96	97	92	111	96	100
large family								
(4+ chn)	113	94	93	96	83	104	93	96

Significance: trend ↘ ****   m.class/w.class ****
family size: large/small ***

experience of linguistic exchange between child and adult in the smaller family, and such an effect would be expected to be particularly marked in performance based on a verbally weighted test.

Of more interest, however, is to look at the relationship between the verbal reasoning scores obtained at eleven and the indices which we had devised to characterise child, mother or both at the age of seven. At the point at which the verbal reasoning scores had been collected for all our children (i.e. when those with the latest birthdates had reached eleven) we did not yet have field data obtained at eleven in a coded form, nor had we yet fully developed our indices for that age-stage. In as much as mothers' styles are consistent from one age-stage to the next – and in so far as we also expect the total situation at seven to bear some relation to the total situation at eleven – it seemed reasonable to make this kind of temporal jump.

Now if child-centredness or home–school concordance (for instance) are both associated with occupational class, and so is verbal reasoning performance, one will expect to find an association between verbal reasoning scores and either of these indices; and so one does, to a very marked degree. Much more enlightening is to hold occupational class constant and look *within* classes at whether these indices obtained at seven are correlated, whether positively or negatively, with verbal reasoning scores at eleven; in this way, the effects of occupational class *per se* are allowed for, and we are now considering separately as factors some of the attitudes and behaviours that go to make up *social-class styles*. Table 36 lists only those indices which are highly significantly related to verbal reasoning when middle-class or working-class affiliation is held constant.

Table 36   *Indices which maintain a correlation with verbal reasoning scores (significant at 0·001) when analysed within middle-class or working-class categories (i.e. which operate in relation to verbal reasoning over and above the occupational class factor)*

Index	Correlation with v.r. scores	m.class/w.class
Child-centredness*	positive	w.class only
Bamboozlement*	negative	both
Temperamental aggression in child*	negative	both
Home literacy	positive	both
Reading/writing competence	positive	both
General cultural interests	positive	both
Home–school concordance	positive	both
Child's liking for school	positive	m.class only

* Main discussion of starred indices will be found in J. and E. Newson, op. cit. (1976*b*).

Among these findings, perhaps the appearance of the first three indices in Table 36 is the most striking. The rest are, after all, more or less directly connected with school and how school activities are backed up at home. But in the first three correlations, we have evidence that children whose parents are child-centred (defined in terms of behaviour in a number of different situations) are at an advantage in verbal reasoning, while children who are themselves aggressive in various ways and children whose parents are prepared in the name of socialisation to 'deceive by trickery, hoax, cozen; to mystify' (*Shorter Oxford English Dictionary*) are at a disadvantage in that respect.

The concepts of advantage and disadvantage thus take on a wider dimension. At this point we are explicitly moving beyond poverty, poor resources and poor understanding of citizens' rights, and saying something about child-rearing as it affects children's competence. Within a working-class milieu, perhaps the child whose parents are child-centred, and who therefore can give him that sense of personal worth and considerability which is (we suggest) the core of being 'advantaged', is compensated further than we have yet fully realised. Within a middle-class environment, perhaps children are more diminished than their mothers intend by the 'bamboozling' technique. Children who have no sense of worth are defeated children; children whose parents attempt to rule them by trickery are defeated in the act of starting a dialogue with those who care for them most, let alone in their transactions with the outside world; aggression, too, may perhaps be regarded as the tactic of the defeated. Social class is of interest in child development and education to the extent that it is associated with attitudes and practices which produce such effects.

. . . insofar as a subculture represents a reaction to defeat and insofar as it is caught by a sense of powerlessness, it suppresses the potential of those who grow up under its sway *by discouraging problem-solving*. The source of powerlessness that such a subculture generates, no matter how moving its by-products, produces instability in the society and unfulfilled promise in human beings (our italics).[9]

Bruner's statement is directly pertinent to our own findings. Already at seven years old there is a chill in the air. Too many of the tender leaves of hope will have withered by the end of the summer of childhood.

NOTES

1 An example of this mother in such a situation is given on page 118, 'Lorry driver's wife'.
2 We have not counted correspondence where the mother says 'university degree' and the child chooses a specific profession.
3 Both quotations from G. A. Kelly, *The Psychology of Personal Constructs*, *Vol. 1: A Theory of Personality* (New York, Norton, 1955).
4 Mary Croxen, op. cit. (1966).
5 Audrey Fessler, op. cit. (1975).
6 Alison Kiln, 'An investigation of factors influencing a child's measured intelligence', undergraduate dissertation, University of Nottingham Psychology Department.
7 John and Elizabeth Newson, Joyce Scaife and Diane Richardson: 'Sex-roles

in adolescence and pre-adolescence', in J. Chetwynd and D. Hartnett, *The Sex Role System*, in press.

8   E. Fraser, *Home Environment and School* (University of London Press, 1959); J. Nisbet, 'Family environment and intelligence', *Eugenics Review*, 45 (1953).

9   J. S. Bruner, *The Relevance of Education* (London, Allen and Unwin, 1972).

Further Reading

There has been a considerable amount of research on different aspects of the relationship between home and school. In presenting our own findings in this volume, we have referred to some of these other studies where it seemed relevant to do so. We decided not to add an extended review of the literature, since that task has already been ably accomplished by Anne Sharrock in her *Home/School Relations* (London, Macmillan, 1970), and by Elizabeth Goodacre in *School and Home* (Windsor, NFER, 1970). Anne Sharrock's *Home and School: A select annotated bibliography* (Windsor, NFER, 1971) is a further valuable source of references and comment on home/school links.

Linking home and school (2nd edn, London, Longman, 1973), edited by Maurice Craft and his colleagues, contains contributions from a number of authorities on research in home/school relations, and on the practical steps that have been taken to bridge the gap. Further practical suggestions are put forward by Lawrence Green in *Parents and Teachers* (London, Allen & Unwin, 1968), Ronald Cave in *Partnership for Change: Parents and schools* (London, Ward Lock Educational, 1970) and Patrick Mc-Geeney in *Parents are Welcome* (London, Longman, 1969).

Further evidence on the nature of the relationship between home background and school performance and adjustment can be obtained from the following sources:

1 Central Advisory Council for Education, *Children and their Primary Schools* (London, HMSO, 1967) (the 'Plowden Report').
2 K. Cullen, *School and Family* (Dublin, Gill & Macmillan, 1969).
3 R. Davie et al., *From Birth to Seven* (London, Longman, 1972).
4 J. W. B. Douglas, *The Home and the School* (London, MacGibbon & Kee, 1968; Panther, 1967).
5 J. W. B. Douglas et al., *All Our Future* (London, Peter Davies, 1968; Panther, 1971).
6 E. Fraser, *Home Environment and the School* (University of London Press, 1959).
7 B. Jackson and D. Marsden, *Education and the Working Class* (London, Routledge & Kegan Paul, 1962; Harmondsworth, Penguin, 1969).
8 G. W. Miller, *Educational Opportunity and the Home* (London, Longman, 1971).
9 S. Wiseman, *Education and Environment* (Manchester University Press, 1964).

Appendix I

The Interview

(*Note:* F in margin denotes a follow-up question tailor-made for the individual child)

UNIVERSITY OF NOTTINGHAM
CHILD DEVELOPMENT RESEARCH UNIT

District.................................
Interviewer at 1:0.................................
Interviewer at 4:0.................................
Interviewer at 7:0.................................
Date.................................

GUIDED INTERVIEW SCHEDULE
(For mothers of children aged 7:0)

A. *BACKGROUND*
   Child's full name ....
   Address ....
   ....
   Date of birth............................. Sex: *Boy/Girl*
   Family size and position (for each child in family, indicate sex and age; include foster children, marked F, and deceased children, marked D)
   sex ... ...
   age ... ...
   MOTHER *Age*............... *Not working/working part-time/full-time*
   Occupation if at work ....

1. Did you train for a job before you had children? (*details, including untrained jobs*)
   FATHER *Age*............... *Precise occupation* ....

2. Does he have to be away from home at all, except just during the day? *Home every night/up to 2 nights away p.w./3 nights + p.w./normally away/separation or divorce/dead/other* ....

Shift work? YES/NO   What shifts?.......................................

3. Does any other adult live here now, apart from your husband and yourself?

    YES............................/NO

    If YES: How does N get on with him/her? Are they good friends?

4. Has N ever been separated from you for more than a day or two since he was four? – has he been in hospital, for instance, or have you been in hospital since then? (*Details: age at separation, how long, etc.*)

B. *GENERAL PERSONALITY*

5. Well, now – it's three years since you last told us about N, and a child can change a lot in that time. How would you describe him now to someone who didn't know him at all?

6. Would you say he was a placid child, or rather temperamental?
    Placid/varies/temperamental

7. Do you find him easy to manage, now he's seven – or is he a bit tricky, do you have to feel your way with him?
    Easy/varies/temperamental

8. Is he the sort of child who usually agrees with what you want him to do, or does he tend to object to things quite a lot?
    Agrees/varies/objects

9. How does he manage in new situations? Does he enjoy them, or is he bothered by what he isn't used to? *Enjoys/varies/bothered*

10. What about new people? Is he shy? *Shy/varies/not shy at all*

11. In general, does he take things as they come, or is he a bit of a worrier? *As they come/varies/worrier*

12. Does he try very hard to understand things that puzzle him, or does he just let things pass over his head if they're difficult?
    Tries/varies/let pass

13. Is he happy to sit still so long as he has something to do, or is he one of those children who can't keep still for a minute?
    Will sit/varies/can't sit still

14. When he's on his own, is he a busy sort of child, or does he easily get bored? *Busy/varies/gets bored*

15. Would you call him an indoor child or an outdoor child?
    In/both/out

C. *ACTIVITIES*

16. We should like to know something now about what sort of things N likes doing when he's not at school. What about in the morning?

Does he have any time to himself between waking up and leaving for school? *YES/NO*
(*If any*): What does he usually do in that time? How does he amuse himself?

17. What about when he comes out of school in the afternoon? Do you fetch him usually? *YES/NO*
    (*If NO*): Does he come straight home, or does he play out or go somewhere else before coming home?
    Straight home first/plays out, unspecified/elsewhere ....
    (*Prompt if necessary*): Do you have any rules about coming straight home? *YES/NO*
    Are you usually here when he gets back from school? (*If not, state arrangements made, if any*)

18. When he gets home, what does he do with his free time until bedtime?

19. Some children seem to spend a great deal of time doing one or two special things, like reading or drawing or making models. Has N a special hobby of this sort? (*specify*)

20. Has he any (other) special toy or game that takes up a lot of his time?

21. Has he anything he collects, or anything that he gradually adds to? (*e.g. Lego, Dinkies, train set, doll's clothes, etc.*)
    (*If bought*): Does he spend his own money on this?
    YES/NO/not bought

22. (*If any siblings*): Some parents like children to have their own special toys, and some think that all the toys should belong to the whole family. How do you feel about that?
    Separate/communal/some of each

23. Do the children (does N) have a special place of their (his) own where they (he) can keep their (his) own things? (*specify*)
    (*If a general room, ask*): Do they keep things in their bedroom?
    YES/NO

24. Does N play there a lot?
    (*prompt if necessary*): Which room does he mostly play in?
    Child's play-space: sep. playroom/bed-playroom/special corner/ no special play-place

25. Is he careful with his toys, or do they seem to get broken rather quickly? *Careful/break/other*

26. Some children seem to enjoy pulling their toys to bits more than actually playing with them – is N like that? *Destructive/not*

27. Some children are careful with their toys when they are using them but they leave them about carelessly so that they get broken that way. Does N do that? *YES/NO*

28. Do you take any trouble to get him to look after his toys? *Much/some/NO*

29. Do you expect him to keep them tidy himself, or do you reckon to tidy up after him?
Himself/M reckons to tidy/M expects but he doesn't/both do it

30. Now that N is at school, does he have enough time to do all the things he wants to do at home? *YES/NO*

31. What about days when there's no school? What does he do with his time mostly? (*Include those occupations which child has on any average weekend, and prompt 'inside?' or 'outside?' as necessary*)
Inside:
Outside:

32. { You've mentioned other children a few times;
    { You haven't mentioned other children very much;
which does N like best – playing with other children, or playing by himself? *Others/alone/equally*

33. Who does he play with mostly?   *Sibs: often/sometimes/never*
                                     Other: often/sometimes/never

34. Has he any special friends? – at school?
                                  at home?

35. Does he see his friends in the weekend?   *YES/NO*
(*If NO*): Any particular reason?

36. Do they come and play at your house?   *Most weeks/sometimes/No*
37. Does he go to theirs?   *Most weeks/sometimes/No*

38. Are you happy about { his friendships ? (*prompt for each*
                        { this friendship ?   *mentioned*)

39. Have you ever tried to discourage any friendship between N and another child?   *YES/NO*
(*If YES*): Any special reason?
(*If NO*): Do you think you would ever do this for any reason? (specify reason)

40. In general, how would you say N gets on with other children? Does he make friends easily?
YES/not very/some difficulty making friends

41. Does he stand up for himself, or does he let other children boss him around? *He's boss/give and take/child prefers to follow/wants to lead but fails*

42. How do you feel about quarrelling at this age? Do you think quarrelling *has* to happen between children?   (*prompt if necessary: between sibs; others*)

Sibs: inevitable at 7/difficult to avoid, but possible/quite unnecessary
Others: inevitable at 7/difficult to avoid, but possible/quite unnecessary

43. Does he do a lot of fighting – do his quarrels often come to blows?
    (*prompt*) *Sibs: often/sometimes/little fighting*
    Others: often/sometimes/little fighting

44. Do you (would you) ever interfere in N's quarrels and arguments
    with other children outside the family?   *YES/NO*

45. Do you ever tell him what he should do in his quarrels, or help
    him to manage them in any way?   (*specify*)

D. *FANTASY AND TENSION*
46. What sort of games does N mostly play with other children?
    (*Place in order of his preference; prompt all if necessary*)
    ....*Rough and tumble, climbing, kicking ball around*
    ....*Construction – building, making*
    ....*Imaginative games: role-playing, 'house', 'school', etc.*
    (*criterion is* plot)

47. Does he ever have play-acting games *when he's on his own* – either
    being someone himself or making up a story with dolls or toy
    animals or puppets?   *YES/NO*
    (*details*)

48. Does he mind you listening to these games, or does he stop when
    you come in?
    Likes audience/doesn't mind/prefers privacy/sometimes each

49. Does he ever make up stories for you about things that haven't
    actually happened?   *YES/NO*
    (*If YES*): Does he tell them as if they were true, or does he explain
    that this is a story?   *As true/as story*

F 50. *Fantasy (follow up for individual child)*:

51. Has N any special fears or worries? (*specify*)   *YES/NO*
    (*If YES*): Has he had that for a long time?   *Since....................*
    Did he come and tell you about it, or could you see that he was
    afraid?

F 52. He used to be afraid of..when he
    was four.
    Is he still afraid of that?

53. Does he ever seem frightened at night?

54. Do you feel that you *know* about most of his thoughts and fears,
    or do you think there's quite a lot that he keeps to himself?

55. We're interested in the various odd habits that children seem to
    have at this age. Does N have any little habits you can think of?
    Does he bite his nails, for instance?   *YES/NO*

F 56. When he was four, he used to suck his thumb. Does he do that now at all?*   YES/NO
(*If NO*): When did he stop doing that altogether?.....................

F 57. Does he ever suck his dummy now?*   YES/NO
(*If NO*): When did he finally give that up?............................
Did you have to do anything about it, or did he just drop it himself?

F 58. Does he ever use his bottle now?*   YES/NO
(*If NO*): When did he give that up finally?............................
Did you have to do anything about it or did he give it up himself?

F 59. *Transitional object* * (*follow up if child had transitional object at four*)

56A, 57A, 58A, 59A *(If YES to any of the follow-ups above)*: Have you tried to stop that, or are you quite happy to let him go on as long as he seems to want it?

60. What about the things children do when they're a bit strung-up? Does he ever clear his throat or swallow as a nervous habit?

61. Does he pull at his ears or mouth, or pick at his face?

62. Does he blink or screw his eyes up?

63. Does he ever stammer or stutter when he speaks?

64. Does he play with his private parts, as far as you know?

65. Is there anything else he does as a habit – when he's overtired or worried, perhaps?

66. (*If ANY HABITS*): Have you noticed whether he.....................
(*prompt back separately for each*) at any special sort of time, or when he's in a particular mood?

67. Have you tried to stop him...............................(*prompt back separately for each*), or are you just expecting him to grow out of it? (*If STOP*): How?

68. Does he ever have a headache or a temperature because he's anxious or excited? (*Prompt*): Is he ever actually sick out of excitement or worry?
(*If YES to either*): Have you tried to do anything about this?

F 69. I think he was still wetting his bed sometimes/quite often when he was four. Does he ever do that now? (*If NO, check*): Never at all? YES/NO
(*If NO*): How long is it since he last wetted his bed?.................
Did you do anything to get him dry at night?
(*If YES*): About how often does he have a wet bed?   *Most nights/1–3 nights p.w./less than once p.w./less than 1 per month*
Are you doing anything about it, or just waiting for him to grow out of it?

F 70. You said he sometimes had wet pants in the daytime when he was four. Does he ever do that now? *YES/NO*
(*If NO*): When did he get quite dry in the day?.......................

F 71. *Soiling (follow up if applicable at four)*

72. A lot of children of this age have their own superstitions – things they must do or mustn't do in order to feel safe, like doing things in a special order, or not walking on the lines of the pavement. Has N any superstitions like that? (*specify*)
(*If YES, prompt for each*): Do you know where he got that from? How long has he had it?
Does it seem very important to him?

73. Does he ever talk to you about magical things happening? (*details*)

F 74. When he was four, you said that at bedtime you always had to
....
Do you still do/say that? *YES/NO*
(*If YES*): Would he mind if you didn't one night?
(*If NO*): Do you do anything else of that sort at bedtime now? (*specify*)

F 75. Does he still take his.............................to bed with him? *YES/NO*
(*If NO*): Does he take anything else instead? (*specify*)

F 76. Does he take anything to bed with him now (instead of his dummy/bottle)?

E. *INDEPENDENCE*
77. Could you tell me now what sort of things N does on his own? Does he ever go on a bus on his own?
Not at all/to school only/otherwise (*specify*).............................

78. Does he play or roam around in the street at all? *YES/NO*

79. Does he go to the shops on his own? *YES/NO*

80. Do you trust him now to cross busy roads on his own? *YES/NO*

81. Can you always find him when you want him?
Always/not always/often can't

82. Do you have any problem over his wandering off so that you don't know where he is?

83. Do you have any rules about telling you where he's going before he goes out? *Yes, firm/would like, but he doesn't/no rules*

84. Have you any rules about how far he can go on his own?
Yes, exact/yes, vague/ad hoc, he'd ask/no rules, up to him

85. Does he ever go to a park or recreation ground by himself?.........

swimming bath alone?................. pictures alone?.................
anywhere else?.................

86. Does he belong to any clubs or organisations like Cubs/Brownies or a church club – anything like that? (*specify*)

87. Does he ever stay the night at someone else's house without you?
YES/NO (*specify*)

88. Does he have any pocket money of his own? (*Prompt: Who gives, how much, regular fixed sum(s)*)? *Exclude school expenses and school savings*)
Is there anyone else who gives him money fairly regularly?.........

89. Does he usually spend his money at once, or does he save any of it?
Does he *have* to save any of it?   *Voluntary saving/compulsory/none*
Is there anything he has to spend it on (like fares or Sunday School collections, etc.)? (*Specify*)
Do you buy him sweets, apart from any he buys with his pocket money?   *YES/NO*

90. If he wants extra money for something, do you give it to him? For what sort of thing?   *Freely, if can afford/no/only less than 6d/ only for..............................*

91. Could he earn extra money from you or his Daddy if he wanted to?
YES/NO
(*If YES*): Does he ever? (*details*)

92. We'd like to know about the sort of jobs children do around the house at this age. Is there any little job you expect N to do now (without being paid)?
(*Prompt for each*): Is that something he does as a regular thing, or just when he feels like it?
Suppose he's too busy doing something of his own one day – what happens?

93. (*If younger sibs*):
Does N ever help you by looking after { his brother/sister?
                                                                    the younger children?
Do you ever leave him in charge of them for a while?
Does he ever take them out with him?   *Only under supervision/ alone in the house for short time/away from house/in sole charge for periods over an hour* (*ref. sibs aged.................*)

94. Has he any animals of his own?   *YES.............................../NO*
(*If NO*): Has the family any pets?   *YES.........................../NO*
Does he look after it/them at all, in the way of feeding and cleaning?
Is that his job, or just a thing he does sometimes?
Responsible/sometimes/NO

F. *SCHOOL AND INTELLECTUAL*

95. We should like to know something now about how N gets on at school. Does he like school?
Very much/well enough/not much/strongly dislikes

96. Which school does he go to?..
(*If M demurs, ask what type*)   *Private/L.E.A./other*.................

97. Does he stay for dinner?   YES.................*per week/NO*
(*If YES*): Does he like that?
(*If NO*): Is that because he doesn't want to?

98. Do you know what he enjoys most at school?

99. Do you know what he *doesn't* like?

100. Does he naturally come and tell you about school, or do you always have to ask him?   *Loves telling/average/have to ask*
(*If ASK*): Does he seem to dislike talking about school?   *YES/NO*

101. Does he seem to get on well with his teacher?   *YES/NO/so-so*

102. Has he changed his class teacher in the last twelve months?
YES/NO
(*If YES*): Did that upset him at all?

103. Does he ever complain about anything special at school? (*specify*)
(*If YES*): What do you say to him about that?

104. Does he ever say he doesn't want to go to school today?   *Often/sometimes/never*

105. What do you do? *or* What do you think you would do if he did?

106. Does he ever pretend he's not well, so as to stay at home from school?   *Often/sometimes/has tried, not in last 12 months/never yet*

107. What do you do? *or* What would you do if he did that?

108. (*If any reluctance to go to school*):
Has he ever *refused* to go to school?
Often/occasionally/not in last 12 months/never yet
(*If YES at all*): Do you know why?
What happened?

109. How do you feel about children's complaints of school? Do you think you should take them seriously?

110. Does he often take things to school to show his teacher?
Often/occasionally/NO
(*If YES*): What sort of things?

111. (*If child does take things*): Do you encourage him in that – would you suggest that he should take something if he didn't think of it?
Encourages/no special encouragement/discourages

112. Does he ever come home and start doing something he's been shown at school?   *YES/NO*

113. Does he ever ask you questions about something he's heard of in class? *YES/NO*
(*If YES*): What sort of things?

114. Apart from school, what sort of questions does he ask you and his Daddy? What interests him?

115. Can you always answer his questions? *YES/NO*
What do you do if you can't? *or* What would you do if you couldn't?

F 116. One question $\left\{\begin{array}{l}\text{you } \textit{didn't} \text{ want to answer}\\ \text{he hadn't yet asked}\end{array}\right\}$ when he was four was where babies come from.
Does N know about that now?

F 117. (*If YES*): Did *you* tell him, or somebody else? *specify*...............
How old was he?..................
(*If NO*): What age do you expect to tell him?..................

118. How good is N's reading? Can he read well enough to enjoy a book for its story? *YES/NO*

119. When he's reading a book to himself, does he say the words aloud or read silently? *Aloud/mouths/silent, no mouthing*

120. Have you tried to help him with his reading at all? In what way?

121. Does he $\left\{\begin{array}{l}\text{read}\\ \text{look at books}\end{array}\right\}$ much at home?

122. (*If he can read*): Does he ever read a book which has more story than pictures? *YES/NO*

123. Does he belong to a library? *YES/NO*

124. $\left\{\begin{array}{l}\text{Has he any books of his own?}\\ \text{Have the children any books of their own?}\end{array}\right.$
About how many?.......................
(*Real books, not comics. Count total of probable interest to N*)

125. Do you get him any comic or magazine regularly? (*specify*)

126. Do you often read to him? About how often? (*Daddy counts, but specify*)

127. What sort of things do you read to him? (*If long books*): Can you tell me some of the books you've read to him which he specially liked?

128. Do you or his Daddy ever help him with other things, like sums or writing, or any other school work?

129. In general, would you say you're pleased with the school N goes to – I don't mean is it a good school, but does it suit N?

130. If he showed the ability, how far would you like him to go with his education?

131. Have you any ideas now about what you would like him to do when he's grown up?

132. Has N any ideas about that?

133. Do you pay for any extra lessons for N – music or dancing or anything else at all? (*specify, and how often*)
Does anybody give him any special lessons that you *don't* pay for?

134. Does he do any drawing or painting at home?
Most days/sometimes/not much

135. What happens to his drawings when he's finished them? (*prompt if necessary*): Do you ever keep any of them yourself?

136. Does he do any writing for his own pleasure? (*If YES*): What does he write?

137. Does he ever write letters to people? *YES/NO*
(*If YES*): What sort of letters does he write – what about?
(*If 'thank-you' letters only specified*): Does he ever write any other letters?
None/'thank-you' or Santa Claus only/occasional others/many
(*If any*): Does he like writing letters, or do you have to go on at him to get them done?

138. Does anyone play a musical instrument in your family? (*any degree of skill counts – specify who and what*)
(*If YES*): Has N learned to play it at all?

139. Do you ever take him to the pictures? (*Daddy counts, but specify*)

140. Have you ever taken him to a theatre or a concert? (*specify*)

141. What about museums and art galleries – has he been to any with you or his Daddy? (*specify*)

142. Is there any other exhibition or show or anything like that which you've taken him to? (*Prompt if necessary*): Has he ever been to a zoo or a circus with you?

143. Does he ever go to a football match, or any other sporting event?

144. Does he ever go to a church service with you or his Daddy?
Regularly................per month/sometimes/NO

145. Does he go to Sunday School?
Regularly/sometimes/used to, not now/NO

146. Do you ever talk to him about religion? *YES/NO* (*specify*)
If NO: What do you tell him if he asks about that sort of thing? (*Prompt if necessary*): Does he say prayers at home at all?
YES/NO

147. Is there any special interest which you and N share – something which you both follow together?

148. Is there anything which he and his Daddy are both specially interested in?

149. Would you say he is closer now to you or to his Daddy?
Mother/father/equally

150. Does your husband like doing things with him?
YES/NO/sometimes
Does he give N a lot of attention?
Very high/average/not much/ignores

151. Is there any outing that N particularly enjoys? (*Prompt*): If you were planning a treat specially for N, what do you think he would choose to do?
About how often do you do that?

152. When you're deciding what to do during the holidays, does N have any say in what you choose?

G. *DISCIPLINE, ETC.*

153. Now that N is seven, what is it about him that gives you most pleasure?

154. Is he a child who shows a lot of affection? (*If not to mother, prompt whether to anyone, including animals if any, and specify*)

155. Do you ever give him a cuddle nowadays, or do you think he's too old for that now?
(*If too old*): Do you kiss him at all now? *No kissing or cuddling/ formal kissing only/frequent informal hugs or cuddling*

156. What about disagreements? What sort of things make you get on each other's nerves now, you and N?

157. Do you find that N takes a long time over doing as you ask him?
Often/sometimes/usually quick

158. What do you do if he is being very slow over this sort of thing?

159. (*If not smack*): What happens if he simply refuses to do something you want him to do? (*or what would*..................?)

160. How do you feel about smacking children of this age?

161. Do you think parents should try to do without smacking altogether, or do you think smacking is a good way of training children?

162. In general, do you think smacking has good results with children of this age? (*specify*)

163. Any bad results?

164. What effect does smacking have on N? (*Prompt if necessary*): Does he behave better? for how long? Does it upset him?

165. What effect does it have on you? Do you feel relieved or upset in

any way, (or is it just a part of the routine?) (*Omit last part if M clearly doesn't smack routinely*)

166. How often does N in fact get smacked?
1 per day +/1 per week +/1 per month +/less

167. (*If any smacking*): Is it just with your hand, or do you use a slipper or a cane or anything like that?
(*If hand only, prompt*): Do you ever *threaten* to use something more? (*specify*)

168. Do you ever $\left\{ \begin{array}{l} \text{take his trousers down} \\ \text{turn her skirt up} \end{array} \right\}$ to smack him/her?
YES/NO

169. (*If any smacking*): Who smacks most, your husband or yourself?
(*ref. to N*)   *Mother/father/equal*
(*If any difference*): Is that because you disagree about smacking, or is it just that you are/he is more often there when it's needed?

170. What sort of thing is N most often smacked for?

171. Of course, there are lots of other ways of dealing with naughtiness, besides smacking; for instance:
Do you ever promise N a reward for being good?
YES/NO/special circumstances.......................

172. Do you ever say that if he's naughty he can't have something he likes – icecream or television, something like that?   *YES/NO*

173. Do you carry out a threat if you've warned him, or do you usually let it go?   *Mostly carries out/sometimes does/lets it go*

174. (*If ch. has pocket money*): Do you ever keep back some of his pocket money?   *YES/NO*

175. Do you ever send him out of the room or put him in a room by himself for a bit?   *YES/NO*

176. Do you ever threaten him with someone else – his teacher or the doctor or a policeman – someone like that?   *YES.............../NO*
(*If YES*): What do you say?

177. Do you ever say he will make you ill if he behaves badly?   *YES/NO*

178. Do you ever threaten to leave him or send him away from home?
YES/NO
(*If YES*): What do you say?

179. Do you tell him you won't love him if he's naughty?   *YES/NO*
(*If YES*): When do you say that?

180. Do you ever hold up another child as an example? What do you say?

(Prompt either way if necessary): What about the other way round?
Do you ever say: 'Look how nicely so-and-so behaves!' *or* 'You
don't want to be like so-and-so, do you?'
Positive example/negative example/both/neither

181. Is there anything else you say to him which stops him being
naughty, or which makes him sorry when he *has* been naughty?

182. Is there any other punishment which you use, or threaten to use,
with N?

183. Some parents find that rudeness and cheekiness are a problem at
this age. Does that happen with N?   *A lot/some/very little*

184. What do you do when he is rude to you? *(specify rudeness)*
Smack/other punishment/rebuke/nothing

185. Has he ever picked up any bad language? *(If YES)*: Can you tell
me what it was? What did you do?
(If NO): What do you think you should do when that happens?

186. Does he ever try to smack you, now he's seven?
Often/sometimes/never

187. What do you do? (What would you do?)
(If disapproved): Is that because you don't like him striking anyone,
or because you don't like him being disrespectful to his mother?
Striking/disrespect/ignored anyway

188. Suppose he tells you he hasn't done something naughty, and you
know quite well that he has. What do you do then?

189. If he tells you something, can you usually take his word for it, or
does he make things up a bit?

190. Does he ever come and tell you he's been naughty, before you
actually find out?   *YES/NO*

191. Does he ever seem to get a kick out of smashing something up?
YES, destructive/only expendables/NO
How do you feel about children doing that sort of thing?

192. Sometimes it's quite easy for high-spirited children to get them-
selves into trouble with neighbours or school or the police. Has
N ever got into that sort of trouble? *(specify)*
(If YES): What did you say to N about it?

193. Does N ever get into a real rage – shouting and stamping and
banging doors? *(Prompt if necessary)*: About how often does it
happen? What usually starts if off?
Do you do anything about it?

194. Do you expect him to say he's sorry to you when he's been naughty
or rude?

(*If YES*): Would you make him do that, even if he didn't want to?
Makes/wouldn't force

195. Do you ever say sorry to *him* for being cross with him?   YES/NO

196. Do you find that how strict you are depends a great deal on your own mood at the time?

197. When do you most approve of yourself – when you're being strict with N, or when you're being easy-going?
Strict/easy-going/other (specify)

198. I think everyone agrees that temperamentally some children are much easier than others. Compared with other children, would you say that N is very easy, or fairly easy, or fairly difficult, or very difficult?   *Very easy/fairly easy/fairly difficult/very difficult*

199. Are there any problems which you've had with N since he was four, which are now over? (*specify, including age and how coped with*)

200. Have you any problems with him now, which you hope to see your way through in the next year or two?

H. PROSPECT

201. One last question: suppose you think ahead a bit, to when N is about sixteen; do you look forward to that time, or do you think they're nicest when they're this sort of age?

HOUSING   *Modern detached/modern semi/Victorian detached/Victorian semi/Victorian terraced/terraced with bays/terraced without bays/self-contained flat/rooms/council house on estate/council (not estate)/council flat/other.......................*
Dirty ?......................

Appendix II

Sampling

1 Constitution

Altogether 697 mothers were interviewed at the seven-year-old stage. Table 37 shows the actual composition of this sample as a function of sex and social class, with, for comparison, the number that would have been expected in a fully random (unstratified) sample of approximately the same size.

Table 37 *Class/sex composition of interviewed sample: compared with (bracketed) expected composition of unstratified sample*

	social class					summary		
	I&II	IIIwc	III man	IV	V	I&II, IIIwc	IIIman, IV, V	Total
	N	N	N	N	N	N	N	N
boys	69	58	105	81	57	127	243	370
	(49)	(45)	(175)	(52)	(27)	(94)	(254)	(348)
girls	65	49	99	75	39	114	213	327
	(49)	(45)	(175)	(52)	(27)	(94)	(254)	(348)
both	134	107	204	156	96	241	456	697
	(98)	(90)	(350)	(104)	(54)	(188)	(508)	(696)
	14%	13%	50%	15%	8%	27%	73%	100%

The discrepancies are partly intentional and partly due to adventitious factors to do with the way the sample was originally drawn and then augmented to replace losses from the four-year-old sample (see section on losses below). As in our previous studies, the avowed aim was to arrive at a stratified random sample using occupational social class as the basis for the stratification. The strategy was to include at least 100 cases in each of the numerically smaller class groups, and as can be seen we fell short of this objective only in as much as we finally saw only 96 families in Class v. The practical problem, both in choosing the sample originally and in making up for losses later, was that the records that we used for our sampling frame did not provide sufficiently accurate or up-to-date information about the father's occupation. In fact they could not have been expected to do so, since from time to time people change their jobs, and sometimes their occupational status in consequence. The final confirmation of occupational social class could therefore only be obtained at the time of the interview itself.

The information contained in Table 37 does, however, enable us to calculate corrected proportions for the sample as a whole and for various sub-groups (such as all the middle-class children) by adopting an appropriate weighting procedure. Given that x per cent of actual respondents answer 'No' to Question Y in specified proportions according to social class, this procedure yields an estimate of what proportions would answer 'No' in a non-stratified random sample. The weighting was undertaken routinely, and thus the data tables throughout include totals in terms of proportions to be expected in a non-stratified sample with equal numbers of boys and girls, as shown in brackets in Table 37.

A further consequence of using a stratified sample obtained in this way is that the tests of significance (using chi-squared) applied to the summary tables could not easily be based upon actual numbers of cases. Instead, therefore, the weighted proportions were referred to a slightly smaller notional sample comprising 600 cases distributed as in Table 38.

Table 38   *Breakdown of the notional sample of 600 cases used as a basis for calculating chi-squared in the summary tables*

(the numbers in brackets indicate the total numbers of children interviewed in fact)

	Middle class I&II, IIIwc	Working class IIIman, IV, V	Both
boys	100 (127)	200 (254)	300 (370)
girls	100 (114)	200 (213)	300 (327)
both sexes	200 (241)	400 (456)	600 (697)

The implication of adopting this procedure is that our conclusions concerning the statistical significances of differences in the summary tables err on the side of caution. Thus the middle-class/working-class differences and the overall sex differences, while correctly represented, tend to be judged slightly less significant that they would have been had we adopted a more sophisticated but less convenient computation procedure which took into account the full number of cases interviewed.

2 *Losses*

Of the 700 children whose mothers we interviewed at four years, we lost 83 cases in the follow-up at seven. This represents an overall loss rate of just under 12 per cent. In Table 39, these losses are analysed as a function both of social class and of reason for loss.

Table 39   *Losses in sample between four years and seven years*

	social class					
	I&II	*IIIwc*	*IIIman*	*IV*	*V*	*Total*
	N	N	N	N	N	N
Outright or implied refusal	6	4	12	14	12	48
Moved away and untraceable (or abroad)	6	2	1	2	1	12
Non-contact, death, protracted illness	2	5	10	5	1	23
Total:	14	11	23	21	14	83
As percentage of interviews attempted	11%	10%	10%	15%	14%	12%

It is clear that more than half the losses were due to refusal or to mothers failing to keep appointments or finding it inconvenient on so many repeated occasions that it seemed obvious that they did not wish to co-operate. At the same time, by no means all these refusals resulted from unco-operative attitudes on the mothers' part. Some were going through genuine family crises at the time, while others were finding their commitments very heavy (sometimes starting new jobs) which made it difficult to find time for a protracted interview during this particular period. Two children were diagnosed as severely handicapped between four and seven, and although the interviews took place, the questions were much less appropriate than they had been for these children at four, and the children were dropped from the sample. One child died, and another was very severely injured and therefore omitted.

Losses were fairly evenly spread across the class spectrum; there were slightly greater losses at the lower end of the scale, but hardly enough to produce any systematic bias in the sample as a whole. The reason for analysing losses must always be to trace any systematic distortion effects, and the losses shown would be unlikely to distort overall results in any very serious way.

References

APLEY, John (1959), *The Child with Abdominal Pains*, Oxford, Blackwell.

APLEY, J. and MACKEITH, R. (1968), *The Child and his Symptoms* (2nd edn), Oxford, Blackwell.

AYERST, David (1967), *Understanding Schools*, Harmondsworth, Penguin Books.

BARNES, Peter (1974), 'Some factors associated with reading ability', unpublished thesis, University of Nottingham.

BENEDICT, Ruth (1935), *Patterns of Culture*, London, Routledge & Kegan Paul.

BENNETT, N. (1976), *Teaching Styles and Pupil Progress*, London, Open Books.

BENSLEY, P. (1970), 'Educational comics', *Where*, 49.

BERNSTEIN, B. (1960), 'Language and social class', *Br. Journ. Sociol.*, XI.

BRUNER, J. S. (1972), *The Relevance of Education*, London, Allen & Unwin.

CENTRAL ADVISORY COUNCIL FOR EDUCATION (1967), *Children and their Primary Schools* (Plowden Report), London, HMSO.

CLARK, M. M. (1970), *Reading Difficulties in Schools*, Harmondsworth, Penguin Books.

CLYNE, Max (1966), *Absent*, London, Tavistock.

CROXEN, Mary (1966), 'Social adjustment of children', unpublished thesis, University of Nottingham.

DAVIE, R., BUTLER, N. and GOLDSTEIN, H. (1972), *From Birth to Seven*, London, Longman.

DIACK, H. (1965), *In Spite of the Alphabet*, London, Chatto & Windus.

DOUGLAS, J. W. B. (1964), *The Home and the School*, London, MacGibbon & Kee.

DOUGLAS, J. W. B. and ROSS, J. M. (1965), 'The effects of absence on primary school performance', *Br. Journ. Ed. Res.*, 38.

DOWNING, J. (1970), 'Relevance versus ritual in reading', *Reading*, 4.

FESSLER, Audrey (1975), 'The development of linguistic skills in primary school children', unpublished thesis, University of Nottingham.

FOGELMAN, K. and RICHARDSON, K. (1974), 'School attendance: some results from the National Child Development Study', in Turner, B. (ed.), *Truancy*, London, Ward Lock Educational.

FRASER, E. (1959), *Home Environment and School*, University of London Press.

GENERAL REGISTER OFFICE (1968), *Classification of Occupations*, London, HMSO.

GREENFIELD, P. M. (1969), 'Goal as environmental variable in the development of intelligence' (Conference on 'Contributions to Intelligence', University of Illinois); quoted in Bruner, 'Poverty and Childhood', essay in op. cit. (1972).

HAUGAARD, Kay (1973), 'Comic books: conduits to culture?', *The Reading Teacher*, 27.

HERSOV, L. (1960), 'Refusal to go to school', *Journ. Ch. Psychol. and Psychiatr.*, I.

ILLICH, Ivan (1974), *After Deschooling, What?*, Writers' and Readers' Publishing Co-operative.

JOHNSON, N. (1966), 'What do children learn from war comics?', *New Society*, VIII, 197.

JONES, J. (1966), 'Social class and the under-fives', *New Society*, VIII, 221.

KAGAN, J. (1971), *Change and Continuity in Infancy*, New York, Wiley.

KAHN, J. (1974), 'School phobia or school refusal?' in Turner, B. (ed.), op. cit.

KELLY, G. A. (1955), *The Psychology of Personal Constructs, Vol. 1: A Theory of Personality*, New York, Norton.

KILN, Alison (1975), 'An investigation of factors influencing a child's measured intelligence', undergraduate dissertation, University of Nottingham Psychology Department.

MCBRIDE, F. (1967), 'The professional preparation of students in colleges of education for the teaching of reading', *Reading*, 1.

MITTLER, P. (1969), 'Towards educational responsibility', *Teaching and Training*, 7.

MORRIS, J. (1966), *Standards and Progress in Reading*, Slough, National Foundation for Educational Research.

NEALE, M.D. (1966), *Analysis of Reading Ability*, London, Macmillan.

NEWSON, J. and E. (1968), *Four Years Old in an Urban Community*, London, George Allen & Unwin; Harmondsworth, Penguin Books.

NEWSON, J. and E. (1976a), 'Parental roles and social contexts'; in Shipman, M. (ed.), *The Organisation and Impact of Social Research: Six original case studies in education and behavioural science*, London, Routledge & Kegan Paul.

NEWSON, J. and E. (1976b), *Seven Years Old in the Home Environment*, London, Allen & Unwin.

NEWSON, John and Elizabeth, SCAIFE, Joyce and RICHARDSON, Diane (in press), 'Sex-roles in adolescence and pre-adolescence', in Chetwynd, J. and Hartnett, O., *The Sex Role System*.

NISBET, J. (1953), 'Family environment and intelligence', *Eugenics Review*, 45.

ORWELL, George (1939), 'Boys' weeklies' in *Critical Essays*, London, Secker & Warburg.

PERRY, G. and ALDRIDGE, A. (1971), *The Penguin Book of Comics*, Harmondsworth, Penguin Books.

PICKARD, P. M. (1961), *I Could a Tale Unfold*, London, Tavistock.

PUMPHREY, G. H. (1964), *What Children Think of their Comics*, London, Epworth Press.

REID, J. (1972), *Reading: Problems and practices*, London, Ward Lock Educational.

ROBINS, S. (1970), 'Comics: the funnies and the weepies', *Where*, Advisory Centre for Education, 48.

ROBINSON, J. H. (1923), *The Mind in the Making*, London, Cape.

SCOTT, T. L. (1974), 'The teaching day as described by some teachers working in ESN(S) schools', MA thesis, University of Nottingham.

SHAW, George Bernard (1910), 'Parents and children' (Preface to *Misalliance*).

TAYLOR, J. J. (1972), 'The reading of comics by secondary school pupils', *Use of English*, 24.

TAYLOR, Mike (1969), 'The machine-minder', in Ronald Fraser (ed.), *Work 2: Twenty personal accounts*, Harmondsworth, Penguin Books.

THOMPSON, G. B. (1975), 'Sex differences in reading attainments', *Educational Research*, 18.

TUCKER, N. (1969), 'Kiddies' cosy corner', *New Society*, XIII, 335.

YOUNG, Michael and MCGEENEY, Patrick (1968), *Learning Begins at Home*, London, Routledge & Kegan Paul.

Index

The reference '1976' denotes that the major discussion of this topic appears in J. and E. Newson, 1976b, op. cit.